URBAN COMPLEXITY AND PLANNING

*To my parents:
Their love and sacrifices*

Urban Complexity and Planning

Theories and Computer Simulations

SHIH-KUNG LAI
*Zhejiang University, Mainland China and
National Taipei University, Taiwan*

and

HAOYING HAN
Zhejiang University, Mainland China

ASHGATE

© Shih-Kung Lai and Haoying Han 2014

All rights reserved. No part of this publication may be reproduced, stored in a retrieval system or transmitted in any form or by any means, electronic, mechanical, photocopying, recording or otherwise without the prior permission of the publisher.

Shih-Kung Lai and Haoying Han have asserted their right under the Copyright, Designs and Patents Act, 1988, to be identified as the authors of this work.

Published by
Ashgate Publishing Limited
Wey Court East
Union Road
Farnham
Surrey, GU9 7PT
England

Ashgate Publishing Company
110 Cherry Street
Suite 3-1
Burlington, VT 05401-3818
USA

www.ashgate.com

British Library Cataloguing in Publication Data
Lai, Shih-Kung.
Urban complexity and planning : theories and computer simulations.
   1. City planning–Computer simulation. 2. Pattern recognition systems. 3. Garbage can models of decision making.
   I. Title II. Han, Haoying.
   307.1'216'0113-dc23

The Library of Congress has cataloged the printed edition as follows:
Shih-Kung, Lai.
Urban complexity and planning : theories and computer simulations / by Shih-Kung Lai and Haoying Han.
   p. cm.
   Includes bibliographical references and index.
   ISBN 978-0-7546-7918-9 (hardback) – ISBN 978-0-7546-9816-6 (ebook) 1. Cities and towns–Computer programs. 2. City planning–Computer programs. I. Haoying, Han. II. Title.
   HT166.S4625 2012
   307.760285'53–dc23

2012022238

ISBN 9780754679189 (hbk)
ISBN 9780754698166 (ebook – PDF)
ISBN 9781409474593 (ebook – ePUB)

Printed in the United Kingdom by Henry Ling Limited, at the Dorset Press, Dorchester, DT1 1HD

Contents

List of Figures		*vii*
List of Tables		*xi*
Foreword by Michael Batty		*xv*
Foreword by Lewis D. Hopkins		*xix*
Preface		*xxi*

1	From Organized Anarchy to Controlled Structure: Effects of Planning on the Garbage-can Decision Processes	1
2	Effects of Planning on the Garbage-can Decision Processes: A Reformulation and Extension	25
3	A Spatial Garbage-can Model	39
4	An Agent-based Approach to Comparing Institutional and Spatial Changes in the Self-organizing City	61
5	On Traction Rules of Complex Structures in One-dimensional Cellular Automata: Some Implications for Urban Change	79
6	Applying Cellular Automata to Simulate Spatial Game Interactions to Investigate Effects of Planning	99
7	Planning for City Safety and Creativity: Two Metaphors	119
8	Emergent Macro-structures of Path-dependent Location Adoptions Processes of Firms	135
9	The Formation of Urban Settlement Systems: Computer Experiments and Mathematical Proofs of the Increasing-returns Approach to Power Law	151
10	Power Law Distribution of Human Settlements: An Explanation Based on Increasing Returns	169

11	A Preliminary Exploration on Self-organized Criticality of Urban Complex Spatial Systems	187
12	Planning in Complex Spatial and Temporal Systems: A Simulation Framework	207
13	Decision Network: A Planning Tool for Making Multiple, Linked Decisions	227
14	Effectiveness of Plans in the Face of Complexity	243

Index *255*

List of Figures

1.1	Simulation design for comparing the generic organization and the land development firm under the garbage-can decision process with and without planning	13
2.1	A conceptual diagram of the garbage-can decision process	26
3.1	A visual representation of the SGC model	47
3.2	System trajectories in time in the energy landscape	48
3.3	Total net energy-time plot for unsegmented structures	49
3.4	Total net energy-time plot for hierarchic structures	49
3.5	Total net energy-time plot for specialized structures	50
3.6	Total net energy-time plot for random structures	50
4.1	Building block of SGCM	64
4.2	Simulation of SGCM	64
4.3	Decision-making rule in the simulation	68
4.4	A snapshot of the simulation	71
4.5	Trajectories of entropy for decision structure	72
4.6	Trajectories of entropy for spatial structure	72
5.1	The NDFA corresponding to rule 76	84
5.2	A DFA corresponding to the NDFA for rule 76	85
5.3	The minimal representation of the DFA for rule 76	93
6.1	Payoff matrix in the simplified prisoner's dilemma game	104
6.2	Evolution pattern of the CA in class 1	108
6.3	Evolution pattern of the CA in class 2	108
6.4	Evolution pattern of the CA in class 3	109
6.5	Evolution pattern of the CA in class 4	109
6.6	Residential-commercial payoff matrix	113
7.1	A sample of illustrations of the simulation runs	128
7.2	Three prototypes of institutional structure	129
8.1	Payoffs resulting from emerging clusters	140
8.2	A map of delineation of regions in Taiwan	142

8.3	Two plots of the R^2 values in relation to distance costs for the random and increasing returns models	146
9.1	An example of attractiveness scores with a single developed cell	155
9.2	An example of attractiveness scores with a regular cluster of developed cells	155
9.3	An example of attractiveness scores with an irregular cluster of developed cells	155
9.4	Examples of simulation results with different attractiveness scores	156
9.5	Stochastic paths of growth in the 9-grid lattice model	162
10.1	The logarithmic linear relation of rank-size	171
10.2	An example of attractiveness scores	173
10.3	An example of the random growth model with an increasing returns mechanism	174
10.4	An example of the random growth model without an increasing returns mechanism	176
10.5	The logarithmic linear relation of the rank-size rule for the US (1890–1970)	183
11.1	Changes in the number of customers in the bar in Arthur's simulation	192
11.2	Procedures for land development in the bounded rationality model	194
11.3	Interaction of cells in Nowak and May's study	196
11.4	Profit-loss matrix for the computer simulation	196
11.5	Spatial patterns and cluster patterns from the simulation (frame 0)	198
11.6	Spatial patterns and cluster patterns from the simulation (frame 1)	198
11.7	Spatial patterns and cluster patterns from the simulation (frame 2)	199
11.8	Spatial patterns and cluster patterns from the simulation (frame 10)	199
11.9	Spatial patterns and cluster patterns from the simulation (frame 100)	199
11.10	Long-term transition of the number of cell clusters	200
11.11	Logarithmic relationship of rank-size for residential land parcels in bounded rationality decision mode	201
11.12	Plot of R2 and adjusted R2	202
12.1	Logic of computing and determining land-use transitions	215

List of Figures

12.2	Sample simulation plot. (Black = road; blue = transit line; I = industrial; C = commercial; R = residential; E = vacant)	216
12.3	Simulation interface. Rules of the genetic algorithm (upper buttons) and the simulated maps and necessary data (lower buttons) are displayed	216
12.4	Simulation framework (complexity 1 through 5 represent degrees of complexity as measured by fractals)	217
12.5	Coupling of a CA model with GIS to explore land use and transportation interaction (yellow = residential; red = commercial; gray = road; blue = river)	218
12.6	Relationship between the garbage can model and the prisoner's dilemma game model (DM = decision maker)	221
13.1	A decision situation	230
13.2	A decision network	230
13.3	The decision network of G_0 for the numerical example	234
13.4	The decision network of G_5 for the numerical example	235
13.5	The decision network of G_8 for the numerical example	236
13.6	A hypothetical example of delineating UCBs	237
14.1	A typology of network topological structures	244
14.2	A simplified circular network of decisions	247
14.3	Networks with different degrees of clustering	248
14.4	How plans of reassigning problems affect the topological structure of the network	251
14.5	The special case of more than one decision with the minimum probability of occurring	252
14.6	Effects of plans as defined here on the total expected utility of the network	252
14.7	Effects of plans on the special case of random network	253

List of Tables

1.1	A typology of planning contexts	2
1.2	The statistics and variable names used in the simulation	9
1.3	The statistics of the garbage-can decision process of the six decision time horizons for the random problem-arrival and one-shot problem arrival scenarios	10
1.4	Comparison of the garbage-can decision processes with and without planning for the generic organization	13
1.5	Effect of energy loads on the garbage-can decision processes with and without planning for the generic organization	14
1.6	Effects of (a) access structures, (b) decision structures, and (c) energy distributions on the garbage-can decision processes with and without planning for the generic organization	16
1.7	Comparison of the garbage-can decision processes with and without planning for the land development firm	17
1.8	Effects of (a) energy loads, (b) access structures, and (c) energy distributions on the garbage-can decision processes with and without planning for the land development firm	17
1.9	Comparison of the decision processes between the generic organization and the land development firm with and without planning	19
2.1	The factors and variables of the simulation design	29
2.2	The statistics and variable names used in the simulation	30
2.3	The ANOVA analysis for the variable of problem persistence (KT)	35
2.4	The ANOVA analysis for the variable of problem latency (KU)	35
2.5	The ANOVA analysis for the variable of problem velocity (KV)	35
2.6	The ANOVA analysis for the variable of problem failures (KW)	35
2.7	The ANOVA analysis for the variable of decision-maker velocity (KX)	36

2.8	The ANOVA analysis for the variable of decision-maker inactivity (KS)	36
2.9	The ANOVA analysis for the variable of choice persistency (KY)	36
2.10	The ANOVA analysis for the variable of choice failures (KZ)	36
2.11	The ANOVA analysis for the variable of energy reserve (XR)	37
2.12	The ANOVA analysis for the variable of energy wastage (XS)	37
2.13	The ANOVA analysis for the variable of problem disutility removal (XT)	37
3.1	Combinations of constraint types with respect to structural variables	52
3.2	The four-factorial design of the 4×4 Graeco-Latin Square	53
3.3	The ANOVA table for the Graeco-Latin Square design	53
4.1	Classification of structural constraints	70
4.2	Numbers of resolution in the decision structure and spatial structure	73
4.3	Tests of between-subjects effects for group 1	74
4.4	Tests of between-subjects effects for group 2	74
4.5	ANOVA for decision and spatial structures in group 2	75
5.1	Classification of transition rules for one-dimensional cellular automata with $k=2$ and $r=1$ by types of rules and classes of structures	87
5.2	The eight transition rules that are semi-lattices and result in class 4 structures	87
5.3	The characteristic transition rule for semi-lattices with complex structures	88
5.4	Classification of transition rules into semi-lattices and trees	94
6.1	Simulation scenarios	106
6.2	Simulation design	106
6.3	Distribution of rules	107
6.4	Classification and numbers of the simulation results	110
6.5	Characteristics of evolution of CA with the interaction of different ranges and neighboring cells	110
6.6	Evolution of the homogeneous agglomeration of C or D and the scopes of b	112
6.7	Rules when $r=1$ and $n=3$	115
6.8	Rules when $r = 2$ and $n = 3$	115

6.9	Rules when $r = 1$ and $n = 5$	116
6.10	Rules when $r = 2$ and $n = 5$	116
7.1	A Summary of effects of different institutional designs	129
8.1	Returns to choosing A or B given previous adoptions	138
8.2	Returns of firms to choosing locations (regions) A, B, C, or D, given previous decisions	139
8.3	The random data of firms entering the market (from 1 to 40 in hundreds)	141
8.4	The real data of firms entering the market (in hundreds)	142
8.5	Lock-in regions for the random and real data with different distance costs (A "-" means no regions dominate; N stands for north; and S for south)	143
8.6	Lock-in regions for random and real data with different initial payoffs by regions (N stands for north; C for central; S for south; and E for east)	143
8.7	Lock-in regions for random and real data with different rates of returns	144
8.8	Lock-in regions for random and real data with different rates of returns by regions	144
8.9	Lock-in regions for random and real data with different rates of returns by industries	144
9.1	Indices for the neighboring attraction model	157
9.2	Indices for the scale-attraction model	157
9.3	Indices for the mixed-relation model of neighboring attraction and scale-attraction	158
9.4	Changes in parameters for different rounds of simulation	159
9.5	Growth of the primary city in three models	160
9.6	Coefficients and R squares in the regression model	163
9.7	Models with and without the consideration of increasing return	163
9.8	Comparison of the models and the real urban settlement systems	165
10.1	The results of the computer simulation	174
10.2	One sample with $N = 5$	175
10.3	The difference between excepted values and actual values	179
11.1	Land development scenarios in the computer simulation	197
11.2	Rank-size classification of land parcels	200
12.1	Payoff matrix	219

13.1	Variables and parameters of the hypothetical decision network problem	233
13.2	The variables and parameters for the hypothetical example of delineating UCBs	238

Foreword:
The Inextricable Duality of Cities and Planning

Michael Batty
CASA, University College London

From classical times, our understanding of cities and their planning have remained largely separate from one another. Although most of us now believe that it is impossible to resolve problems in cities or to achieve the ideal city or the city beautiful without some basic understanding of their current state, plans still tend to be fashioned with little understanding of whether or not they are realizable in terms of how cities actually function. Moreover, our understanding of cities often sees plans as something imposed on top of and not an intrinsic part of the functioning of cities, hence being separate from all other processes that determine how cities are organized and how they evolve. Since planning has been institutionalized in many countries as part of the social functions of government over the last 100 years, this schism has been exacerbated. The city has become a focus for all kinds of ills that might be resolved by politically expedient solutions; and often, policies and plans fly in the face of the fact that many of the unintended consequences of such interventions are simply never anticipated. In parallel fashion, those intent on an understanding of cities tend to see such systems as external to our self, akin to the remoteness of phenomena in the physical sciences, to be studied passively rather than actively. To an extent, this dichotomy between cities and planning is now the subject of intense scrutiny, but so far there are few insights into how our understanding of cities might be informed by their planning and vice versa.

In the last 20 years, complexity theory has come under the broad canvas of urban and regional planning. In general terms, such approaches do tend to grapple with the notion that decision processes are the defining instruments of such understanding and in this sense planning is but one of many processes that determine the functioning of systems such as cities. Yet most research into complexity theory as applied to cities has not explicitly broached the notion of planning. In some senses, the same divisions between aggregate social physics and more micro individual behaviours that exist in economics have come to characterize the structure of this theory. Ideas about how cities evolve from the bottom up quickly generate aggregates that show signatures and patterns such as self-similarity, self-organization, emergence, path-dependence, and a host of generic characteristics that serve to define complexity. New approaches to modelling such patterns and morphologies using bottom-up structures such as those embodied in individual or agent-based models do offer the prospect of integrating planning processes with many others that serve to determine how cities are structured and how they evolve. But to date, the schism still exists, particularly when ideas about complexity theory are thought about in the context of institutionalized planning processes. If you were to open a book about "complexity science and cities" and one about "complexity science and planning," and such books do exist, you would be forgiven for wondering how they are related to one another. Apart from the term complexity, there would be little common material. The challenge is to enable a proper synthesis: to establish what is in essence an inextricable duality between cities and planning in terms of complexity and this has never been more urgent. In fact the field will not progress unless this kind of synthesis becomes central to our thinking.

What is interesting and insightful about Shih-Kung Lai and Haoying Han's new book is that they broach this problem head on. The essence of their argument is that they propose simple but tractable organizational decision processes that look both to ideas about how to generate good solutions to urban problems through planning but which build on ideas about how cities evolve from the bottom up. In short, they have written a book on a complexity theory of cities *and* city planning. This is no mean feat because, as I have implied when one looks at planning, it is but one of many processes that determine how cities function. But to make progress in understanding how these particular processes differ from the myriad of other decision-making structures that determine how cities function and evolve, we need to somehow distinguish "planning processes" of the kind that we use professionally to redesign the city from all those other processes affected by planning but do not have any synoptic perspective or goal about the state of the city in general. This poses an asymmetry that in a sense has stopped the field from progressing. Merging top-down "public" planning processes with the many other "private" ones which tend to cover the range from top down to bottom up has been quite difficult, while at the same time embedding such logics into the approaches that see the city as a complex phenomenon in more aggregate terms has proved somewhat intractable. This is the reason why books on complexity and cities differ so much from those on complexity and planning. The former deal with cities *per se*, while the latter deal only with planning *per se*, and never the twain shall meet.

In fact Shih-Kung Lai and Haoying Han tackle this issue by assuming a generic organizational model which Michael Cohen and his colleagues called the "garbage-can model" (GCM). An unusual, somewhat evocative term perhaps, but one that focuses directly on the fact that complex decision-making problems form an "organized anarchy" of parallel, simultaneous, and sequential processes that exist both dependently and independently of one another but operate at different speeds with different goals. The GCM is a model that can be elaborated in many ways and the authors first generalize it to spatial concerns and then illustrate how it can be applied to cities in terms of different foci—land development, individual firms, and related activities. They then translate this model into slightly more familiar terms, developing agent-based and one-dimensional cellular automata equivalents which serve to ground the decision structures in more traditional complexity theory, involving ideas about the organization of cities in terms of size and agglomeration whose signatures are power laws. In a sense, their thesis works backwards from planning to cities, but in taking a manifestly complex decision-making structure to begin with, they succeed in showing how planning can be embedded in ideas about how cities function and evolve.

This is not an easy book to read. It switches the focus from the comfortable, more conventional ways of planning based on communicative and learning processes dominated by diverse stakeholder interests, and from standard ideas about cities as complex systems which show emergence, fractality, and so on, to the ground between. This is difficult terrain and it forces the reader to think long and hard about the goals of planning and the way cities respond to these in terms of the way they evolve. In the last three chapters, they pull these ideas together, proposing a more generic framework for planning and design. Throughout the book, they provide tantalizing glimpses of theories and methods that inform the debate—issues about creativity, links between problem-solving and decision-making, ideas about how these problems might be formulated using the theory of games. There is much food for thought here and I urge readers to pursue these arguments with diligence for there is much to be learnt from these chapters. But even more important is that fact that any treatise on complexity theory in cities and planning can only provide snapshots of such complexity and it is the tools that are introduced here that readers should grasp, extend, and apply to new kinds of planning problems at different scales and in different cultures.

Foreword

Lewis D. Hopkins
University of Illinois at Urbana-Champaign

Planning is often seen as unable to cope with complexity. Planning as design—figuring everything out ahead of time and then doing it—cannot cope with complexity because it is impossible to fully understand complex systems. Shih-Kung Lai and Haoying Han have challenged this traditional view by framing planning as a systemic behavioral pattern embedded within complex systems. In their framing, the fundamental property of planning is that planning considers more than one decision at a time. In their extensions of the garbage-can model, they have shown that we can learn through simulations about the effects of planning in complex systems. Expanding the scope of decisions considered at any one time and expanding the scope of problems considered at any one time can affect whether problems are resolved and how well they are resolved, objectives that may compete with each other.

Lai and Han have linked ideas about cities as systems with ideas about planning. They consider planning as part of the spontaneous order created within systems behavior rather than an external control. This approach contrasts with the frequent confounding of planning with regulation, which is usually framed as a set of external restrictions on available actions. So, rather than thinking in equilibrium terms about the outcomes of spontaneous behaviors, as in neoclassical markets, with and without certain regulations, these models imagine many actors, each of whom is planning and thus considering expanded scopes of decisions before acting. Each actor may expand this consideration of actions to other, future actions of its own and actions of other actors. Thus, as in simulations that consider path-dependence and increasing returns to scale, these simulations are able to consider plan-dependence over time and among actors.

The proposed decision network tools attempt to extend decision theory and decision analysis to consider multiple decisions in situations less structured than those addressed in traditional game theory. When reframing problems, such as when considering two problems together instead of one, expressed preferences may change. A sequence of choices and outcomes creates a path of experience that may affect preferences, making preferences themselves endogenous. The focus of simulations then becomes trying to understand how particular planning behaviors can affect trajectories rather than trying to choose optimal trajectories ahead of time. When we do not know what will happen or even what we will prefer, then we need understanding of general principles for behavior. For example, we need to understand how robustness, adaptability, portfolio, and just-in-time strategies work in general. We need to learn how to imagine multiple futures and what to observe as futures unfold.

Lai and Han's simulations of urban systems, plans, and decision-making are contributing to this new view of plans as inherent and endogenous attributes of systems of behavior rather than as separate, external controls on a system.

Preface

The inspiration for this book can be traced back to a talk given by Professor Michael Batty about fractal cities at the University of Illinois, where the author was a PhD student in the late 1980s and to Professor Lewis Hopkins who introduced us to the idea of complexity in 1994. Since that time, the authors have come to believe that cities are complex systems that defy any form of deductive analysis derived from mathematics. As such, producing comprehensible representations of cities requires a new, non-mathematical approach.

In response to this need, computer simulation, particularly cellular automata (CA), has become an important tool to understand how cities work. Unlike many current researchers however, we view CA not as a language for the iconic modeling of cities, but rather as an abstract modeling language reminiscent of mathematics that can describe urban complexity effectively and succinctly. It is beyond the scope of this book to discuss the epistemological implications of computer simulation; however, we are confident that the models we present go a long way toward portraying how cities work and revealing how planning affects spatially complex systems such as urban development.

This work is based on the assumption that independent decision-making is insufficient to deal with the complexities of the modern world. Dealing effectively with complex systems requires that decisions be made within the context of plans. We believe that traditional decision theory has inherent structural and arguably fundamental flaws. First, the theory assumes an invariant utility function for the decision-maker, such that actions are selected according to their ability to maximize the expected utility. In contrast, we argue that the utility function is frame-dependent and changes according to how decision situations are framed. Secondly, the theory assumes that every decision is made independently, as if the decision-maker were acting as a discrete entity. Although this approach can be effective in a simple world, in more complex situations, decisions are interdependent. Thus, linked decisions (plans) are the only way to overcome problems of complexity and produce the desired results. This book introduces a series of computer simulations addressing the characteristics of complex systems in urban and regional development, both in hypothetical and actual spatial settings.

In the last two chapters, we propose a novel planning tool derived from our experience with computer simulation. The results obtained from these simulations prove that the formulation of plans to deal with complexity is a worthwhile endeavor. This book is targeted at theorists and practitioners involved in decision-making processes and planning.

The challenge for planning is to reconcile two types of order in cities: the undirected "natural" order and the deliberate man-directed order. Planning structures imposed upon the undirected natural order (what we call the garbage can model) and the directed actions of individuals creates choice opportunities so that the decision making process itself becomes more orderly. It is conventional to say that planning makes it possible to coordinate the actions of diverse actors and give greater predictability to the consequences of their actions. Here, in our models, we see how that actually happens. Other simulations suggest how cities tend to self-organize themselves into a "critical state," that is, order at a higher level spontaneously emerges from the natural and man-directed processes, and it is the role of planning to reconcile those decisions and actions and make that higher-level order more desirable.

The author is one of the few scholars to begin a career writing a PhD dissertation on decision theory in a planning program, and we have been pondering the relationship between decision-making and planning ever since. Not until recently, with the rise of the complexity movement, developments in the logic of making plans (Professor Lewis Hopkins), and insights into the science of cities (Professor Michael Batty), has it become clear to us that plan-based decision-making is the most powerful thinking mode we have developed to deal with the complex world in which we find ourselves. We will leave the reader to judge whether we have made our case.

This book represents a collective effort of more than 15 years. We would like express our profound gratitude to former students and all others who helped to make this work possible, including Chih-Ger Chen, Chuan-Yuan Chen, Tzen-Lon Chen, Yo-Jen Chen, Hong-Hsen Gao, Po-Chien Ko, Shiu-Chien Kuo, Chiu-Yi Tang, Li-Guo Wang, Yu-Chie Wang, Chi-Hsu Yeh, and Ju-Ling Yu. We are particularly grateful to the Ashgate team for their careful editorial help in preparing the book, including Claire Bell, Matthew Irving, and Valerie Rose. We acknowledge full responsibility for any errors found in the book.

Chapter 1
From Organized Anarchy to Controlled Structure: Effects of Planning on the Garbage-can Decision Processes[1]

1 Introduction

Planning occurs in an uncertain world in which events and outcomes arise in an unpredictable way. Planners realize this fact but sometimes believe unrealistically that they can control the processes as well as the outcomes. There is little backing for this overconfidence. Planning is thus carried out by planners overlooking or simplifying the complexity of relationships among intertwined events that are analytically inextricable. Recent approaches to planning methods attempt to cope with this complexity by drawing on methods of operations research to manage uncertainty rather than providing ultimate solutions to planning problems (Friend and Hickling, 1987). These approaches are claimed to be effective based not on some well-designed research methodology but on the users' confidence or satisfaction in applying these approaches. The effectiveness of these approaches must be examined through careful research designs for dealing with ill-defined problems (Hopkins, 1984). Computer simulations provide a useful means for such explorations in that they can easily draw, from a particular population, large samples of data by manipulating experimental variables with a much lower cost than if real human subjects were used (e.g., Lee and Hopkins, 1995).

Most planning takes place in organizational contexts, such as corporations, firms, and governments. It is difficult to define planning in any exclusive way but we can at least identify that planning enhances decision-making by reducing uncertainty (Friend and Hickling, 1987; Hopkins, 1981). Organizations are artifacts designed for coordinating actions: that is, arranging sequences of actions to achieve certain goals. A plan is a set of related contingent decisions; therefore planning and organization are in part interchangeable (Lai and Hopkins, 1995). It is crucial, however, to distinguish between planning with respect to substantive decisions and planning with respect to planning activities (Hopkins, 1981). The first involves gathering information about related decisions made either by other decision-makers or by the same decision-maker with respect to various issues,

---

[1] This chapter has been published in *Environment and Planning B: Planning and Design* 1998, Vol. 14, pages 85–102.

whereas the latter concerns decisions to plan made either by other decision-makers or by the same decision-maker with respect to these issues. Though the study on planning with respect to decisions to plan or planning activities has not been well formulated, it could have implications on how planning activities should be organized and it thus worth pursuing (the exceptions include Sheshinsky and Intriligator,1989). For convenience, I shall call the latter type of planning metaplanning. Table 1.1 shows planning and metaplanning as occurring in different organizational contexts. In reality, however, planning can progress through intertwined planning and metaplanning behaviors. A firm gathering information about another decision-maker's decision to reduce uncertainty for improving decisions to maximize its profits is a manifestation of planning with respect to substantive decisions (type 3 planning), whereas a local government coordinating decisions to plan among its planning departments with respect to various issues to improve actions for resolving external problems imposed by the environment is an example of planning with respect to planning behavior (type 8 planning). In this chapter, the focus is on type 5 planning, namely, coordinating the actions or decisions of a single decision-maker or organizational entity to resolve problems external to the organization. This type of planning is most relevant to the assumptions of the standard theory of choice from which the garbage-can model of organizational choice was developed (Cohen et al., 1972).

I will present a partial computer simulation exploring the effects of planning on organizational decision processes based on the framework proposed by Lai and Hopkins (1995). In the framework, research design exploring planning effectiveness in spatial, temporal, and complex contexts was suggested based on three models: the garbage-can model (Cohen et al., 1972), the prisoner's dilemma game (Nowak and May, 1993), and fractal space (Mandelbrot, 1983). In particular, planning behavior was introduced into the garbage-can model to compare its effects on the random decision-making sequences of the model. Therefore I will focus here on the garbage-can model by considering the effects of planning on the model under different planning investments. Planning investments are represented by the time periods in which related choices are compared and selected for enactment. To lend a concrete example to the simulation and show how this research can be related to

Table 1.1 A typology of planning contexts

	Action			
	Same decision-maker		Different decision-makers	
	Decision-making	Decisions to plan	Decision-making	Decisions to plan
Coordinating actions for resolving problems:				
Internal to the organization	Planning (type 1)	Metaplanning (type 2)	Planning (type 3)	Metaplanning (type 4)
External to the organization	Planning (type 5)	Metaplanning (type 6)	Planning (type 7)	Metaplanning (type 8)

land development, a survey was conducted on seven local land development firms to construct a prototypical organizational structure of the land development firm. Based on that structure, the effects of planning on the decision processes of that firm and on the generic organization were compared. A pilot study extending such simulation to incorporate important decision factors into the model was conducted and will be discussed in Section 6. I will first introduce the garbage-can model and consider how planning can be introduced in it. The simulation designs and results based on the designs are then depicted.

2 The Garbage-can Model

Departing from the standard theory of organizational choice of a closed rational cycle connecting individual actions to environmental changes through organizational decisions, Cohen et al. (1972) proposed a behavioral theory of organized anarchy drawing on observations they made about how organizations, in particular public, educational, and illegitimate ones, make their decisions. The behavioral theory, or garbage-can model, they developed takes into account three general properties of such organizations. The first property is problematic preferences, meaning that the organizational actions are taken through ambiguous preferences. The second is unclear technology, indicating that the organizational decision processes are usually not understood by its members. The third is fluid participation, where the participants' attention to the decision processes varies. Instead of providing a normative theory of decision-making for such an organization, Cohen et al. invented the garbage-can model of simulation to investigate how organizations make decisions under such ambiguous circumstances characterized by the three general properties.

In brief, the garbage-can model views the decision-making process of a decentralized organization, or organized anarchy, as random combinations of four elements: decision-makers, solutions, problems, and choice opportunities or garbage cans (Cohen et al., 1972). Each combination of four elements provides a decision context to produce outcomes. Problems and choice opportunities (garbage cans or choices) arise randomly with the other two elements thrown into these garbage cans in given organizational structures and something happens.

According to Lai and Hopkins's definitions (1995), choices are situations in which decisions can be made, that is, commitments to actions to be taken. In organizations, votes to spend money or signatures on forms to hire or fire persons are examples of choices. Solutions are alternative actions that might be taken, such as persons who might be hired, tax schedules that might be lived, or land developments that might be approved. Solutions are things that choices can commit to enact, things we have the capacity to do directly. Problems are issues that are likely to persist and that decision-makers are concerned to resolve, such as homelessness, unfair housing practices, congested highway, or flooding. Note that choices enact solutions through decisions; they do not solve problems. We cannot merely choose not to have homelessness. We cannot "decide a problem." We can choose to spend money on shelters or to hire social workers, which may or may not affect the persistence of homelessness as a problem. Decision-makers are units of capacity to take action in choice situations.

A garbage can is a choice opportunity where the elements meet in a partially unpredictable way. Solutions, problems, and decision-makers are thrown into a garbage can, resulting in complex outcomes. There is, however, no simple mapping of decision-makers to problems or of solutions to problems. Further, an organization has many interacting garbage cans, many interacting choice opportunities. The original model was used to investigate universities as an example of "organized anarchy." Structure can be increased from this starting point, however, which enables the investigation of a wide range of types and degrees of organizational structure (e.g., Padgett, 1980). Planning and organizational design are at least partially substitutable strategies for affecting organizational decision-making. They are both means for "coordinating" related decisions.

The major assumption in the models is that streams of the four elements are independent of each other. Solutions may thus occur before the problems these solutions might resolve are organized. Choice opportunities may occur because regular meetings yield decision-maker status, independent of whether solutions are available.

With this general conceptual formulation, Cohen et al. (1972) ran a simulation addressing four variables: net energy load, access structure, decision structure, and energy distribution. Net energy load is the difference between the total energy required for a problem to be resolved and that available from decision-makers. Different net energy loads, roughly analogous to organizational capacity in the form of decision-makers relative to organizational demand, should yield differences in organizational behavior and outcomes. Access structure is the relationship between problems and choices. A zero-one matrix defines which problems can be resolved by which choices. Different access structures vary in the number of choices that can resolve particular problems. Decision structure defines which decision-makers can address which choices and thus how the total energy capacity of the organization can be brought to bear in resolving choices. For example, there were three types of access structures, unsegmented, hierarchical, and specialized, as shown in matrices A_0, A_1, and A_2, and, respectively:

	Choices		
Problems	1111111111	1111111111	1000000000
	1111111111	1111111111	1000000000
	1111111111	0111111111	0100000000
	1111111111	0111111111	0100000000
	1111111111	0011111111	0010000000

	Choices		
Problems	1111111111	0011111111	0010000000
	1111111111	0001111111	0001000000
	1111111111	0001111111	0001000000
	1111111111	0000111111	0000100000
	$A_0=$ 1111111111	$A_1=$ 0000111111	$A_2=$ 0000100000
	1111111111	0000011111	0000010000
	1111111111	0000011111	0000010000
	1111111111	0000001111	0000001000
	1111111111	0000001111	0000001000
	1111111111	0000000111	0000000100
	1111111111	0000000111	0000000100
	1111111111	0000000011	0000000010
	1111111111	0000000011	0000000010
	1111111111	0000000001	0000000001
	1111111111	0000000001	0000000001
	(unsegmented structure)	(hierarchical structure)	(specialized structure)

In the unsegmented structure, any active problem had access to any active choice; in the hierarchical structure, important problems (upper part of the matrix) had access to many choices; in the specialized structure, each problem had access to only one choice. The decision structures were classified in the same way except that there were only ten decision-makers. As to energy distribution, the model also assumed three types: important people-less energy, equal energy, and important people-more energy, with the total amount of energy loads: light (1.1 required per problem); moderate (2.2 required per problem); and heavy (3.3 required per problem). Solutions were represented through flows of solution coefficients serving as discount rates of effective energy. There were totally 3^4 (81) types of organizational situations obtained by taking all possible combinations of the values of the four variables.

In the simulation, there were in all 20 problems, ten choices, and 20 time steps. At each of the of the first ten time steps, two problems and one choice "arrived" according to respective random sequences. Decision-makers and problems were associated with each choice and the energy required to resolve the problems and that available from decision-makers were compared to determine if a decision could be made at each choice. If the amount of energy available was greater than that required for resolving the problems, the decision was made for that choice; otherwise the choice and the associated problems persisted in time, looking for appropriate decision-makers in future time steps to resolve these persisting problems.

Cohen et al. (1972) reported their results by focusing on four statistics: decision style, problem activity, problem latency, and decision difficulty. The three decision styles were resolution, oversight, and flight. Resolution meant that a choice taken resolved all or part of the problems that were thrown into the garbage can of that choice opportunity. If a decision was taken for a choice to which no problems were attached, it was classified as oversight. All other situations constituted flight. Cohen et al. were able to demonstrate the sensitivity of organizational behavior to various access structures and decision structures. For example, the decision process was quite sensitive to net energy load and to combinations of access and decision structures.

Extensions of the garbage-can model have been made by incorporating hierarchical structures of organization (Padgett, 1980); by exploring the behavioral merit of the model among publishers (Levitt and Nass, 1989); and by constructing computer simulations based on artificial intelligence (Masuch and LaPotin, 1989). Despite these later developments, the model seems to suffer from lacking external validity because there is no evidence yet showing that the garbage-can model is "the" behavioral theory of organizational choice. Even Cohen et al. (1972) admitted that the model did not describe all activities of any organization. Given its persuasive internal validity and the reasons depicted earlier, the garbage-can model simulates a microcosm in which uncertainty and ambiguity pervade, reminiscent of the uncertain world in which urban planning occurs. Thus it provides a useful starting point for the investigation of planning in organizations, and possible extensions could be made into modeling planning behavior in wider contexts, such as cities.

3 Planning in the Garbage-can Model

The original garbage-can model implied that the organization did not have control over the occurrence of problems and choices. Decisions incurred no cost and were not made mainly to resolve problems. In particular, the organization was not capable of generating choice opportunities to deal with problems that had arisen in a given time step. The arrival of choice opportunities and the arrival of problems were each random. One way of introducing a type of planning to the model is to allow the organization purposefully to create choice opportunities for resolving problems. This choice-problem dependence is a matter of degree with one extreme being the original garbage can and the other extreme a complete mapping of arriving problems to crated choice opportunities. This dependence can be represented by assigning weights to disutilities incurred by problems in the decision rule, as will be depicted in Section 6. This is equivalent to being able to compare garbage cans and choose one to act in at each time period of the simulation. What effect would the capability to choose among choice opportunities over time so as to match current problems have on the simulation results?

Lai and Tang (1995) ran a prototypical simulation to illustrate this approach. They assume that, at a given time step, the planner is able to acquire complete information about the structure of the organization except for the arrival of problems in that time period. The planner knows the decision structure and access structure and thus the relationships among the elements. Thus the planner can predict which decision-makers and problems will be in which garbage cans (i.e., choice opportunities) and how much energy will accumulate and be sent by decision-makers in each choice opportunity. Choice opportunities in this case are related choices from which the planner can select based on the difference between the energy required to make a decision and the energy available from decision-makers. The planning criterion is thus to select the choice opportunity (the garbage can) that results in the smallest energy deficit. Planning thus defined involves choosing the entry times for choices, but not for problems, decision-makers, or solutions. Simulation results were sensitive to interventions based on this definition of planning. In the pilot study, such planning resulted in increased efficiency of making choices, that is, more choices with less energy expended, but resolved fewer problems. Problems, choices, and decision-makers tended to remain attached to each other in the planning case more than in the case without planning.

These results are still only tentative because of the small size of the simulation. This definition is only one way of introducing planning to the original model. Control over other elements could also be considered. A combination of partial controls on the four elements might yield a definition of planning that would result in more useful analyses of simulation results. Regardless, the possibility of instructive results is demonstrated by the pilot study because it shows that we might add structure to decision-making without increasing the ability of organizations to resolve problems. This result suggests that this modeling approach incorporates sufficient degrees of freedom to discover counterintuitive results.

4 Simulation 1: Effects of Planning on the Garbage-can Model

The objective of the first simulation is the same as that of the simulation depicted in Lai and Tang (1995) in that it addresses the effects of planning on the garbage-can decision processes. I will focus here, however, on planning investments; that is, I will investigate the effects of decision time horizons over which planning takes into account related choices in making decisions at a particular time step. The decision time horizons are not merely those considered in temporal decision-making as discussed by Keeney and Raiffa (1976) because in the current formulation the horizons take into account related decisions, not just independent consequences. The relatedness among choices is central to planning and is embedded in the garbage-can model through the decision and access structures, that is, enacting one choice changes the outcome resulting from enacting another. Though under stringent conditions, comparing decisions is equivalent to comparing consequences

(Savage, 1972). Delving into such issues may deviate from the main purpose of this research.

Another issue is that the time horizons could be variable, fixed, certain, or uncertain. The problem of optimal time horizons for planning can best be addressed by means of economic theory (e.g., see Sheshinsky and Intriligator, 1989), but it is a question beyond the scope of this research. I am interested mainly in the sensitivity of the garbage-can model to variations of decision time horizons in which related choices are considered. With such time horizons under consideration, the more comparisons among choices or computations the decision-maker has to make. Based on the simulation discussed in Lai and Tang (1995), we can compare how different time horizons would affect the garbage-can process.

4.1 Simulation Design

Because in the garbage-can model exactly one choice opportunity occurs at each of the first ten of 20 time steps, increasing the decision time horizons implies that more choices are taken into account. For example, decision time horizon 2 takes into account the choices to appear two time steps ahead of each time step when the decision is made (including the current time step). Decision time horizon 0 takes whichever choice opportunity occurs at each time step when the decision is made without taking into account the upcoming choices. For simplicity and without loss of generality, we compare decision time horizons 0, 2, 4, 8, and 10. Note that decision time horizon 10 is equivalent to the simulation conducted by Lai and Tang (1995) in which all ten choices were considered at the same time. The result for time horizon 10 obtained here are slightly different from those in Lai and Tang because a computational error was found and fixed in the computer code when running the present simulation. Two scenarios were considered in the simulation design: (1) random arrival of problems, and (2) one-shot arrival of problems. In the first scenario, two of the 20 problems arrived at each of the first ten of 20 time steps as proposed in the simulation of Cohen et al. (1972). In the second scenario, all 20 problems arrived at the first time step simultaneously. Only the compulsory rule was considered because it conformed more closely to real planning situations. That is, at each time step through the simulation, a choice opportunity must be enacted until all choices are exhausted.

4.2 Results

Following Cohen et al. (1972), we focus on four statistics that characterize the garbage-can decision processes: problem activity, problem latency, decision-maker activity, and decision difficulty. Decision style will be discussed in the future. Problem activity measured the degree to which problems are active within the organization and reflects the degree of conflict or articulation of problems. As shown in Table 1.2, three statistics were used for this measure: problem failure

(K_W), problem velocity (K_V), and problem persistence (K_T). Problem latency measures the degree to which problems are active but not attached to any choices. The measure is reflected by K_U in Table 1.2. The decision-maker activity measure is reflected by decision-maker inactivity (K_S). Decision difficulty is measured by choice failures (K_Z) and choice persistence (K_Y).

The simulation results based on the design specified are shown in Table 1.3 for the random and one-shot problem arrival scenarios. Note that the statistics in the table are averaged over all 81 possible structural combinations of access structure, decision structure, energy distribution, and net energy load.

When problems arrived in a random sequence, as is shown in Table 1.3 that, in general, the total number of time periods when a choice was activated, summed over all choices (K_Y), and that of time periods any decision-maker shifted from one choice to another (K_X) decreased with an increase in planning investment (or decision time horizon). In addition, the total number of time periods when a decision-maker was not attached to a choice, summed over all decision-makers (K_S), also increased with an increase in planning investment. Three other statistics showed similar patterns with an increase in planning investment. Three other statistics showed similar patterns with respect to decision time horizons: the total

Table 1.2 The statistics and variable names used in the simulation

Statistics	Variable[a]	Interpretation
Problem persistence	K_T	The total number of time periods a problem is activated and attached to a choice, summed over all problems
Problem latency	K_U	The total number of time periods a problem is activated, but not attached to a choice, summed over all problems
Problem velocity	K_V	The total number of times any problem shifts from one choice to another
Problem failures	K_W	The total number of problems not solved at the end of 20 time periods
Decision-maker velocity	K_X	The total number of times any decision-maker shifts from one choice to another
Decision-maker inactivity	K_S	The total number of time periods a decision-maker is not attached to a choice, summed over all decision-makers
Choice persistence	K_Y	The total number of time periods a choice is activated, summed over all choices
Choice failures	K_Z	The total number of choices not made by the end of 20 time periods
Energy reserve	K_R	The total amount of effective energy available to the system but not used because decision-makers are not attached to any choice
Energy wastage	K_S	The total effective energy used on choices, in excess of that required to make them at the time the choices are made

[a] These variables were used originally by Cohen et al. (1972).

Table 1.3 The statistics of the garbage-can decision process of the six decision time horizons for the random problem-arrival and one-shot problem arrival scenarios

Horizon	K_Z	K_Y	K_X	K_W	K_V	K_U	K_T	K_S	X_R	X_S
Random problem arrival										
0	1	29	60	11	61	55.50	174	88	28.49	13.45
2	1	28	60	13	51	60.80	180	97	32.08	11.23
4	1	27	58	13	50	57.90	186	102	33.31	9.95
6	1	30	58	14	51	64.00	193	105	34.63	10.86
8	1	26	55	13	55	76.20	182	107	33.51	10.02
10	1	22	45	14	45	97.50	167	120	37.43	8.89
One-shot problem arrival										
0	1	42.8	63	11	110	30	291	72	24.11	13.96
2	1	44.1	66	12	76	41	291	86	29.26	10.42
4	1	43.8	58	12	58	62	270	91	31.20	8.68
6	1	41.7	56	12	50	80	249	100	33.59	8.04
8	1	44.2	57	11	46	100	221	94	30.52	8.69
10	2	45.4	52	12	35	116	205	103	33.46	7.41

Note: See Table 1.2 for explanation of variables.

number of problems not solved at the end of the 20 time periods (K_w); the total number of time periods a problem was activated, but not attached to a choice, summed over all problems (K_U); and the total amount of effective energy available to the system but not used because decision-makers were not attached to any choice (X_R).

For the one-shot scenario, the patterns were somewhat different. The K_U value increased with an increase in decision time horizons (planning investments). Similar patterns were found for K_S and X_R. Two new patterns were found in the total number of times any problem shifted from one choice to another (K_V) and the total number of time periods when a problem was activated and attached to a choice, summed over all problems (K_T), in that the values of these variables decreased with increase in decision time horizons.

On the face of it, it can be inferred that planning investment speeded up the decision-making processes in the random arrival case; that is, decisions were made more quickly than the arrival of the problems so that problems arriving later formed a queue and decision-makers did not have many chances to be attached to choices and thus these problems could not be resolved. In the one-shot arrival case, because problems arrived at the beginning of the decision processes, decisions were made at much later times (K_Y values were much greater) and the numbers of problems unresolved (K_w) were not as sensitive to planning investments as in the case of the random arrival case, but the patterns of the changes in the statistics with respect to planning investments remained similar. In both cases, the total effective energy (X_s) used on choices, in excess of that required to make them at the time they were made, tended to be lower for greater planning investment.

It can be argued from the simulation that planning increased the speed of decision-making and saved more energy but did not necessarily resolve more problems. Most such decisions were made either by flight or oversight, that is, not because these decisions could resolve problems but because there was accidentally enough energy from available decision-makers for making decisions in existing choices. Planning seemed to enhance such a tendency. In the one-shot arrival case, because problems accumulated in the beginning, the time periods required for decisions to be made were longer, but the patterns of changes in the values of these variables remained similar with respect to decision time horizons. One useful insight based on the observations is comparison among related choices; we can observe not only how that insertion alters the system behavior but also, by adding the structure incrementally, how the system reacts to such increments.

5 Simulation 2: A Case Study of Land Development Firms

To lend a concrete application of the garbage-can model to the type of simulations exposited in this research, in the second simulation we compare the garbage-can decision processes between generic and prototypical organizations; namely, the averaged behavior of the organizations across all combinations of the values of the four simulation variables and a sample of real land development firms. Through a questionnaire survey we constructed the prototypical organizational structure of land development firms in Taipei in terms of the access and decision structures and examined whether the decision processes in these firms fulfill the characteristics of the garbage-can decision process. Using this prototypical structure, we compare the garbage-can decision process under that structure with those under the averaged structure used in the first simulation.

5.1 The Organizational Structure of the Land Development Firm

Seven land development firms were selected as a sample for the questionnaire survey. The purposes of the survey were: (1) to investigate whether the decision process in these firms could be characterized by the garbage-can model; and (2) to determine which decision and access structures in the garbage-can model could characterize the organizational structures of the land development firms. The questionnaire was divided into two parts. In the first part, respondents' responses to questions one through ten were used to infer whether the decision processes in their firms could be characterized by ambiguous preferences, unclear technologies, and fluid participants. In the second part, questions one and two were asked to elicit from the respondents the access and decision structures of their decision processes, respectively. In addition to the three types of structures [unsegmented, hierarchical, and specialized, as originally proposed by Cohen et al. (1972)], a random structure was proposed in case none of the three structures applied. In the random structure there is no fixed pattern of mapping between problems (or decision-makers) and choices as shown in matrices A_0, A_1, and A_2.

After a pretest of the questionnaire by two respondents with experience in land development, 45 questionnaires were mailed out to the seven non-randomly selected land development firms, with 40 of them returned and 35 effective. Of the respondents, 80% expressed explicitly and implicitly that decisions were made under unclear objectives, and 91% showed that they did not share the same interests and perspectives on problems among their co-workers. Most decision-makers indicated that experiences might affect their decisions (86%) which in turn might make preferences unclear (Levitt and Nass, 1989) and that decisions were made under conflicting opinions (94%). Of the respondents, 80% showed that they were not aware of the overall decision processes when making decisions and all of them made decisions based on past experiences or the trial-and-error method resulting from unclear decision processes (Cohen et al., 1972). All respondents were unclear about the method for achieving goals, and 89% of them did not take into account available information, which might result from irrational decision processes (Levitt and Nass, 1989). Almost half of the respondents (45%) noticed that participants in certain decision-making processes changed over time. We can conclude, based on the results from the survey, that the decision processes in these land development firms can be characterized by the garbage-can model of unclear technologies, ambiguous preferences, and fluid participants.

In addition, 37% of the respondents considered their access structures as hierarchical, compared with 29%, 14%, and 20% as unsegmented, specialized, and random, respectively. Of the respondents, 66% indicated that their decision structures were hierarchical, compared with 25%, 0%, and 9% as unsegmented, specialized, and random, respectively. We can conclude that the access structure of the land development firms can be represented by either an unsegmented or a hierarchical structure and the decision structure can be represented by a hierarchical structure. In the following simulation design, the land development firms are therefore characterized by the combination of the unsegmented or hierarchical access structure and the hierarchical decision structure.

5.2 Simulation Design

The simulation design for comparing the generic organization and the land development firms was similar to that in simulation 1, in that only the original garbage-can decision process and the decision process with planning under compulsory rule were considered. The decision time horizon for planning was set to ten time steps. We ran the comparison for both the generic organization and the land development firms in order to discover differences between the decision processes for the two types of organizations. The simulation design is depicted in Figure 1.1.

From Organized Anarchy to Controlled Structure 13

	Organization	
	Generic organization	Land development firm
Garbage can without planning	Simulation type 1	Simulation type 2
Garbage can with planning	Simulation type 3	Simulation type 4

Figure 1.1 Simulation design for comparing the generic organization and the land development firm under the garbage-can decision process with and without planning

Given the simulation design, it is possible to compare decision processes with and without planning within each organizational type. That is, we can compare between type 1 and type 3 simulations and between type 2 and type 4 simulations. We can also compare decision processes with and without planning across organizational types, that is, between type 1 and type 2 simulations and between type 3 and type 4 simulations.

5.3 Results

Let us consider first the comparison of simulations within organizational types. Table 1.4 shows the simulation results of planning effects for the generic organization based on the ten statistics defined in Table 1.2. The numbers in Table 1.4 are the means of the variables averaged across 81 combinations of the 4 experimental factors: 3 energy loads, 3 energy distributions, 3 decision structures, and 3 access structures. A t test was chosen for such a comparison with a degree of freedom of 80%.

Following Cohen et al. (1972), the variables can be grouped into four categories: problem activity (problem persistence K_T, problem velocity K_V, and problem failures K_W); problem latency (K_U); decision difficulty (choice persistence K_Y, and choice failures K_Z); and decision-maker activity (decision-maker velocity K_X, decision-maker inactivity K_S, energy reserve X_R, and energy wastage X_S). Except for problem persistence and choice failures, all other statistics indicated that planning affected significantly the decision process. Fewer problems changed from one choice to another in the planning case than in the original model. However,

Table 1.4 Comparison of the garbage-can decision processes with and without planning for the generic organization

	K_Z	K_Y	K_X	K_W	K_V	K_U	K_T	K_S	X_R	X_S
Without planning	0.90	29.17	59.59	11.25	61.47	55.52	174.07	87.86	28.49	13.45
With planning	1.01	21.90	45.50	14.15	44.77	97.51	167.33	120.25	37.43	8.98
t statistic	-0.62	2.29	2.71	-2.54	4.75	-4.55	0.44	-4.13	-3.20	3.72
P value	0.54	0.023[a]	0.01[a]	0.01[a]	0.00[a]	0.00[a]	0.66	0.00[a]	0.00[a]	0.00[a]

Note: See Table 1.2 for explanation of variables.
[a] Statistically significant at $\alpha = 0.05$.

the number of problems resolved at the end of the 20 times steps decreased in the planning case. More problems were activated but not attached to any choices in the planning case. The number of choices that were activated, through the 20 time steps, decreased significantly in the planning case. Decision-makers tended to shift less frequently between choices in the planning case. As a result, the number of decision-makers not attached to any choices was significantly greater in the planning case: so was the amount of energy not used in making decisions. Energy was used more efficiently in the planning case in that significantly less energy was wasted relative to that required to make decisions. In general, the key reason for these observations was that decisions in choices were made more quickly in the planning case, resulting in a problem queue in later time steps, and decision-makers had fewer opportunities to attach themselves to these choices.

Table 1.5 shows the comparison of four statistics with respect to the effects of net energy load on the garbage-can decision process with and without planning: choice persistence (K_Y), decision-maker velocity (K_X), problem latency (K_U), and problem persistence (K_T). These four statistics indicate the four characteristics of organizational choice behavior; namely, decision difficulty, decision-maker activity, problem latency, and problem activity. A one-way analysis of variance was conducted for testing differences among means for each statistic.

It can be shown from Table 1.5 that the effects of net energy load were significant in decision difficulty and problem activity in that increase in net energy load increased the degree of decision difficulty and problem activity in the cases with and without planning. Change in net energy load did not affect problem latency and decision-maker activity.

Table 1.5 Effect of energy loads on the garbage-can decision processes with and without planning for the generic organization

	K_Y	K_X	K_U	K_T
Without planning				
Light	17.67	58.48	64.63	105.56
Moderate	32.44	59.63	52.04	187.74
Heavy	37.41	60.67	49.89	228.93
F	6.90	0.02	0.38	10.97
P value	0.00[a]	0.98	0.68	0.00[a]
With planning				
Light	15.11	46.56	97.70	133.78
Moderate	23.41	45.15	95.52	176.93
Heavy	27.19	44.48	99.30	191.30
F	3.15	0.03	0.04	3.52
P value	01048[a]	0.97	0.96	0.03[a]

Note: See Table 1.2 for explanation of variables.

[a] Statistically significant at $\alpha = 0.05$.

Table 1.6(a) indicates the effects of access structure on the garbage-can decision process with and without planning for the generic organization. It can be shown for the case without planning that decision difficulty and problem latency increased significantly with the segmentation of access structure, whereas problem activity decreased significantly with that segmentation. Decision-maker activity was not sensitive to the segmentation of access structure. In the case of planning, the effects of access structures on the four variables were similar except that decision-maker activity increased significantly with that segmentation of access structures.

Table 1.6(b) shows the effects of decision structures on the characteristics of the garbage-can decision process with and without planning. In the cases with and without planning, the segmentation of decision structures affected significantly decision difficulty, decision-maker activity, and problem activity. Problem latency was insensitive to the segmentation of decision structures. In particular, both decision difficulty and problem activity increased significantly with the segmentation of decision structures, whereas decision-maker activity decreased significantly with that segmentation.

Table 1.6(c) shows the effects of energy distribution on the garbage-can decision processed for the generic organization. It is clear that none of the three types of energy distribution—important people with less energy, all decision-makers with equal amounts of energy, and important people with more energy—affected the four statistics significantly.

For the land development firm, the garbage-can decision processes, with and without planning and with respect to the ten statistics, are compared in Table 1.7. Seven of the ten statistics showed significant differences between the cases with and without planning (decision-maker velocity K_X, problem failures K_W, problem velocity K_V, problem latency K_U, decision-maker inactivity K_S, energy reserve X_R, and energy wastage and problem persistence K_T) and were not sensitive to planning effects.

As in the analysis for the generic organization, these ten statistics can be grouped into four categories representing the characteristics of the garbage-can decision process: problem activity (K_T, K_V, and K_W), problem latency (K_U, decision difficulty (K_Y and K_Z), and decision activity (K_X, K_S, X_R, and X_S). The number of problems shifting from one choice to another was significantly smaller in the case of planning than in the case without planning, whereas the number of problems not resolved at the end of the 20 time steps increased significantly in the first case. Decision difficulty (K_Y and K_Z) was not sensitive to planning. As regards decision activity, decision-maker velocity decreased significantly as planning was introduced into the decision process. The number of decision-makers not attached to any choices was significantly greater in the case with planning without planning; as a result, the total amount of unused effective energy was significantly greater in the case with planning. The amount of energy exceeding that which was required in making decisions was significantly smaller in the planning case. In comparison with the generic organization, planning effects on the garbage-can decision process for the land development firm are similar except that change in choice persistence is insignificant in the planning case.

Table 1.6 Effects of (a) access structures, (b) decision structures, and (c) energy distributions on the garbage-can decision processes with and without planning for the generic organization

	K_Y	K_X	K_U	K_T
Access structures				
Without planning				
Unsegmented	17.22	54.22	0.00	245.41
Hierarchical	30.44	57.00	21.37	203.48
Specialized	39.85	67.56	145.19	73.33
F	8.81	1.05	657.23	31.67
P value	0.00[a]	0.35	0.00[a]	0.00[a]
With planning				
Unsegmented	9.96	30.37	80.89	192.96
Hierarchical	16.96	44.59	48.85	237.85
Specialized	38.78	61.22	162.78	71.19
F	30.98	7.88	563.25	85.56
P value	0.00[a]	0.00[a]	0.00[a]	0.00a
Decision structures				
Without planning				
Unsegmented	16.85	100.59	64.22	129.63
Hierarchical	24.48	61.07	59.26	151.19
Specialized	46.19	17.11	43.07	241.41
F	19.22	493.98	0.75	9.49
P value	0.00[a]	0.00[a]	0.48	0.00[a]
With planning				
Unsegmented	14.04	70.59	91.89	132.44
Hierarchical	20.70	48.41	101.41	169.52
Specialized	30.96	17.19	99.22	200.04
F	6.48	40.15	0.26	4.62
P value	0.00[a]	0.00[a]	0.77	0.01[a]
Energy distributions				
Without planning				
Important people-less energy	29.11	59.26	55.78	178.30
equal distribution	29.37	59.70	56.15	172.41
Important people-more energy	29.04	59.81	54.63	171.52
F	0.002	0.002	0.004	0.030
P value	0.998	0.998	0.996	0.970
With planning				
Important people-less energy	23.44	40.52	100.67	165.52
equal distribution	21.15	47.70	96.30	168.56
Important people-more energy	21.11	47.96	96.56	167.93
F	0.14	0.49	0.08	0.01
P value	0.87	0.61	0.92	0.99

Note: See Table 1.2 for explanation of variables.
[a] Statistically significant at $\alpha = 0.05$.

Table 1.7 Comparison of the garbage-can decision processes with and without planning for the land development firm

	K_Z	K_Y	K_X	K_W	K_V	K_U	K_T	K_S	X_R	X_S
Without planning	0.70	24.48	61.07	9.48	58.07	59.26	151.19	77.63	23.47	14.49
With planning	0.96	20.70	48.41	14.89	44.07	101.41	167.52	119.96	38.12	8.35
t statistic	-1.24	1.03	3.28	-2.85	2.50	-2.65	-0.74	-4.31	-4.13	5.55
P value	0.22	0.31	0.00[a]	0.01[a]	0.02[a]	0.01[a]	0.47	0.00[a]	0.00[a]	0.00[a]

Note: See Table 1.2 for explanation of variables.
[a] Statistically significant at $\alpha = 0.05$.

Table 1.8 Effects of (a) energy loads, (b) access structures, and (c) energy distributions on the garbage-can decision processes with and without planning for the land development firm

	K_Y	K_X	K_U	K_T
Energy loads				
Without planning				
Light	13.44	60.78	67.67	73.56
Moderate	27.00	63.44	56.44	163.56
Heavy	33.00	59.00	53.67	216.44
F	11.10	0.62	0.10	7.25
P value	0.00[a]	0.55	0.90	0.00[a]
With planning				
Light	12.44	45.11	107.33	132.33
Moderate	22.89	49.78	98.44	184.44
Heavy	26.78	50.33	98.44	191.78
F	2.54	0.21	0.09	1.36
P value	0.10	0.81	0.91	0.28
Access structures				
Without planning				
Unsegmented	16.44	56.22	0.00	224.67
Hierarchical	23.56	56.67	28.11	166.67
F	3.51	0.04	19.13	1.98
P value	0.08	0.85	0.00[a]	0.18
With planning				
Unsegmented	11.00	42.00	90.00	220.00
Hierarchical	15.89	39.33	51.89	225.22
F	18.53	0.17	43.34	0.08
P value	0.00[a]	0.68	0.00[a]	0.78

Table 1.8 Concluded

	K_Y	K_X	K_U	K_T
Energy distributions				
Without planning				
Important people-less energy	28.00	59.22	56.33	166.78
equal distribution	23.56	61.89	61.33	146.33
Important people-more energy	21.89	62.11	60.11	140.44
F	0.60	0.31	0.01	0.17
P value	0.56	0.73	0.99	0.85
With planning				
Important people-less energy	24.11	33.00	108.33	170.11
equal distribution	20.00	55.67	98.44	172.00
Important people-more energy	18.00	55.56	97.44	166.44
F	0.38	7.10	0.13	0.01
P value	0.68	0.00[a]	0.87	0.99

Note: See Table 1.2 for explanation of variables.
[a] Statistically significant at $\alpha = 0.05$.

Table 1.8(a) shows the effects of net energy loads on the garbage-can decision processes with and without planning. In the case without planning, the numbers of choices that were activated and of problems that were activated and attached to choices increased significantly when the net energy load increased; decision-maker velocity and problem latency were not sensitive to changes in the net energy load. This observation implies that increase in net energy load increased decision difficulty and problem activity. In the case of planning, the characteristics of the garbage-can decision process were not affected by changes in net energy load.

Table 1.8(b) shows the effects of access structure on the characteristics of the garbage-can decision processes with and without planning. In the case without planning, only problem latency was affected significantly by the segmentation of access structures in that problem latency increased significantly with the segmentation. The other three statistics were not sensitive to the segmentation of access structures. In the case with planning, choice persistence and problem latency were affected significantly by the segmentation of access structure. In particular, the number of choices activated through the 20 time steps increased significantly with the segmentation of access structures, whereas the number of problems not attached to any choices was significantly smaller in the hierarchical access structures than in the unsegmented access structures. The other two statistics, K_X and K_T, were not sensitive to the segmentation of access structures.

Table 1.8(c) depicts the effects of energy distributions on the garbage-can decision processes with and without planning. In the planning case, only the decision-maker velocity was affected significantly by the three energy distributions. More specifically, the energy distribution of important people with less energy resulted in a significantly smaller number of decision-makers shifting from one choice to another in the planning case. The remaining statistics were not affected by the energy distributions in the cases both with and without planning.

Table 1.9 summarizes the comparison between the garbage-can decision processes with respect to the four statistics for the cases with and without planning. No significant differences in terms of the four statistics were found between the two organizational structures in both cases.

In general, the garbage-can decision processes without planning seemed chaotic; planning imposed some order on the process. Decisions were made quickly in planning, resulting in a queue of problems, and decision-makers without appropriate choices to be attached to. When control was brought into the garbage-can process, decision-makers tended to shift less frequently from one choice to another; problems tended to be associated with choices; energy was used more efficiently; problems tended to remain unsolved; and decision-makers tended to be inactive. However, the order brought in by planning did not imply that the performance of the organization as a whole was better. Saving more energy and making decisions more efficiently were achieved at the cost of resolving fewer problems.

The sensitivity of the garbage-can decision process to the control variables—net energy load, access structure, decision structure, and energy distribution—varied. The process was not sensitive to variation in energy distribution. It was highly sensitive to the access and decision structures, whereas moderate process sensitivity was observed with respect to net energy load. No significant difference was found for the garbage-can decision processes between the generic organization and the land development firm for the cases both with and without planning. The garbage-can decision process for the land development firm seemed less sensitive to control variables than that for the generic organization.

Table 1.9 Comparison of the decision processes between the generic organization and the land development firm with and without planning

	K_Y	K_X	K_U	K_T
Without planning				
Generic organization	29.17	59.59	55.52	174.07
Land development firm	24.48	61.07	59.26	151.19
t statistic	-1.40	0.35	0.25	-0.96
p value	0.17	0.70	0.80	0.34
With planning				
Generic organization	21.90	45.40	97.51	167.33
Land development firm	20.70	48.41	101.41	169.52
t statistic	-0.30	0.61	0.36	0.12
p value	0.76	0.54	0.72	0.91

Note: See Table 1.2 for explanation of variables.

6 Discussion

In the simulations, decisions were considered costless and problems did not incur disutility. In reality, these two are important factors affecting planning behavior. Decisions are normally made for status building as well as problem-solving purposes (March, 1995). Decision-makers make decisions as a symbol of their status in a power structure. Decisions thus made do not necessarily resolve problems and usually little cost is incurred in reversing a decision. But for most planning situations, decisions are costly and the ultimate goal is to eliminate problems. Cost is incurred both in implementing and in reversing decisions just made. In particular, the more durable the effects of decision are, the greater the cost of reversing it, for example, the so-called sunk costs or capital investments in engineering projects. Costs of implementing and reversing a decision can be blended into a cost index associated with that decision. Problems resulting from the gaps between what is expected and what is actually perceived by the problem owners impose disutility in these owners. At an abstract level, problems can be represented by a scale of disutility similar to that of utility (Saaty et al., 1983). The more significant the problem is, the greater the amount of comparison of utility and temporal change of preferences for reasons depicted earlier.

A pilot study on simulating the garbage-can decision process taking into account decision cost and problem disutility was conducted (Lai, 1996). In this simulation, planning was defined as control over entry times of choice opportunities in the garbage-can model, but instead of ignoring decision cost and problem relevance, they were both considered. Each decision made in a garbage can was assumed to incur some cost between zero and one associated with that garbage can because decisions were made only in garbage cans and there were no explicit variables representing decisions. These costs are assigned randomly *a priori* to the ten choice opportunities, each arriving at each time step. Each problem was associated with an amount of disutility between zero to one, which is also assigned randomly *a priori*. Such random assignments allow us to produce large samples of different populations for analysis. In the simulation, the ten randomly generated decision costs were 0.70, 0.84, 0.72, 0.31, 0.16, 0.33, 0.47, 0.25, 0.83, and 0.28, and the 20 randomly generated problem disutilities were 0.23, 0.03, 0.86, 0.20, 0.27, 0.67, 0.32, 0.16, 0.37, 0.43, 0.08, 0.48, 0.07, 0.84, 0.06, 0.29, 0.92, 0.37, 0.78, and 0.33. Planning investments were represented by the numbers of time periods or choice opportunities considered for comparison. Choices that had not arisen or been activated were compared based on a criterion of energy deficit to be activated or enacted for each time period. There were thus three control factors in this design: planning investment, decision cost, and problem significance. Different weights were assigned to decision costs and problem disutilities associated with the choice opportunities and problems, respectively, to indicate the relative importance of decision cost and problem disutility in making decisions. These weights are set to real numbers between 0 and 1, with increments of 0.2. Thus we had decision and problem weights set to 0.0, 0.2, 0.4, 0.6, 0.8, and 1.0. There are in total $6 \times 6 \times 6 = 216$

combinations of different levels of the three factors (6 decision horizons, 6 decision weights, and 6 problem weights). Each combination represents a set of particular levels of planning investment, decision cost, and problem significance.

Because of the complex structure of the garbage-can model, it was difficult to come up with clear explanations for the results without more rigorous research designs. The results obtained from the simulation were at best tentative. The partial simulation might, however, provide some clues to how effects of planning could be investigated realistically and tested statistically. Neither decision cost nor problem significance seemed to have all the attributes desired from the planner's point of view of increasing organizational performance in the garbage-can decision processes. Though focusing on decision cost tended to reduce problem latency and increased decision-maker activity, it also tended to increase problem activity and decision difficulty. Focusing on problem significance tended to have the reverse effect. The effects of planning seemed to depend on relative importance placed on decision cost and problem significance. An organization emphasizing decision cost and ignoring problem significance might not perform better than the one taking an opposite position. It is possible that, from a normative point of view, the organization could be improved and that planning can claim to be effective.

This possibility could be explored with a more rigorous computer simulation design. Consider the combinations of the levels of the three factors, that is, $6 \times 6 \times 6 = 216$. For each combination, we draw a large sample composed of random assignments of problem disutilities and costs of choices in which decisions are made, forming a $6 \times 6 \times 6$, three-factorial, design. The confounding effects among the three factors can be tested statistically and conclusions about how decision cost and problem significance may affect planning effects can be drawn.

In short, preliminary results showed that the three factors (planning investment, decision cost, and problem disutility) confounded each other, with the possibility that the latter two were more closely correlated. Insights into the characterizations of a normative theory of planning could be derived from a more rigorous computer simulation design. Understanding of how organizations should balance the relative importance between decision cost and problem significance and how planning would affect organizational performance in garbage-can decision processes could be enhanced by similar simulations.

7 Conclusions

Within the current formulation of the simulations, we have shown that imposing some order on the garbage-can model did affect the decision processes and outcomes. More surprisingly, planning as we defined here did not improve the organizational performance. It resulted in more efficient decision-making activities but at the cost of reducing the organizational performance, that is, resolving fewer problems. This finding seemed counterintuitive to our presumption that planning makes things better. The simplicity of the model and the narrow definition of planning might render our results unrealistic or even invalid but the message is clear: effectiveness of planning is a fundamental question to the planning professional, and more rigorous research designs should be tested to verify our overconfident presumption that planning works. One possible design toward the incremental improvement of such understanding was proposed by extending the current simulations by considering decision cost and problem disutility. The research approach illustrated here is promising in that interaction or relatedness among decisions made by different stakeholders with various interests can be observed through similar simulations. We can learn from such research when and how planning would achieve what it intended to accomplish.

Acknowledgements

The author thanks Chu-I Tang for her assistance in analyzing the simulation results. The comments from three anonymous reviewers, the editor, and Professor Lewis D Hopkins are acknowledged. The research was supported by the National Science Council of the Republic of China (NSC83-0301-H005A-014 and NSC84-2411-H005A-007).

References

Cohen, M.D., J.G. March, and J.P. Olsen. 1972. "A garbage can model of organizational choice." *Administrative Science Quarterly* 17: 1–25.

Friend, J., and A. Hickling. 1987. *Planning Under Pressure: The Strategic Choice Approach*. Pergamon, New York.

Hopkins, L.D. 1981. "The decision to plan: planning activities as public goods." In *Urban Infrastructure, Location, and Housing*, eds W.R. Lierop, P. Nijkamp (Sijthoff and Noordhoff, Alphen and den Rijn) pp 273–96.

———. 1984. "Evaluation of methods for exploring ill-defined problems." *Environment and Planning B: Planning and Design* 11: 339–48.

Keeney, R.L., and H. Raiffa. 1976. *Decisions with Multiple Objectives: Preferences and value Tradeoffs*. John Wiley, New York.

Lai, S.K. 1996. "Effects of planning on the garbage can decision process in consideration of decision cost and problem disutility." Paper presented at Association of Collegiate Schools of Planning and Association of European Schools of Planning Joint International Conference, Toronto, Canada; copy available from the author.

Lai, S.K., and L.D. Hopkins. 1995. "Planning in complex, spatial, temporal systems: a simulation framework." Paper presented at Association of Collegiate Schools of Planning Meeting, Detroit, USA; copy available from the author.

Lai, S.K., and C.I. Tang. 1995. "Effects of planning in a garbage can decision process: a simulation comparison." Proceedings of the Fourth International

Conference on Computers in Urban Planning and Management (Volume Two) University of Melbourne, Parkville, Australia pp 1−12.

Lee, I.S., and L.D. Hopkins. 1995. "Procedural expertise for efficient multiattribute evaluation: a procedural support strategy for CEA," *Journal of Planning Education and Research* 14: 255–68.

Levitt, B., and C. Nass. 1989. "The lid on the garbage can: institutional constraints on decision making in the technical core of college-text publishers." *Administrative Science Quarterly* 34: 190−207.

Mandelbrot, B.B. 1983. *The Fractal Geometry of Nature.* W H Freeman, New York.

March, J.G. 1995. *A Primer on Decision Making: How Decisions Happen.* The Free Press, New York.

Masuch, M., and P. LaPotin. 1989. "Beyond garbage cans: an AI model of organizationl choice." *Administrative Science Quarterly* 34: 38–67.

Nowak, M.A., and R.M. May. 1993. "The spatial dilemmas of evolution." *International Journal of Bifurcation and Chaos* 3(1): 35−78.

Padgett, J.F. 1980. "Managing garbage can hierarchies." *Administrative Science Quarterly* 25: 583–604.

Saaty, T.L., L.G. Vargas, and R.E. Wendell. 1983. "Assessing attribute weights by ratios." *Omega* 11: 9−13.

Savage, L.J. 1972. *The Foundations of Statistics.* Dover, New York.

Sheshinsky, E., and M.D. Intriligator. 1989. "Cost-Benefit analysis with switching regimes: application of the theory of planning." *Computers Mathematical Applications* 17: 1317–27.

Chapter 2
Effects of Planning on the Garbage-can Decision Processes: A Reformulation and Extension[1]

1 Introduction

Though faced with a bewildering set of decisions, planners are confident in many cases that planning affects not only behaviors of organizations, but also outcomes. There is, however, little backing for this confidence. It is particularly true in urban planning. Both organizations and cities are complex systems and we are just beginning to understand their emergent properties. We know surprisingly little about planning processes and how they affect organizations and urban development (Hopkins, 2001). One approach to gaining understanding of planning in organizations and urban development, or complex systems generally, is to develop and analyze simulation models. The simulation presented here builds on the garbage-can model of organizational choice behavior presented by Cohen, March, and Olsen (1972) because that model describes realistically "an environment characterized by complex interactions among actors, solutions, problems, and choice opportunities" (March, 1994) and can be extended to represent real planning situations (Hopkins, 2001). The objective of the book is to develop simulations sufficient to investigate the implications of introducing planning behaviors into complex systems evolving in time, but not space. The primary focus is on devising simulations from which we might discover general principles about the effects of planning phenomena on systems behavior. Though I could construct from scratch new, simpler models other than the garbage-can model for the purpose of specifically examining the effects of planning, such models might lack internal and external validity of complex environments as the garbage-can model seems to possess. I will discuss in Section 5 how such a dilemma can be resolved.

I consider, therefore, the book as a sequel of my previous work on planning effects on garbage-can decision processes by reporting the results from a simulation proposed in that work (cf. Lai, 1998, pp. 100–101). In contrast to that work emphasizing on organizational choice behavior where decision-making

---

[1] This chapter has been published in *Environment and Planning B: Planning and Design* 2003, Vol. 30, pages 379–89.

and implementing incur no cost and problems do not harm, my focus here is to relax that assumption by simulating the same garbage-can model, but with some modifications and different interpretations. The next section depicts conceptually the working of the garbage-can model. For detailed descriptions of how the garbage-can model works and how planning can be incorporated into that model, the reader is recommended to consult the Cohen et al.'s original article (1972) and my previous work (Lai, 1998), respectively. I will then introduce the simulation design for the present purposes, and report the results, as well as discuss some implications in the next three sections.

2   The Garbage-can Model

The garbage-can model was originally designed to describe organizational choice behavior under three conditions: problematic preferences, unclear technology, and fluid participants (Cohen et al., 1972). Put simply, four streams of elements flow into the organizational system in a relatively independent way with problems, decision-makers, and solutions thrown into choice opportunities or garbage cans, and decisions are made. No cost and harm as measured by disutility are incurred by decisions and problems in the original formulation. Figure 2.1 shows a simplified, conceptual diagram of the garbage-can model where DM stands for decision-makers.

In the simplified diagram, the inputs of the model are the sequences of problems, solutions, and choice opportunities, while the outputs are decisions. A system of organization composed of decision-makers is facing incoming problems, solutions, and choice opportunities in time. Once the three streams of elements flow into the system in an unpredictable, random way, decision-makers, solutions, and problems are thrown into garbage cans where decisions may or may not be made. If a decision is made in a garbage can as an output of the system, problems and choice opportunities attached to the garbage can disappear and leave the system.

In the original garbage-can model, decisions and problems incur no cost and harm. This is not the case in the real world situations. Making and implementing decisions are costly and problems reduce persons' levels of satisfaction. Making

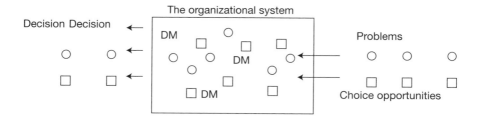

Figure 2.1   **A conceptual diagram of the garbage-can decision process**

decisions to build highways and infrastructures costs, among others, time, money, and energy. Floods may kill households or render them as homeless. If we incorporate, however, some variation of cost indices into these elements, the garbage-can model captures, at least partially if not completely, some characteristics of the realistic complex planning processes.

3 Simulation Design

Similar to the previous work (Lai, 1998), I define, narrowly, planning here in part as controlling over entry times of choice opportunities in the garbage-can model, but instead of ignoring decision cost and problem disutility as in the original garbage-can model, they are both considered in the present simulation. In addition to the four internal variables originally considered in Cohen et al.'s formulation (i.e. net energy load, access structure, decision structure, and energy distribution, which will be explained shortly) forming 81 ($3\times3\times3\times3 = 81$) stereotypes of simulation runs, in the present simulation I add three control factors to investigate their effects on the system; namely decision cost, problem disutility, and planning investment, forming a three-factor factorial design with the observation number equal to one for each combination of the six levels of the three factors. Garbage cans, choice opportunities, and decision situations are used interchangeably in the following depiction.

Energy load implies the amount of resources measured as energy required to solve a problem. There are three types of energy load: light, medium, and heavy. Access structure describes which problem could be solved in which decision situation. Decision structure regulates which decision-maker is able to participate in which decision situation. There are three types of access structure and decision structure, respectively: hierarchical, unsegmented, and specialized. Energy distribution prescribes how resources are allocated to decision-makers. Three types of energy distribution available to decision-makers are considered: more important people with more energy (i.e. energy available decreases from the first to the last decision-maker), less important people with more energy (i.e. energy available increases from the first to the last decision-maker), and equal energy (i.e. all decision-makers have the same amount of energy). The combination of the levels of the internal variables is reminiscent of the typology of various organizations with different characteristics. For example, problems are more easily solved in one organization, such as a university, than in another, such as a construction firm. Sampling across these various typical organizations, as done in the present simulation, may yield generalizable explanations.

The logic of the simulation design is equivalent to that of the design of factorial experiments with three factors, each combination of the control factors having only one observation, which can be found in any experimental design text (e.g., Winer, 1971 and Kirk, 1982). Therefore, the validity of that experimental design and the associated analyses apply here (e.g., Scheffé, 1959, pp. 98–106). Instead of using real subjects, in the simulation design for each combination of the levels of the three factors each set of the 81 stereotypes of the simulation are run once, given a predetermined sequence of problems and choice opportunities. The values of 11 statistics, which will be discussed shortly, are recorded across the 81 stereotypes, forming one set of observations concerning the characteristics of the organization. A three-way ANOVA analysis can be carried out for each statistic to examine the main effect of each factor. Note, however, that the interaction term is neglected in the statistic model for simplicity; "hence all sources of variation other than main effects are considered to be part of the experimental error" (Winer, 1971, p. 394). Thus the conclusions obtained from the proposed simulation can be generalized.

More specifically, assume that each decision made in a garbage can incurs some cost between zero and one associated with that garbage can. These costs are assigned randomly *a priori* to the ten choice opportunities, each arriving in each of the first ten time steps respectively. Assume also that each problem is associated with an amount of disutility between zero and one which is also assigned randomly *a priori*. The ten randomly generated decision costs are 0.70, 0.84, 0.72, 0.31, 0.16, 0.33, 0.47, 0.25, 0.83, and 0.28, whereas the 20 disutilities are 0.23, 0.03, 0.86, 0.20, 0.27, 0.67, 0.32, 0.16, 0.37, 0.43, 0.08, 0.48, 0.07, 0.84, 0.06, 0.29, 0.92, 0.37, 0.78, and 0.33. One might argue that the random assignment of costs and utilities can best be characterized by a Monte Carlo simulation. I suspect that this would make the simulation more complicated without gaining more useful insights, given the validity of the experimental design as just depicted.

Planning investment is represented as the number of time periods and choice opportunities considered for comparisons. In particular, choice opportunities that have not been activated or have not arisen, but are within the time horizon of the prediction, are compared based on a criterion of energy deficit to be activated or enacted for each time period. Thus some degree of interdependence among decisions is reached through this formulation. Energy deficit is the difference between the amount of energy required to make a decision and that available from the associated decision-makers in the previous time step.

Following the previous work (Lai, 1998), in the present simulation there are, in total, ten choice opportunities each occurring in each of the first ten time steps, respectively. Five levels of planning investment are considered in the present simulation; that is, 0, 2, 4, 6, 8, and ten time step decision horizons in which choice opportunities coming in the system are compared. Decision horizon is defined here as the number of time steps that the planner can look ahead from the current time step. In order to evaluate, as a way of controlling, how the variations of focus on the two additional factors of decision cost and problem disutility would affect the system's behaviors, different weights are assigned to decision cost and problem disutility. These weights can also be considered as relative importance between the two factors placed by the planner, and set to real numbers between zero and one with 0.2 increments. Thus we have decision and problem weights set to 0.0, 0.2, 0.4, 0.6, 0.8, and 1.0, respectively.

There are, in total, 216 (6×6×6) combinations of different levels of the three factors (six decision horizons or planning investments, six decision weights, and six problem weights). Each of the 216 combinations represents a set of particular levels of planning investment, decision cost weight, and problem significance weight. Statistics are recorded by summing across all 81 stereotypes of simulations for all 216 combinations of the factorial levels. Table 2.1 summarizes the simulation design.

Table 2.1 The factors and variables of the simulation design

Controlling factors	Internal variables	Number of levels	Total number of observations
Planning investment decision horizons	Net energy loads (three types) Access structures (three types) Decision structures (three types) Energy distributions (three types)	6: 0, 2, 4, 6, 8, and 10 (across all 81 combinations of values of internal variables)	6×6×6 = 216 combinations of levels (across all 81 combinations of values of internal variables)
Decision cost weights	Net energy loads (three types) Access structures (three types) Decision structures (three types) Energy distributions (three types)	6: .0, .2, .4, .6, .8, 1.0 (across all 81 combinations of values of internal variables)	
Problem disutility weights	Net energy loads (three types) Access structures (three types) Decision structures (three types) Energy distributions (three types)	6: .0, .2, .4, .6, .8, 1.0 (across all 81 combinations of values of internal variables)	

4   Simulation Results

Following Cohen et al. (1972), in the analysis of the results I focus on four sets of statistics that characterize the garbage-can decision processes: problem activity, problem latency, decision-maker activity, and decision difficulty. These statistics are necessary to provide an overview as to how the organizational systems perform. Problem activity measures the degree to which problems are active within the organization and reflects the degree of conflict within the organization or the degree of articulation of problems. As shown in Table 2.2, four statistics are used for this measure: disutility removal (XT), problem failures (KW), problem velocity (KV), and problem persistence (KT). Problem latency measures the degree to which problems are active, but not attached to any choice opportunities. The measure is reflected by KU in Table 2.2. The decision-maker activity measure is reflected by decision maker-inactivity (KS), decision-maker velocity (KX), energy reserve (XR), and energy wastage (XS). Decision difficulty is measured by choice failures (KZ) and choice persistence (KY). A statistic of the total amount of problem disutility removed (XT) is considered here in addition to the original ten statistics proposed in the original model.

Based on the simulation design, a three-way ANOVA analysis is conducted for the 216 simulation runs for each statistic as shown in Tables 2.3 through 2.13 in the Appendix. Due to the limitation of space, the simulated data are not reported here. Because each combination of the levels of the three factors is composed of one simulation run, that is, one set of data, the confounding effect or the interaction term of the statistic model is ignored for simplicity. We can test, however, the main effects of the three control factors on the organizational behavior for the 11 statistics, respectively. According to the results from Tables 2.3 through 2.13, except for the main effect of problem disutility for KX, namely decision-maker velocity, as shown in Table 2.7, all other main effects on the system's behavior of the three factors with respect to all the 11 statistics were statistically significant at the level where p is equal to 0.05.

A closer examination of the simulated data showed the following findings. In terms of problem activity, the focus on decision cost and that on problem disutility yielded similar tendencies. The heavier the weight placed on decision cost or problem disutility, the more disutility was removed, but an increase in planning investment had the reverse effect. More planning investment tended to result in less amount problem disutility removed. Increase in the weight on problem disutility resulted in more problems resolved, but increase in planning investment and decision cost led to fewer problems solved. Different tendencies were found in problem velocity

Table 2.2 The statistics and variable names used in the simulation

Statistics	Variables[†]	Interpretation
Problem persistence	KT	The total number of time periods a problem is activated and attached to a choice, summed over all problems
Problem latency	KU	The total number of time periods a problem is activated, but not attached to a choice, summed over all problems
Problem velocity	KV	The total number of times any problem shifts from one choice opportunity to another
Problem failures	KW	The total number of problems not solved at the end of 20 time periods
Decision-maker velocity	KX	The total number of times any decision-maker shifts from one choice to another
Decision-maker inactivity	KS	The total number of time periods a decision-maker is not attached to a choice, summed over all decision makers
Choice persistence	KY	The total number of time periods a choice opportunity is activated, summed over all choice opportunities
Choice failures	KZ	The total number of choice opportunities not made by the end of the 20 time periods
Energy reserve	XR	The total amount of effective energy available to the system but not used because decision-makers are not attached to any choice opportunity
Energy wastage	XS	The total effective energy used on choice opportunities in excess of that required to make them at the time they are made
Disutility removal	XT	The total amount of disutility removed at the end of the 20 time steps

Note: [†] Except for disutility removal (XT), these variables were used originally by Cohen et al. (1972).

and problem persistence in that these measures increased (respectively, decreased) with the increase in the weight of decision cost (respectively, problem disutility). Planning tended to decrease problem velocity and problem persistence.

In terms of problem latency, the focus on decision cost and that on problem disutility yielded tendencies counter to each other: the heavier the weight placed on decision cost (respectively, problem disutility), the smaller (respectively, larger) the number of latent problems. Planning tended to increase the number of latent problems.

The measures of decision-maker activity indicated profound effects of decision cost and problem disutility. In terms of decision-maker velocity, the focus on decision cost increased the degree to which decision-makers shifted from one choice to another, while planning investment had the reverse effect in that increase in planning investment decreased decision-maker velocity. But for decision-maker inactivity, the measure yielded tendencies counter to each other for the focus on decision cost and that on problem disutility. Increase in the weight of decision cost (respectively, problem disutility) tended to decrease (respectively, increase) the number of decision-makers not attached to choice opportunities. Increase in planning investment resulted in more such decision-makers. As a result, the total energy not used for decision-making presented the same pattern. Increase in the weights of decision cost and problem disutility resulted in increase in energy wastage, while increase in planning investment decreased energy wastage.

As to the measures for decision difficulty, for choice failures, the focus on decision cost (respectively, problem disutility) tended to increase (respectively, decrease) the number of choice opportunities in which no decisions were made, and planning investment had a similar effect in that increase in planning investment resulted in increase in decision difficulty. Choice persistence showed a similar pattern in relation to decision cost and problem disutility. Increase in planning investment resulted in decrease in choice persistence.

On the face of it, the effects of decision cost and problem disutility seemed counter to each other. Increase in the weight of decision cost (respectively, problem disutility) tended to increase (respectively, decrease) problem activity, decrease (respectively, increase) problem latency, increase (respectively, decrease) decision-maker activity, and increase (respectively, decrease) decision difficulty. However, increase in either decision cost weight or problem disutility weight would remove more problem disutility. Planning rendered less amount of problem disutility removed, but increased decision-making efficiency. Compared to the previous results of the earlier simulation, the effects of planning remained the same in the present simulation, regardless of whether decisions were costly and problems caused harm. The three factors all mattered in affecting the organizational choice behavior independently.

5 Some Implications

From the results derived in the previous and present simulations concerning the effects of planning on complex systems, we can conclude that making plans matters in complex systems. Planning imposes some degree of order on the seemingly chaotic garbage-can decision processes in that problems and decision-makers tend to stick to the same decision situations. On the other hand, planning tends to solve fewer problems. The question of immediate interest is: how much planning should we invest to gain better outcomes? The conventional wisdom of idealized rational, comprehensive planning paradigm implies that the planner should acquire all information and evaluate all alternatives to seek the actions that bring about optimal outcomes. This approach is equivalent to an attempt to fully control the dynamic processes of a complex system. Regardless of whether one can accomplish this objective, the simulations presented here and earlier suggest that neither zero planning investment nor making plans with a complete scope is desirable. There might be an optimal level of planning investment between the two extremes. How much planning investment a planner should make in a particular situation is a question of theoretical and practical importance, and needs further rigorous investigation.

In the present simulation, there are two interpretations of weights associated with decision cost and problem disutility. The first interpretation is that they represent the planner's trade-off judgments between the two factors: the more weight that is imposed on problem disutility, the more attention that is focused on solving these problems. The more weight that is given to decision cost, the more attention that is focused on making these decisions. Decisions made may not, however, solve problems. Depending on the planner's preferences, whether the organization is to solve problems without worrying about how resources are spent or to make efficient decisions is a subjective judgment. The simulation implies that the two objectives seem conflicting. The second interpretation is that they represent the hypothesized change in the amount of cost and disutility. Regardless of which interpretation is adopted, decision cost and problem disutility seem to have counter effects on the garbage-can decision processes. More focus on or increase in decision cost results in more problems and decision-makers shifting among decision situations and thus makes decision-making more difficult, while problem disutility has the counter effects. There is a need for a balance between how much emphasis should be put on problem-solving and decision-making to promote the overall performance of the garbage-can organization.

The present simulation showed that planning investment, decision cost, and problem disutility all matter; that is, they all affect how the garbage-can decision processes evolve. Planning seems, however, quite distinct from the other factors because decision cost and problem disutility seem correlated in terms of the effects on the statistics. I suspect that though all three factors matter, planning affects the dynamic processes through control while the other two factors only have partial impacts on these processes. Making plans is only one way of affecting outcomes. Other characteristics of organizations, such as their designs and objectives, may also affect how the organizations perform. How to make effective use of different organizational factors collectively to gain what we want is a challenging task.

One might argue that in order to test the effects of planning directly, a totally different, simpler simulation should be designed and run by addressing patterns of interdependence among decision situations and the resulting effects. This simple design can then focus solely on how cost and disutility of decisions and problems affect the system's behavior, without referring to seemingly irrelevant variables, such as decision structure and energy load. These variables may digress from the research objectives. Though simplicity is of course desired in modeling, it is sometimes at the cost of realism. The garbage can model is at least simple enough to understand conceptually. That model is a descriptive one for complex decision environments with plausible internal and external validity. Simulating that model would result in useful conclusions. One way to resolve this dilemma, however, is to conduct another simpler Monte Carlo simulation, taking into account different streams of decision situations with respect to different patterns of interdependences, and comparing effects of various amounts of cost, disutility and planning investment. We can then apply the "alignment of computational models" approach as suggested by Axtell et al. (1997) to examine whether the two simulations produce the same results. Such a comparison is beyond the scope of the present book and begs future work.

6 Conclusions

I have shown a simulation based on the garbage-can model to consider planning, decision cost, and problem disutility. The simulation results showed that all the three factors affected the system's behavior in a statistically significant way. The main effects of the three factors with respect to almost all the statistics under consideration were significant. Each factor matters in affecting the organizational choice behavior with planning effects quite distinct from the other two factors.

The simulation results showed that neither decision cost nor problem disutility had all the attributes desired from the planner's point of view of increasing the organizational performance in the garbage-can decision processes. Though focusing on the decision cost tended to reduce problem latency and increase decision-maker activity, it also tended to increase problem activity and decision difficulty. The focus on problem disutility tended to have the reverse effects. The effects of planning were similar to those derived from the previous simulation in that it resulted in fewer problem resolutions, but more efficient decision-making. An organization emphasizing decision cost but ignoring problem disutility might not perform better than the one taking an opposite position. It might be that, from a normative point of view, the organization needs to balance or make value trade-offs between the two so that the overall performance of the organization could be improved and that planning has its claim to be effective. We may not be sure under what conditions planning may yield better outcomes, but one thing we can be sure of, based on the simulation results, is that making plans and acting accordingly in the narrow sense defined here does matter in a complex system characterized partially by chaotic interactions of components. Insights into the characterizations of a normative theory of planning could be derived from a more rigorous axiomatic analysis based on the result, such as the four I's conditions for planning argued by Hopkins (2001).[2] Additional work will be necessary to determine the external validity of these simulations, that is, to interpret concrete situations in terms of such principles.

Acknowledgements

The author thanks Dr Hong-Long Wang and Miss Ju-Ting Cheng (National Taipei University, Taiwan) for their assistance in running and analyzing the ANOVA tables. An earlier version of the work was presented at CUPUM in Hawaii, 2001. The author is grateful to two anonymous reviewers for their useful comments on an earlier version of the book.

References

Axtell, R., R. Axelrod, J.M. Epstein, and M.D. Cohen. 1997. "Replication of agent-based models." In R. Axelrod. 1997. *The Complexity of Cooperation* Princeton University Press, Princeton, New Jersey pp. 183–205.
Cohen, M.D., J.G. March, and J.P. Olsen. 1972. "A garbage can model of organizational choice." *Administrative Science Quarterly* 17: 1–25.
Hopkins, L.D. 2001. *Urban Development: The Logic of Making Plans*. Island Press, London.
Kirk, R.E. 1982. *Experimental Design Second Edition*. Brooks/Cole Publishing Company, Monterey, California.
Lai. S-K. 1998. "From organized anarchy to controlled structure: effects of planning on the garbage-can decision processes." *Environment and Planning B* 25: 85–102.
March, J.G. 1994. *A Primer on Decision Making: How Decisions Happen*. The Free Press, New York.
Scheffé, H. 1959. *The Analysis of Variance*. John Wiley & Sons, Inc., New York.
Winer, B.J. 1971. *Statistical Principles in Experimental Design Second Edition*. McGraw-Hill Book Company, New York.

---

2   Hopkins (2001) argues that the urban development processes can be characterized by 4 conditions among decisions under which making plans can gain benefits, that is, to seek actions that result in better outcomes: interdependence, indivisibility, irreversibility, and imperfect foresight, or the 4 I's. Interdependence means that the outcome of one decision affects that of another; indivisibility requires that increments of a physical investment cannot be made in arbitrary amounts; irreversibility implies that decisions, once made, are costly to change; and imperfect foresight simply recognizes the fact that prediction is not complete. Under these conditions which defy iterative adjustments assumed in the economic literature, making plans by considering related decisions may yield better outcomes. It is worth proving axiomatically, however, that Hopkins's argument is true.

Appendix: The ANOVA tables

Table 2.3 The ANOVA analysis for the variable of problem persistence (KT)

Factor	DF	SS	MS	F	P
Decision cost	5	54906684	10981336	384.03	0.000
Problem disutility	5	42038900	8407780	294.03	0.000
Planning investment	5	53307428	10661485	372.85	0.000
Error	200	5718930	28595		
Total	215	155971936			

Table 2.4 The ANOVA analysis for the variable of problem latency (KU)

Factor	DF	SS	MS	F	P
Decision cost	5	81092960	16218592	293.96	0.000
Problem disutility	5	650187	130037	2.36	0.042
Planning investment	5	113282776	22656556	410.65	0.000
Error	200	11034384	55172		
Total	215	206060304			

Table 2.5 The ANOVA analysis for the variable of problem velocity (KV)

Factor	DF	SS	MS	F	P
Decision cost	5	100208640	20041728	503.05	0.000
Problem disutility	5	527966	105593	2.65	0.024
Planning investment	5	28492375	569848	14.30	0.000
Error	200	7968026	39840		
Total	215	111553872			

Table 2.6 The ANOVA analysis for the variable of problem failures (KW)

Factor	DF	SS	MS	F	P
Decision cost	5	28485	5697	4.83	0.000
Problem disutility	5	262006	52401	44.42	0.000
Planning investment	5	272294	54459	46.16	0.000
Error	200	235951	1180		
Total	215	798736			

Table 2.7 The ANOVA analysis for the variable of decision-maker velocity (KX)

Factor	DF	SS	MS	F	P
Decision cost	5	17122228	3424445	127.12	0.000
Problem disutility	5	21291	4258	0.16	0.977
Planning investment	5	4921405	984281	36.54	0.000
Error	200	5387909	26940		
Total	215	27452832			

Table 2.8 The ANOVA analysis for the variable of decision-maker inactivity (KS)

Factor	DF	SS	MS	F	P
Decision cost	5	38717772	7743155	212.42	0.000
Problem disutility	5	6535899	1307180	35.86	0.000
Planning investment	5	36378568	7275713	199.60	0.000
Error	200	7290435	36452		
Total	215	88920672			

Table 2.9 The ANOVA analysis for the variable of choice persistency (KY)

Factor	DF	SS	MS	F	P
Decision cost	5	51406300	10281260	1678.98	0.000
Problem disutility	5	2057397	411479	67.20	0.000
Planning investment	5	5836151	1167230	190.61	0.000
Error	200	1224704	6124		
Total	215	60524552			

Table 2.10 The ANOVA analysis for the variable of choice failures (KZ)

Factor	DF	SS	MS	F	P
Decision cost	5	41094.2	8218.8	574.09	0.000
Problem disutility	5	9031.6	1806.3	126.17	0.000
Planning investment	5	4608.2	921.6	64.38	0.000
Error	200	2863.3	14.3		
Total	215	57597.3			

Table 2.11 The ANOVA analysis for the variable of energy reserve (XR)

Factor	DF	SS	MS	F	P
Decision cost	5	2155737	431147	176.75	0.000
Problem disutility	5	701772	140354	57.54	0.000
Planning investment	5	3486094	697219	285.82	0.000
Error	200	487869	2439		
Total	215	6831471			

Table 2.12 The ANOVA analysis for the variable of energy wastage (XS)

Factor	DF	SS	MS	F	P
Decision cost	5	254593	50919	66.04	0.000
Problem disutility	5	61132	12226	15.86	0.000
Planning investment	5	1312748	262550	340.52	0.000
Error	200	154207	771		
Total	215	1782680			

Table 2.13 The ANOVA analysis for the variable of problem disutility removal (XT)

Factor	DF	SS	MS	F	P
Decision cost	5	2471.0	494.2	2.31	0.045
Problem disutility	5	47579.7	9515.9	44.55	0.000
Planning investment	5	35241.3	7048.3	33.00	0.000
Error	200	42721.5	213.6		
Total	215	128013.5			

Chapter 3
A Spatial Garbage-can Model[1]

1 The City as an Organized Anarchy

The urban development, or spatial, process is composed of at least two sets of interrelated spatial decisions: investments in facilities and activities taking place in and between these facilities. In addition, there exists a set of rules, formal/informal and spatial/non-spatial, as the constraints imposed on the discretion of these decisions. There are of course many interacting actors making these decisions. It should be arguably true that cities are collectives of accumulated stock of such facilities, resulting from numerous interacting development decisions made by both the public and private sectors. These decisions are interrelated functionally, geographically, and institutionally. Various activities that take place in cities are affected by the locations, densities, and types of these developments, and influence, in return, where development decisions are implemented, when, and how. There is no apparent order and collective intention as to how these decisions are made and how they interact with each other. Modeling such mechanisms based on a conceptually sound framework may help not only understand how the urban development process comes about, but also provide useful insights into how to make effective plans for the process.

Traditional transportation/land-use mathematical models treat all the actors of these decisions, such as households and landowners, the same and apply statistical techniques, such as regression analysis, to construct and calibrate an aggregate, representative behavioral model to fit the empirical data. Though these models are useful to some extent in making forecasts about the urban development process, the underlying mechanisms of how these actors interact in cities and how individual differences play out in the evolution of urban development are largely ignored.

The recent surge of the agent-based modeling approach provides a useful alternative for urban modeling, thanks to the advance of computing technology, in that the spatial interaction among these actors is explicitly recognized and the emerging properties of urban spatial evolution are simulated, observed, and interpreted (e.g., Parker et al., 2003; Benenson and Torrens, 2004). Though the agent-based modeling approach to urban phenomena looks promising, most works in this line of research focus on the investment decisions of cities, such as where and what type of land use to develop, ignoring activities decisions of the

---

[1] This chapter has been published in *Environment and Planning B: Planning and Design* 2006, Vol. 33, pages 141–56.

actors as to where and what actions to take. The model presented in this book is to provide a simulation framework where both investments and activities decisions and their interactions are accounted for, given some institutional structures that set the constraints for how these decisions interact. The model presented is by no means complete in modeling urban phenomena, but shows how investments and activities decisions within some institutional structures can be blended into a coherent whole that captures the essence of the urban development process.

To elaborate the urban development process in more detail, consider first investments decisions. The complexity of intertwined development decisions defies any theoretical explanation that focuses only on orderly sequences, but we can at least understand the process by viewing the emergent development pattern as derived from the interplay among five almost independent streams of elements; namely decision-makers, solutions, problems, decision situations, and locations (e.g., Cohen et al., 1972). Decision-makers are actors or developers in the public or private sector who seek appropriate lands to develop. Solutions are lands and capitals or any other resources that can help realize the development decisions. Problems are the gaps between what decision-makers anticipate and what the current status of the situations is under consideration. Decision situations are occasions where development decisions are attended to and may or may not be made. Locations are associated with lands where developed facilities are built. An emergent development decision is derived from a seemingly random meeting of decision-makers, solutions, problems, and locations in a particular decision situation where all the other four elements happen to match each other to reach a consensus among the decision-makers involved. A developer might initially have lands available, but would not know what to do about them. When opportunities arise, such as low interest rates, emerged accessibility to major streets, and increased land values, the developer with other participating partners, such as landowners, might decide in a meeting to develop the land in that particular location in the hope to yield profits. There is no clear, definite, and causal relationship between the elements, due to the complexity of the interaction among them. Solutions might already exist before problems would arise at later times. Decision-makers look for work. Problems look for decision situations where they could be discussed.

Now consider activities decisions. Cities are full of changing events, which can be seen as changes in status quo. Events trigger activities. The events of initiatives of services provided by business owners affect households to determine where to locate, which store to go to, where to work, which restaurant to dine in, which movies to go to, which hospital to visit, which route to take, and which school to attend, to name just a few. Each emergent activity, routine or non-routine, is also derived from a complex of intertwined decision-makers, solutions, problems, decision situations, and locations. In deciding where to shop and what to buy, for example, the household might first have funds available and be looking for stores offering different goods in various locations. With traveling capability through network facilities and in a particular store, he or she would select a particular good with a reasonable price that meets his or her needs, and an exchange decision is made. When decision-makers, solutions, problems, and decision situations meet in a seemingly random form in a particular decision situation, an activity decision may or may not be made, depending on whether the four elements match each other in that particular decision situation. The crux is that there is no clear, definite, and causal relationship between the five elements, due to the complexity of the interaction among them. Each stream of elements seems independent of the others. Chances reign in part in the occurrences of such events and thus the making of activities decisions.

Investments decisions and activities decisions interact with each other. A successful highway investment would attract more travel activities of trips, which in turn affect the land uses near the interchanges located along the highway. The traditional dilemma of transportation and land-use planning is a case in point.

Given the same interpretational elements of how investments and activities decisions emerge, at a more fundamental level, the urban development process as a whole can be characterized by decision-makers, solutions, problems, and locations meeting in particular decision situations, and something happens, whether a development of facilities or an initiative of activities. Note that investments and activities decisions are constrained by a set of formal or informal rules or institutions. Zoning is a good example. It specifies what type of development is allowed where and with what densities, which in turn determines what activities can be carried out in that particular location. For example, in a residential zone, only apartments or similar facilities can be built for dwelling purposes, with other uses prohibited.

With such a simplified conception of the urban development process in mind, the simulation presented in the present book is grounded on the presumption that a city can be viewed as an organized anarchy of loosely coupled components where five streams of elements, including decision situations, decision-makers, problems, solutions, and locations, interact in an unpredictable way in time within certain organizational or institutional structures. Decision situations and choice opportunities as well as problems and issues are used interchangeably. This conception is based on Cohen et al.'s (1972) garbage-can model of organizational choice behavior. Though the garbage-can model was created to explain descriptively how decisions are made in organizations, its framework is being applied in other complex systems, mainly in public administration of political systems, where the interaction of the elements in these systems seems random and chaotic (e.g., Kingdon, 2003). Unlike cities, there is no consideration, however, of spatial elements in these complex systems, such as agenda setting in a political system.

With the simplified mindset about the urban development process, I formulate a simulation about the dynamics of the spatial evolution of the city based on the garbage-can model, which will be called spatial garbage can or SGC model. I treat each actor as a decision-maker who encounters a stream of problems, such as where to shop or look for housing; a stream of solutions so that these problems can be attached to suitable solutions, such as shopping malls and apartments; a stream of decision situations where decisions are made, such as regular meetings and informal encounters with colleagues; and a stream of locations where activities or investments might be located as a result of decisions. This conception is arguably a too simplified view of the city, but rather than decomposing the urban system into independent, functional parts as most traditional models usually do or regard the actors and their environment as separate entities, the simulation attempts to blend all the seemingly unrelated elements into a coherent framework through which interesting, counterintuitive phenomena could be uncovered. Therefore, the present chapter focuses on how urban dynamics can be perceived descriptively, rather than how we should plan for improving situations. Such attempts are reported elsewhere based on the original garbage-can model (e.g., Lai 1998, 2003), and will be made in the future based on the proposed SGC model.

The present chapter will construct the elements of this simulation framework in sequence and report the results. Section 2 describes the garbage-can model. Section 3 explains how the spatial elements can be incorporated in the garbage-can model. Section 4 reports the design and results of the simulation. Section 5 discusses some implications, possible applications, and future extensions of the SGC model. In particular, suggestions of how planning is defined and incorporated into the SGC model will be discussed. Section 6 concludes.

2 The Garbage-can Model

The original formulation of the garbage-can model of organizational choice considers four independent elements: choice opportunities, solutions, problems, and decision-makers (Cohen et al., 1972). Choice opportunities are situations in which decisions can be made, that is, commitments to actions are taken. In organizations, votes to spend money or signatures on forms to hire or fire persons are examples of choice opportunities. Solutions are actions that might be taken, such as persons who might be hired, tax schedules that might be levied, and land developments that might be approved. Solutions are things that choice opportunities can commit to enact, things we have the capacity to do directly. Problems are issues that are likely to persist and that decision-makers are concerned to resolve, such as homelessness, unfair housing practices, congested highways, or flooding. Note that choice opportunities enact solutions and that they do not solve problems. We cannot merely choose not to have homelessness. We cannot "decide a problem." We can choose to spend money on shelters or to hire social workers, which may or may not affect the persistence of homelessness as a problem. Decision-makers are units of capacity to take action in decision situations (Lai and Hopkins, 1995).

A garbage can is a choice opportunity where the elements meet in a partially unpredictable way. Solutions, problems, and decision-makers are thrown into a garbage can and something happens. There is, however, no simple mapping of decision-makers to problems or of solutions to problems. Further, an organization has many interacting garbage cans, many interacting choice opportunities. The original model was used to investigate universities as an example of "organized anarchy." Structure can be increased from this starting point, however, which makes possible the investigation of a wide range of types and degrees of organizational structure (e.g., Padgett, 1980). Planning and organizational design are at least partially substitutable strategies for affecting organizational decision-making. They are both means for "coordinating" related decisions. Thus the garbage-can model provides a useful starting point for investigating planning in organizations (Lai, 1998, 2003). The major assumption of the model is that the streams of the four elements are independent of each other. Solutions may thus occur before the problems these solutions might resolve are recognized. Choice opportunities may occur because regular meetings yield decision-maker status, independent of whether solutions are available.

With this general formulation, Cohen et al, (1972) ran a simulation addressing four variables: net energy load, access structure, decision structure, and energy distribution. Net energy load is the difference between the total energy required for a problem to be resolved and that available from decision-makers. Different net energy loads, roughly analogous to organizational capacity in the form of decision-makers relative to organizational demand, should yield differences in organizational behavior and outcomes. Access structure is the relationship between problems and choices or choice opportunities. A zero-one matrix defines which problems can be resolved by which choices. Different access structures vary in the number of choices that can resolve particular problems. Decision structure defines which decision-makers can address which choices and thus how the total energy capacity of the organization can be brought to bear in resolving choices.

Cohen et al. (1972) reported their results by focusing on four statistics: decision style, problem activity, problem latency, and decision difficulty. The three decision styles were resolution, oversight, and flight. Resolution meant that a choice taken resolved all the problems that were thrown into the garbage can of that choice opportunity. If a decision was taken for a choice to which no problems were attached, it was classified as oversight. All other situations constituted flight. Cohen et al. were able to demonstrate the sensitivity of organizational behavior to various access structures and decision structures. For example, the decision process was quite sensitive to net energy load. The reader is encouraged to consult Cohen et al. (1972) for the detailed working of the garbage-can model in a computer program written in FORTRAN.

3 Incorporation of Spatial Relationships

Planning in the context of urban development, both physical and social, must acknowledge the significance of spatial effects of association, cooperation, and competition. Recent work on spatial evolution behavior characterized as cellular automata provides one popular alternative for incorporating space in the kinds of simulations developed here. These models represent spatial clusters of cities or regions in either Euclidean or fractal geometry (e.g., Allen and Sanglier, 1981; Batty and Longley, 1994). They tend to view urban change from a global point of view and planners can manipulate parameters or objects in the models in order to affect how cities evolve. The SGC model developed here takes a different spatial perspective of urban processes in that the actors experience urban processes from a local point of view, and intend to solve problems incrementally through making related decisions as will be discussed in more detail in Section 5.

In his recent book based on a metaphor of canoeing on a river, Hopkins (2001) argues for the adoption of the garbage-can model to describe the situations faced by a planner or stream of opportunities model. In that model, decision situations are choices about actions the planner has the capacity, authority, and opportunity to take; issues are things the planner cares about; solutions are things the planner knows how to do; and decision-makers are the people with authority, capacity, and opportunity to take actions. These four streams of elements are floating around in a relatively unstructured way and the chance meeting of these things may lead to decisions and actions. Hopkins explains how the metaphor of canoeing on a river is compared to the stream of opportunities model and how planning situations can be described in this way. A fifth element can be added to the intermingling patterns of the above relatively independent phenomena floating in a stream, namely locations of lands and facilities.

In the traditional spatial modeling concept, from a global point of view, locations where actions are taken are fixed. For example, certain activities, such as shopping mall retailing, are carried out in a particular location, such as a building on a parcel of land in the suburbs. Choice opportunities or decision situations in combination with other elements must be about certain locations so that decisions can be made about investments and activities occurring at these locations. Locations are thus an additional element that becomes available in the model in the same way that problems, issues, and decision situations do. Thus, as Hopkins (2001) argues, "a stream of opportunities model, built on the garbage can model of Cohen et al. (1972), provides one way to think about plans in complex systems: A plan-making situation is a collection of interdependent, indivisible, and irreversible decisions looking for issues; a collection of issues looking for interdependent decision situations in which they might be pertinent; a collection of solutions looking for issues to which they might be an answer; and a collection of planners looking for work." It is also a collection of locations looking for decision situations where these decisions, issues, and actors can be brought to bear.

To make the spatial garbage-can model more concrete, define a decision structure of relationships in terms of a matrix between decision-makers and choice opportunities, an access structure of relationships between problems and choice opportunities, a solution structure between solutions and problems, and a spatial structure between choice opportunities and locations. These zero-one matrices of relationships have the same meaning and range of forms as in the original garbage-can model and are givens external to each simulation run. The meanings of decision structure, access structure, and solution structure are given in the original garbage-can model. For example, assuming that there exist 20 problems and ten choice opportunities, there are three types of constraints in access structures, unsegmented, hierarchical, and specialized, as shown in matrices A_0, A_1, and A_2, respectively. A 1 in the matrices means that the problem in the corresponding row can be attended to in the choice opportunity for the corresponding column, while a 0 means that there is no such relationship. In the unsegmented structure, all active problems have access to any active choice opportunities; in the hierarchical structure, important problems (upper part of the matrix) have access to many choice opportunities; in the specialized structure, each problem has access to only one choice opportunity.

	Choice opportunities		
Problems	1111111111	1111111111	1000000000
	1111111111	1111111111	1000000000
	1111111111	0111111111	0100000000
	1111111111	0111111111	0100000000
	1111111111	0011111111	0010000000
	1111111111	0011111111	0010000000
	1111111111	0001111111	0001000000
	1111111111	0001111111	0001000000
$A_0=$	1111111111 $A_1=$	0000111111 $A_2=$	0000100000
	1111111111	0000111111	0000100000
	1111111111	0000011111	0000010000
	1111111111	0000011111	0000010000
	1111111111	0000001111	0000001000
	1111111111	0000001111	0000001000
	1111111111	0000000111	0000000100
	1111111111	0000000111	0000000100
	1111111111	0000000011	0000000010
	1111111111	0000000011	0000000010
	1111111111	0000000001	0000000001
	1111111111	0000000001	0000000001

Similarly, the spatial structure can be constructed by the zero-one matrices as shown in B_0, B_1, and B_2. A 1 in these matrices means that a choice opportunity, such as deciding to construct a sewer line, can occur at a particular location, such as a transportation corridor, while a 0 indicates that such association does not exist.

		Locations				
Choices		1111111111		1111111111		1000000000
		1111111111		0111111111		0100000000
		1111111111		0011111111		0010000000
		1111111111		0001111111		0001000000
	$B_0 =$	1111111111	$B_1 =$	0000111111	$B_2 =$	0000100000
		1111111111		0000011111		0000010000
		1111111111		0000001111		0000001000
		1111111111		0000000111		0000000100
		1111111111		0000000011		0000000010
		1111111111		0000000001		0000000001

To "visualize" the SGC model and to make the concept more concrete, consider a grid system where the five elements flow to and mix with each other (see Figure 3.1). Note that the grid system does not have any physical meanings. It is only created for visualization purposes for the process. There are five types of elements: decision situations (choice opportunities), decision-makers, solutions, issues (problems), and locations; with access structure linking issues to decision situations, solution structure linking solutions to problems, decision structure linking decision-makers to choice opportunities, and spatial structure linking choice opportunities to locations. At each time step, an element of each type emerges, located randomly in the grid system, and these elements flow randomly to four different directions, one cell further for the next time step. When the supply of energy provided collectively by decision-makers, solutions, and locations, exceeds the demand required collectively by problems and choice opportunities at a particular location for a particular choice opportunity, a decision is made. If there are problems associated with the choice opportunities and the criterion of energy requirement is met, these problems are then solved.

Cities are complex spatial systems where actors interact with each other spatially, and spontaneous order thus emerges regardless of the patterns of such interaction (Webster and Lai, 2003). Viewing the complex spatial systems of cities as collections of elements interacting in an unpredictable, random way, I formulate a framework as described above for computer simulations to examine the effects of the structures on the system's behavior. Put differently, following Cohen et al.'s (1972) garbage-can model, I consider the complex spatial system as a loosely coupled organization composed of five independent streams of elements: solutions, problems, decision-makers, decision situations, and locations (see Figure 3.1). These random walk elements interact with each other in the two-dimensional grid system, and decisions may get made. Though the assumption of randomness of the five interacting streams might be too strong, the observation that the dynamics of the complex spatial system is usually considered as chaotic supports, at least partially, such a conception. Concrete examples as manifested in the SGC model are found in many occasions in the city as sketched in Section 1.

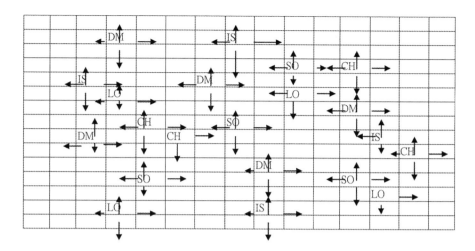

Figure 3.1 A visual representation of the SGC model

4 Simulation Design and Results

A simulation design of Graeco-Latin Square (Kirk, 1982) was run using the formulation discussed in the previous section. In particular, the grid system was composed of 50×50 cells, with 500 decision-makers and 500 locations randomly occupying these cells initially. Solutions, problems, and choice opportunities were added to the system, one of each at a time, for the first 500 time steps. Decision-makers, solutions, and locations were energy suppliers, while problems and choice opportunities were energy demanders. When at least each of the five elements met in a particular cell and the amount of energy supply associated with these elements was greater than that of energy demand, a decision was made. The associated problem(s) was solved and disappeared, and so did the associated choice opportunity (opportunities).

To visualize the temporal trajectories of the evolution of the complex spatial system, define a three-dimensional energy landscape space where the total net energy, the number of decisions made, and the number of problems solved form the three axes, as shown in Figure 3.2. The total net energy of the system is computed by summing up all the energy supplied and subtracting all the energy needed across all elements at a time step. In Figure 3.2, curves A and B represent two dynamic trajectories of the complex spatial system in the energy landscape.

The amount of energy supply was given randomly from 0 to 1 to each solution. The amounts of energy supplied by each decision-maker and location were set to 0.55 and 2.55, respectively, while the amounts of energy demanded by each problem and choice opportunity were both set to 1.1. These numbers were chosen according to Cohen et al.'s (1972) original simulation, except that the energy

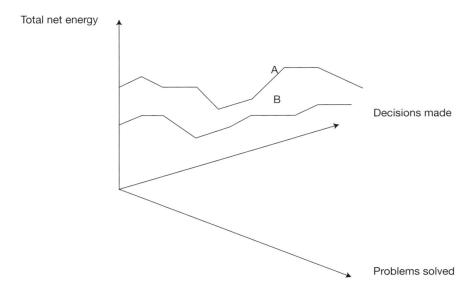

Figure 3.2   System trajectories in time in the energy landscape

supplied by each location was set to a higher value to reflect the importance of this element. Since these numbers were fixed in all simulations in the research design and thus not treated as a control variable, a different set of these numbers would not have affected the simulation results. Total net energy refers to the difference between the total amounts of energy associated with all demanders and suppliers. The simulation was programmed using Visual Basic and run on a Windows 2000 platform.

Figures 3.3 to 3.6 show the preliminary results from a pilot simulation based on the total net energy-time plot of the system. Figure 3.3 shows the result run for the unsegmented type of constraint in access, solution, decision, and spatial structures. Figure 3.4 is for the hierarchic type of constraint in structures. Figure 3.5 is for the specialized type of constraint in structures. Figure 3.6 is for random type of constraint in structures. Each simulation was run for 20,000 time steps. Note that for each total net energy-time plot, we can compute statistically an asymptotic value that sets approximately the upper limit for the curve.

All trajectories showed skewed "v" shape curves in that the total net energy decreased dramatically in the early time steps, and then regained its amount slowly in later time steps. This characteristic "v" shape results mainly from the inflow pattern of the elements in that problems and decision situations arrive initially, causing a drop in the total net energy because few decisions are made to reduce energy demand in the early stage. When more decisions are made and problems solved in later time steps, the system regains its total net energy because demand for energy levels decreases. A change in the pattern of arrival of problems and decision

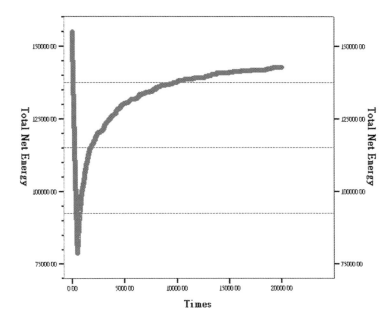

Figure 3.3 Total net energy-time plot for unsegmented structures

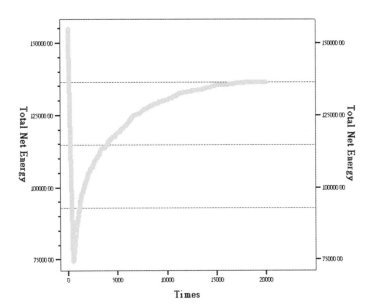

Figure 3.4 Total net energy-time plot for hierarchic structures

50   *Urban Complexity and Planning*

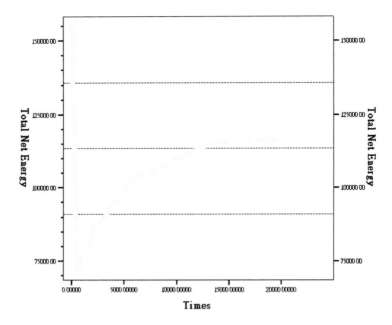

Figure 3.5   Total net energy-time plot for specialized structures

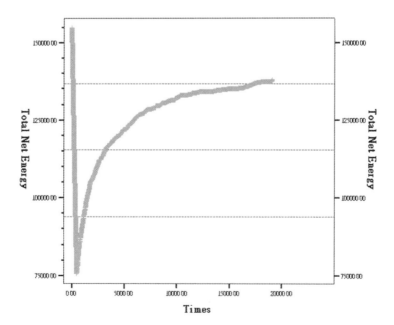

Figure 3.6   Total net energy-time plot for random structures

situations or a change in the access or decision structures can be considered as a disturbance as will be discussed in more detail in Section 5. The only difference between these curves was the steepness of the "v" curves after the lowest point had been reached. The "v" curves for the unsegmented structures seemed the steepest among all four structures, while those for the specialized structures were the flattest. Energy demanders, including problems and choice opportunities waiting to be solved and made, were added to the system incrementally, decreasing the amount of the total net energy sharply in the beginning. At later time steps, when sufficient numbers of elements were added to the system resulting in decision-making being more likely, the total net energy increased because more and more decisions were made and problems solved, which in turn lessened the demand for energy. Structural constraints did seem to affect the shapes of the trajectories. In particular, more stringent structural constraints rendered the system less capable of adapting to the inflow of disturbances of problems, choice opportunities, and solutions. Put differently, more stringent structural constraints, such as the specialized structural type, reduce the likelihoods that the five elements meet with each other and thus decrease the opportunities of making decisions to solve problems. The system becomes more insensitive to the effects of the inflow of elements. In the real world, this observation can be likened by the contrast between a free development market and a regulated development market. In the free development market where exchanges are not constrained, reminiscent of an unsegmented structural type, the effects of external disturbances can be absorbed more quickly by the system, making it more resilient than the regulated one. The observation that more stringent structural constraints render the system less able to adapt seems to be also implied by the original garbage-can model in that the specialized access structure results in a higher proportion of choice opportunities where decisions are made only to resolve problems, which is more difficult than other types of decision style (Cohen et al., 1972).

For completeness, I designed a simulation of a Graeco-Latin Square of 16 orthogonal combinations of the four types of constraints (unsegmented, specialized, hierarchic, and random) with respect to the four structures (access, spatial, solution, and decision structures). The 16 orthogonal combinations of the constraint types with respect to the four structural variables are given in Table 3.1. Unsegmented, specialized, hierarchic, and random constraints are denoted as 1, 2, 3, and 4, respectively. A random constraint means that the 1s in a matrix are randomly assigned to the elements in that matrix.

A 20,000 time-step simulation was conducted for each of the 16 combinations of the constraint types with respect to the four structural variables shown in Table 3.1. For each of such simulation runs, I was able to compute, using the SPSS statistics package, the asymptotic value of the total net energy at the end of 20,000 time steps as an upper limit. These values are given in the four-factorial design of the 4×4 Graeco-Latin Square as shown in Table 3.2. Note that a, b, c, and d denote access structure, spatial structure, solution structure, and decision structure, respectively, and that 1, 2, 3, and 4 denote unsegmented constraint, specialized constraint, hierarchic constraint, and random constraints, respectively. For example, d_2 represents the decision structure with a specialized constraint. The number in each cell represents the asymptotic value of the total net energy for the simulation after 20,000 time steps, given the combination of different structures and constraints. For example, the number of 154783 in the cell of a_1b_3 in row 2 (c_2) and column 2 (d_2) is the total net energy of the simulation result considering the combination of access (a), spatial (b), solution (c), and decision (d) structures with unsegmented (1), hierarchic (3), specialized (2), and specialized (2) constraints, respectively, and coded as 1322 in Table 3.1.

Following Kirk's (1982, pp. 314–6) computational procedure for a 4×4 Latin Square, I was able to compute the ANOVA table for this design as shown in Table 3.3. Note that since there is only one observation in each cell, the significance of the effect of the interaction term cannot be tested.

According to the ANOVA table, the main effect of access structure was statistically significant at $p < 0.05$, while the main effects of the other three structures were insignificant. We can conclude that the relationship between problem and choice opportunities is of paramount importance in determining how the system behaves, while spatial structure, solution structure, and decision structure do not affect the performance of the system in terms of the total net energy. This conclusion is made partly because problems and choice opportunities are the only two energy demanders, and the relational structure between the two elements, that is, the access structure, plays a central role in determining whether a decision is made in a particular choice opportunity and the associated problems

Table 3.1 Combinations of constraint types with respect to structural variables

Access structure	Spatial structure	Solution structure	Decision structure
1	1	1	1
2	4	2	1
3	2	3	1
4	3	4	1
2	2	1	2
1	3	2	2
4	1	3	2
3	4	4	2
3	3	1	3
4	2	2	3
1	4	3	3
2	1	4	3
4	4	1	4
3	1	2	4
2	3	3	4
1	2	4	4

resolved to reduce the amount of energy demand, thus increasing the amount of total net energy. As depicted earlier, a change in energy levels set initially would not change the simulation result because these values are constant across all combinations of structures in the simulations. Similarly, different types of access structure would not change the result as long as they and other structural constraints are held as constant throughout the simulations. The implications of this result will be elaborated in more detail in Sections 5 and 6.

Table 3.2   The four-factorial design of the 4×4 Graeco-Latin Square

	d_1	d_2	d_3	d_4
c_1	a_1b_1 143440	a_2b_2 117499	a_3b_3 135603	a_4b_4 137877
c_2	a_2b_4 135417	a_1b_3 154783	a_4b_2 138176	a_3b_1 134963
c_3	a_3b_2 137576	a_4b_1 137106	a_1b_4 141200	a_2b_3 117070
c_4	a_4b_3 135603	a_3b_4 131700	a_2b_1 117004	a_1b_2 137702

Table 3.3   The ANOVA table for the Graeco-Latin Square design

Source	SS	df	MS	F
Access structure (a)	1062967500	3	354322500	15.1420[†]
Spatial structure (b)	43093200	3	14364400	0.6139
Solution structure (c)	233988500	3	77996167	3.3333
Decision structure (d)	87632700	3	29210900	1.2483
Residual	70199800	3	23399933	
Total	1497881700	15		

Note: [†]Significant at $p < 0.05$.

5   Discussion

The original garbage-can model is concerned with decision-making in an organizational setting. It differs from traditional decision theory in that it is descriptive rather than normative. It is grounded on limited rationality of decision-making rather than perfect rationality. It addresses organizational choice behavior rather than individuals making decisions. It tries to make sense of the seemingly chaotic, collective processes of fragmented decision-making in an organizational setting where central planning is absent. In sum, it describes how an organized anarchy adapts to the changing environment in order to survive, albeit without central planning.

The intermixing of the elements in the garbage-can model is not purely random; there are some structures imposed on their chance meeting, namely access structures and decision structures. An access structure determines which problem can be attended to in which decision situation, while a decision structure specifies which decision-maker can join which decision situations to make decisions. The combination of the two can be viewed as an institutional structure that allocates the rights as to which decision-maker has what authority to resolve which problem through which decision situation. Thus a decision-maker in the context of the garbage-can model is not exposed to any solutions, any options. His or her discretion of making decisions is somewhat constrained.

The extension of the garbage-can model to a spatial context, as proposed in this book, is not meant to model planning behavior itself, but to model urban development processes. These two phenomena beg two different theoretical underpinnings, but elaborating on the distinction between the two is beyond the scope of the book. Put simply, the SGC model can be treated as a descriptive manifestation of how urban spatial dynamics evolves, while a planning theory can be narrowly thought of as a behavioral theory of how to make interdependent decisions, or plans. Given this simple distinction, we can thus provide a theoretical basis, using the SGC model, on which effectiveness of different planning theories can be examined. For example, is incrementalism (focusing on no rationality) that renders planning as useless, as suggested by some scholars in public administration, more effective in solving urban problems than comprehensive rationalism (focusing on perfect rationality), as suggested by conventional planning theorists? By imposing different degrees of structure or control on the dynamics of the SGC model representing the incremental-rational spectrum, we might find that something in between the two extremes (focusing on bounded rationality) might be more effective (Hopkins, 2001). Conventional planning decision-making models are essentially normative and based on perfect rationality, by assuming that actors have clear preferences, known technology, and a complete set of alternatives to choose from; while the garbage-can model is in effect descriptive and based on bounded rationality in that actors' preferences are problematic, technology is unclear, and alternatives are created. That is, the garbage-can model is designed based on empirical observations on how organizations *do* make decisions, rather than how they *should* make decisions. From a descriptive point of view, the garbage-can model is therefore behaviorally more telling than conventional, normative planning decision-making models. In making a development decision, can the developer know for certain what other actors would do when and where, and how, they interact? In addition, conventional planning theories do not seem to take into account the differences among behaviors of spatially disaggregate actors because the urban models based on which these theories are developed tend to assume homogeneous actors. The SGC model proposed here decomposes the urban system into individual actors and related elements that mimic the real world situations. Loosely speaking, the SGC model is reminiscent of an agent-based modeling approach to urban phenomena, so the main logic of such an approach in contrast to the traditional, mathematical urban modeling approach applies here (e.g., Parker et al., 2003; Benenson and Torrens, 2004).

The mechanisms underlying the model might sound counterintuitive at first to traditional decision theorists and planners, but empirical findings have shown that the model at least captures well the essence of the fragmented agenda setting processes in the federal government of the US (e.g., Kingdon, 2003). Whether this same theoretical framework works empirically for the urban development process remains as an interesting future research question, but I suspect that, as described in Section 1, cities could be viewed as spatial organized anarchies characterized by the garbage-can decision processes. For example, if we replace the agendas of a political system in Kingdon's model of agenda setting with development decisions of an urban system, some of Kingdon's explanations of how agendas emerge in a complex system could be applied to describe, at least in part, how development decisions emerge in the urban development process. For example, a city manager may have development proposals available looking for a "policy window" as a decision situation comes up, so that a development project is approved. However, a crucial distinction between an agenda and a physical facility is reversibility in that the cost of reversing an agenda might be much lower than reversing a building. Regardless, the dynamic processes of the two systems might share some common theoretical underpinnings characterized by the garbage-can model.

If my presumption is true as set out in Section 1, that cities are spatial, organized anarchies, we can start looking for ways to explain plan-making behavior consistent with the garbage-can notions. Lai (1998, 2003) has tried to do so in an organizational, not spatial, setting. In these two works based on the original garbage-can model, he considered planning as predicting the occurrences of the upcoming choice opportunities and intentionally selecting the ones that maximize the net energies in the associated decisions. Energy used in the SGC model could be explained as benefits, profits, revenues, utilities, labors, capitals, or any other measurable resources in urban development situations. This strategy of incorporating planning into the garbage-can model is consistent with the idea that making plans implies evaluating related decisions and acting accordingly in light of the relationship between current and future decisions (Hopkins, 2001).

Decision-making focuses on choosing the best alternative from a given set, while planning, narrowly defined here, arranges for a contingent path of related decisions in time and space, or linked decisions. Though decision theorists recognize the importance of considering linked decisions, little has been said on how and under what situations a set of linked decisions should be analyzed (Keeney, 2004). Planning is thus obviously more challenging than decision-making because it deals with uncertainties, values, and conflicting objectives much more complex than the latter.

Given this narrow definition of planning, there are at least two ways for the planner to make progress in the SGC model to affect the system's performance.

On the one hand, the planner could focus on anticipating possibilities of the occurrences of choice opportunities, arranging them in time and space before taking the first action; that is, making plans before acting. For example, to resolve a transportation/land-use problem in an urban area where negative externalities pervade, such as congestion and pollution, the planner could look for decision situations where decisions can be made regarding the construction of transportation networks that could alleviate the congestion issues, while taking into account the decision situations where rezoning is possible to mitigate the pollution issues. He or she could even intentionally create other decision situations, such as budgeting of appropriate timing, if necessary, to address the pressing issues by persuading relevant governmental officials, citizens, and developers to resolve collaboratively other problems in sequence or jointly, leading to resolution of the two problems under consideration. On the other hand, the planner could make changes in institutional structures to reassign rights to limit actions, which in turn affects the outcome of the urban development process. For example, to create walkable communities of a city as claimed by the New Urbanist to increase social capital, changes in institutional structures might be a more effective means than physical designs. We could enhance social equity, not simply by providing approximately equal, physical accessibility to streets, but by allocating rights-of-way to all individuals equitably through regulations so all individuals have approximately equal rights to travel through the network, leading in turn to approximately equal authorities using facilities through accessibility and thus approximately equal chances of carrying out activities to meet personal needs. The implication is, as derived from the simulation result, that spatial issues, such as the transportation/land-use problems and the New Urbanist's claim of walkable communities, could be addressed more effectively through design of institutional structures than merely focusing on physical layouts. Note that the institutional structures implied by the unsegmented, specialized, hierarchic, and random structural types do not fully carry realistic connotations in the simulation. They are designed mainly to distinguish different patterns of structures and test the significance of structural effects on the system's evolutionary outcomes. It is arguably true that zoning and permit systems are sufficiently distinct and lead to different patterns of urban development.

The "v" shape of the trajectories in the energy landscape can be seen as a result from external disturbances to the system. When problems, choice opportunities, and solutions are added to the system incrementally, this sequence of elements flowing into the system can be considered as external disturbances to the system, resulting in a dramatic drop in the total net energy. Eventually, when decisions are being made and problems solved, the system regains its stability to sustain itself to function smoothly again, as evidenced by the slow increase asymptotically in the total net energy to a steady level. This behavioral characteristic can be used to model a wide range of external disturbances to the complex spatial system, such as changes in institutional structures through regulation implementations. When the land control measure of an urban area is shifted from zoning to permit systems, the system may undergo a sea change in the underlying structures of the system, such as access structure, spatial structure, solution structure, and decision structure, perhaps from a hierarchic to random structural type. The random nature of the interaction among the elements remains, however, the same. We can test using the SGC model how well the system adapts to these disturbances to sustain its level of total net energy, given these structural changes, and what structural schemes of the system would result in minimum disturbances in terms of energy fluctuations.

Finally, the simulations presented here and elsewhere by Lai (1998, 2003) assume that the structural constraints are fixed and given externally, limiting the explanatory power of the SGC model. Regulations emerge as cities evolve, so it is arguably true that these structures co-evolve with the system being simulated. That is, these structures are at present, fixed at the unsegmented, specialized, hierarchic, and random types. If left to be co-evolving with the system, the spatial structure might result in spontaneous order as a form of spatial correlation of decision situations. Similar effects might happen if we introduce the notion of transaction cost in making decisions in garbage cans. That is, if decisions are costly in combining decision-makers, problems, solutions, decision situations, and locations, reducing that cost is desirable, resulting in systematic, rather than random, behaviors of actors. These systematic behaviors might be reflected in the structural patterns in the constraints in the form of association, cooperation, or even competition if these structures are left to co-evolve with the system. However, the underlying chance meeting characteristic among the elements remains the same. Lai (2003) extended the garbage-can model into a consideration of decision cost, similar to the notion of transaction cost in the combination of elements, based on a three-factorial simulation design, and the results showed that all three factors, that is planning investment, decision cost, and problem disutility, matter in affecting the system's behavior. However, transaction cost is more pertinent to the spatial context formulated here (Webster and Lai, 2003), and can be incorporated into the model in the future.

6 Conclusions

Traditional and recent spatial modeling considers adaptive actors separately from their environment. In the simulation presented here, the spatial elements of the environment and the actors are blended into a partially random formulation so that they co-evolve. The SGC model provides a new way of looking at the urban spatial process. Its descriptive validity begs further deductive and empirical investigations, but the model serves as a starting point for much richer interpretations of the urban spatial process than can be depicted here. The simulation results indicate that different structures have different effects on the total net energy of the system. In particular, the relationship between problems and choice opportunities, reminiscent of constraints of institutions, dominates the outcomes, while the effects of spatial, solution, and decision structures are insignificant. One would expect that the spatial structure, highly correlated to the physical environment, matters in the system, but the simulation results suggest that it does not. This counterintuitive finding may prompt a reconsideration of the extent to which the physical environment can improve human conditions, and to which the institutional structures can be helpful.

Acknowledgements

The conception of the SGC model presented in this work was initiated when the author was a visitor at Centre of Advanced Spatial Analysis (CASA) of University College London in 2001. The author is grateful to the assistance provided by CASA. The author thanks Professor Lewis Hopkins of the Department of Urban and Regional Planning at the University of Illinois at Urbana-Champaign for his helpful clarification of the ideas and examples in developing the SGC model. The research is partially funded by the National Science of Council of the Republic of China (NSC92-2415-H-305-008). The author also thanks Chi-Hsu Yeh and Kenny Perng for their assistance in statistical analysis and computer programming, respectively. An earlier version of the book was presented at the Centennial Meeting of the Association of American Geographers and at the Department of Urban and Regional Planning at the University of Illinois at Urbana-Champaign in 2004. The author is grateful to three anonymous reviewers for their very constructive comments.

References

Allen, P.M., and M. Sanglier. 1981. "Urban evolution, self-organization, and Decision-making." *Environment and Planning* A 13: 167–83.
Batty, M., and P. Longley. 1994. *Fractal Cities*. Academic Press, New York.
Benenson, I., and P.M. Torrens. 2004. *Geosimulation: Automata-Based Modeling of Urban Phenomena*. John Wiley & Sons, West Sussex, England.
Cohen, M.D., J.G. March., and J.P. Olsen. 1972. "A garbage can model of organizational choice." *Administrative Science Quarterly* 17: 1–25.
Hopkins, L.D. 2001. *Urban Development: The Logic of Making Plans*. Island Press, Washington.
Keeney, R.L. 2004. "Making better decisions." *Decision Analysis* 1(4): 193–204.
Kingdon, J.W. 2003. *Agendas, Alternatives, and Public Policies*. Longman, New York.
Kirk, R.E. 1982. *Experimental Design: Procedures for the Behavioral Sciences*. Brooks/Cole, Monterey, CA.
Lai, S-K. 1998. "From organized anarchy to controlled structure: effects of planning on the garbage-can decision processes." *Environment and Planning* B 25: 85–102.

Lai, S-K. 2003. "Effects of planning on the garbage-can decision processes: a reformulation and extension." *Environment and Planning* B 30(3): 379–89.

Lai, S-K., and L.D. Hopkins. 1995. "Planning in complex, spatial, temporal systems: a simulation framework." Paper presented at the Association of Collegiate Schools of Planning, Detroit.

Padgett, J.F. 1980. "Managing garbage can hierarchies." *Administrative Science Quarterly* 25: 583–604.

Parker, D.C., S.M. Manson, M.A. Janssen, M.J. Hoffmann, and P. Deadman. 2003. "Multi-agent systems for the simulation of land-use and land-cover change: a review." *Annals of American Association of Geographers* 93(2): 314–37.

Webster, C., L.W-C. Lai. 2003. *Property Rights, Planning and Markets: Managing Spontaneous Cities*. Edward Elgar, Northampton, MA.

Chapter 4
An Agent-based Approach to Comparing Institutional and Spatial Changes in the Self-organizing City

1 Introduction

Complexity theory has been a new paradigm to study urban development since the founding of the Santa Fe Institute in the 1980s. Considering the interaction of different types of agents in urban development, it can simulate many aspects of urban development that are characterized by cities in the real world and explain urban phenomena that cannot be described or solved by traditional mathematical models. Although the models based on complexity theory could display self-organization to some extent, no model of complexity, however, can perfectly restore the process or explain the mechanism of urban development until now. That is mainly because a city is a very complex system, which comprises almost an infinite number of elements and agents, interacting with each other. Therefore, a conceptual framework rather than a large and comprehensive model is needed to simulate and explain urban development in research.

The spatial garbage-can model (SGCM) looks at urban development from a particular perspective. It considers cities as collectives of accumulated stocks of buildings, which result from numerous interacting development decisions made both by the public and private sectors. These decisions are interrelated functionally, geographically, and institutionally (Lai, 2006). It also views the emergent development pattern as being derived from the interplay among five almost independent streams of elements, namely decision-makers, solutions, problems, decision situations, and locations (see, e.g., Cohen et al., 1972). Those five elements flow and mix with each other. In specific occasions, decisions are made and activities take place. The structural constraints (to be explained shortly) are the crux in determining whether decision can be made through the interactions of agents, which move according to some rules in a fictitious hyper-space, similar to the concept of agent-based modeling (ABS). What differentiates mostly the SGCM from traditional urban development models is that the former focuses mainly on the impact of structural constraints, such as the institutional and spatial designs, on urban development, while the latter on the explanation of the patterns and changes of urban space, without regard to intangible impacts, such as institutions.

In the previous SGCM simulation, the structural constraints, reminiscent of institutions to some extent, were given externally and fixed (Lai, 2006), which actually evolve slowly over time in the real world (North, 1998). This design has limited the validity of the simulation in relation to reality. Lai (2006) proposed that the structural constraints may evolve with the system, reminiscent of the emergence of regulations in cities. In the present chapter, we examine this proposition by integrating the concept of self-organization or evolution of the system and ABM into a computer experiment. More specifically, we intend to test two hypotheses:

1. The structural constraints would evolve with the system when they are not given externally and fixed; they self-organize themselves.
2. The impact of institutional design on urban development is more significant than that of spatial design in the self-organizing system.

In Section 2, we review some ideas about Agent-based Modeling and the spatial garbage-can model. In Section 3, we depict the research design, followed by the simulation results in Section 4. In Section 5, we conclude.

2 Literature Review

2.1 Agent-based Modeling in Urban Studies

The history of ABM can be traced back to the von Neumann machine and cellular automata (von Neumann, 1966). After that, game of life (Conway, 1970) was developed with similar ideas except that interesting dynamic patterns were found. Distinct from cellular automata, ABM in its current form enables agents to move across cells rather than being fixed in space. The basic characteristics for an agent include: (1) activity: agents can decide and act; (2) autonomy: agents have the ability to decide by themselves; (3) interaction: agents can interact with each other; (4) sociality: agents can communicate with each other at short distance; (5) responsiveness: agents can act according to their surrounding environment; (6) durative: the agents' actions will continue if not stopped by the modeler(s); (7) adaptability: agents can grow smarter by learning; and (8) mobility: agents can move unconditionally within the system (Batty, 2003).

Now ABM is becoming the dominant paradigm in social simulations due primarily to its priority on reflecting agents' choices in complex systems. Researchers employed ABM for planning support and decision-making on urban policies. One example was a role-playing approach introduced by Ligtenberg, in which a complex spatial system including a multi-actor spatial planning process can be simulated for spatial planning support (Ligtenberg, 2001). Furthermore, in regard to the highly complex process of making urban policy decisions, a multi-agent paradigm has been built to develop an intelligent and flexible planning support system, within which three types of agents, including interface agents who improve the user-system interaction, tool agents to support the use and management of models, and domain agents to provide access to specialized knowledge, were created (Saarloos et al., 2008). Researchers also utilize ABM to simulate urban development processes. As described by a CityDev model, the economic activities of agents (e.g., family, industrial firms, and developers) that produce goods by using other goods and trade their goods on the markets have been simulated to visualize urban development processes resulting from urban policies (Semboloni et al., 2004).

In recent years, ABM has been widely applied in the study of land development. For example, using ABM, Benenson (1998) and Benenson et al. (2002) simulated the self-organization of urban development and the spatial differentiation of residence based on the data of economic development, real estate prices, and cultural identification. Ligtenberg (2001) created an integrated model of ABM and CA with consideration of the impacts of plans led by the local government. Li et al. (2007) simulated the urban development of Haizhu District in Guangzhou China. Hanley and Hopkins (2007) analyzed the choice of location and timing of single-family house development, taking into account the interaction of land owners and land developers.

2.2 Spatial Garbage-can Model (SGCM)

The spatial garbage-can model was first developed by Lai (2006). It adds the element of place and two structural constraints (solution and spatial structures) into the traditional garbage-can model to simulate and explain the process of urban development. The SGCM views cities as organized anarchy. In the system with these organized or regular structures, there are five elements: decision situations, decision-makers, issues (problems), solutions and places (Figure 4.1). These elements flow independently in a hyperspace (Figure 4.2). There is no clear, definite, and causal relationship between the five elements, owing to the complexity of the interaction among them. When all the five elements (at least one of each type) meet in a particular cell and the amount of energy supply associated with these elements is greater than that of energy demanded, a decision is made.

Taking the decision-making in a land development as an example, decisions are unpredictably made in this process. A decision-maker may have usable land at the beginning, but does not know how to use it. When the interest rate decreases or the land value increases due to the construction of new roads, the decision-maker(s) may decide to develop the land to gain profits. That means solutions (land available) may exist before problems (development intended). In addition, a decision made may not result in a resolution of the problem(s). In the decision-making process, problems are sometimes, but not always, solved. New problems will also be brought out after the resolution of some problems.

The SGCM can further explain the occurrence and evolution of urban events. A city comprises all types of continuously changing events, which brings out activities. The supply of public services in cities will influence the activities of families, for instance, the places constructed for housing, shopping, working, walking, recreation, watching movies, hospitals and schools, and so on. No matter whether plans are followed or not, decision-makers, solutions, problems, decision situations and places will interact with each other, and produce complex outcomes. A family will have a budget for shopping, search for the commodities in the stores of different locations, and find the most favorite one(s) in a specific store. The shopping decision relies on the meeting of different elements. When decision-makers, solutions, problems, and locations meet in a specific decision situation, whether a decision can be made will depend first on the structural constraints. Such structural constraints include both formal and informal rules and institutions. An apparent example of such type of structural constraint is zoning, which prescribes what type of development is permitted where, for instance, the location and density of construction. It also demands what type of use is prohibited; for example, facilities other than apartments, town houses, single-family houses or similar residential use are not allowed to be constructed in a residential area.

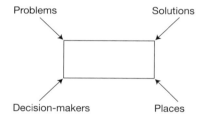

Figure 4.1   Building block of SGCM

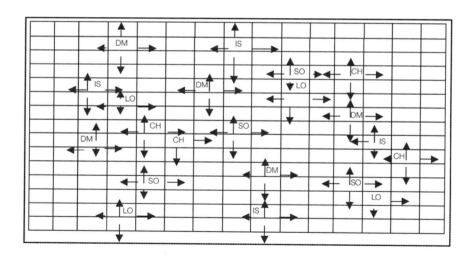

Figure 4.2   Simulation of SGCM

3 Research Design

We set four structural constraints in the simulation of this research: decision structure, access structure, solution structure, and spatial structure. Consistent with the settings in the SGC model, a decision structure of relationship is defined in terms of a 0-1 matrix between decision-makers and choice opportunities, an access structure of relationship between problems and choice opportunities, a solution structure between solutions and problems, and a spatial structure between choice opportunities and locations. The decision structure is reminiscent of an institutional constraint, while the spatial structure represents a spatial constraint. Both of the structures are adaptive in this simulation, capable of evolving with the change in the system over time. The access and solution structures each have three forms of constraint: unsegmented, hierarchical, and specialized as depicted in Section 3.2. These three forms are fixed and do not evolve with the change in the system over time.

3.1 Parameters

We use a grid of 50×50 = 2,500 cells in this computer experiment, in which five types of elements move and interact, including decision situations (choice opportunities), decision-makers, solutions, issues (problems), and locations.

(1) Agents, Grids and Time Frame At the beginning of the simulation, 500 decision-makers and 500 locations are randomly distributed on the grid. At each ensuing time step, a new solution, issue, and decision situation are added into the system. No new elements will be added in when the number of elements of any type reaches 500. The simulation stops at the 2,000th time step.

(2) The Energies of Agents In the spatial garbage-can model, each element is allocated an amount of energy, which represents the relative contribution to make a decision. The energy can have either a positive or a negative value. A positive one indicates the amount of supplied resources, such as time and labor, while a negative one represents the amount of resources demanded. In the present simulation, we use the same energy levels set in the spatial garbage-can model. The amount of energy supplied was given randomly from 0 to 1 for each solution. The amounts of energy supplied by each decision-maker and location were set to 0.55 and 2.55, respectively, and the amounts of energy demanded by each problem and choice opportunity were both set to 1.1. These figures do not correspond to any empirical meanings of decision-making in the real world; they are specified for computational purposes so that generalized observation can be derived from such computation.

(3) ID of the Agents For data structure design purposes, each agent is allocated an ID when it enters into the system. Different types of agents are numbered

separately. For example, a decision-maker and a choice opportunity could both have an ID of ten, symbolizing the tenth decision-maker and the tenth choice opportunity, respectively. However, they will be calculated in different situations and will not cause double counting. In addition to the energy attached, a choice opportunity includes three attributes: decision array, spatial array, and whether a decision has been made. The decision array shows the relationship between decision-makers and choice opportunities, while the spatial array indicates the relationship between choice opportunities and locations. Both of the arrays are composed of strings of 500 numbers with a value of either 0 or 1: 1 means that a decision-maker or location can appear at the corresponding choice opportunity, while 0 means that it cannot. The values of the 500 numbers in the arrays are allocated randomly. The probabilities for the appearance of 0 or 1 are set initially to 0.5 each at the beginning of the simulation. Moreover, whether a decision has been made is also symbolized by 0 or 1: 0 indicates that a decision had not been made, while 1 indicates the opposite.

3.2 Structural Constraint

When at least all the five elements, each of which from a different type, meet in a particular cell and the amount of energy supply associated with these elements is greater than that of energy demand, a decision is made. Whether a decision can be made also depends on the structural constraints. If the value of the corresponding number in the array was 0, a decision cannot be made, meaning that the element cannot appear in the corresponding choice opportunity or location. Otherwise, a decision can be made if the value was 1. The settings for different structural constraints are as follows.

$$A_0 = \begin{bmatrix} 1 & 1 & 1 & 1 & 1 \\ 1 & 1 & 1 & 1 & 1 \\ 1 & 1 & 1 & 1 & 1 \\ 1 & 1 & 1 & 1 & 1 \\ 1 & 1 & 1 & 1 & 1 \end{bmatrix}, A_1 = \begin{bmatrix} 1 & 1 & 1 & 1 & 1 \\ 0 & 1 & 1 & 1 & 1 \\ 0 & 0 & 1 & 1 & 1 \\ 0 & 0 & 0 & 1 & 1 \\ 0 & 0 & 0 & 0 & 1 \end{bmatrix}, A_2 = \begin{bmatrix} 1 & 0 & 0 & 0 & 0 \\ 0 & 1 & 0 & 0 & 0 \\ 0 & 0 & 1 & 0 & 0 \\ 0 & 0 & 0 & 1 & 0 \\ 0 & 0 & 0 & 0 & 1 \end{bmatrix}$$

(1) Access Structure There are three prototypical types of constraint in access structures: unsegmented, hierarchical, and specialized, as shown in matrices $_{A0}$, $_{A1}$, and $_{A2}$, respectively [see equation (1)] (Cohen et al., 1972). A "1" entry in the matrices means that the problem in the corresponding row can be attended to in the choice opportunity for the corresponding column, whereas a "0" means that there is no such relationship.

In the unsegmented structure, all active problems have access to any active choice opportunities; in the hierarchical structure, important problems (upper part of the matrix) have access to more choice opportunities; in the specialized structure, each problem has access to only once choice opportunity. The application of a hierarchical structure means that more important problems can enter into more choice opportunities than less important problems. Following Fioretti and Lomi (2008), in the present chapter this structure is constructed through a comparison of the IDs between problems and choice opportunities. Before its movement, a problem would search for whether there is any choice opportunity in its eight neighboring cells. If no choice opportunity is found, it moves one step randomly toward one of its eight neighboring cells. If a choice opportunity is found, a comparison between the ID of the problem and that of the choice opportunity is made first. If the former is smaller, the problem moves at that time step, meaning that decision-making is possible. Otherwise, it stops to render decision-making impossible. The same rule applies to the choice opportunity. If the ID of the choice opportunity is greater, it moves. Otherwise, it stops. In the specialized structure, a choice opportunity can only meet a specific problem. If the ID of a problem is equal to that of a choice opportunity, the problem moves. Otherwise, it stops. The rule for the movement of agents in the solution structure was similar to that in the access structure.

(2) Decision Structure Similar to the agents in access structure, a decision-maker will search for whether there is any choice opportunity in its eight neighboring cells before its movement. If no choice opportunity is found, it moves one step randomly toward one of its eight neighboring cells. If a choice opportunity is found, the decision array of the decision-maker is examined. If the corresponding number of the decision array associated with a decision-maker is 1, that decision-maker moves. Otherwise, it stops. For the choice opportunities, there is no such restriction. The rule for the movement of agents in the spatial structure is similar to that in decision structure.

3.3 Rules for Decision-making

In addition to the decisions in the spatial garbage-can model, the present simulation distinguishes oversight decisions in the original garbage-can model. An oversight decision means that if a choice opportunity is activated when problems are attached to other choice opportunities and if there is energy available to make the decision quickly, it will be made without any attention to existing problems and with a minimum of time and energy. In other words, if a decision is made when the four types of elements other than problems meet at a particular cell, the problem(s) is not resolved. Therefore, oversight decisions can be regarded as an inefficient way of decision-making.

Whether a decision has been made is judged at the cells (Fioretti and Lomi, 2008). At each time step, a judgement will be made at all the cells based on the following rules (Figure 4.3):

1. If at least one decision-maker, one choice opportunity, one solution, and one location meet at a particular cell, no problem exists, and the total net energy of all those agents is positive, an oversight decision will be made. If there is more than one decision-maker at a particular cell, all these decision-makers will participate in the decision-making. If there is more than one choice opportunity, solution, or location at a particular cell, one of them will be randomly selected.
2. If at least one decision-maker, one choice opportunity, one problem, one solution, and one location meet at a particular cell, and the total net energy of all those agents is positive, a resolution decision will be made.
3. After a decision is made, the problem and solution will be thrown out of the system, while the decision-maker, choice opportunity, and location will remain within the system. Moreover, the energy of the choice opportunity will be set to be 0 and marked so that it will not participate in the future decision-making and the calculation of entropy, which will be discussed shortly in the next section.

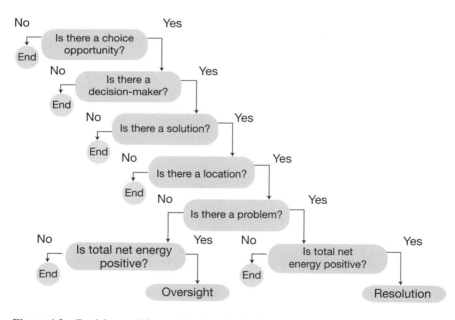

Figure 4.3 Decision-making rule in the simulation

In the present research, we hypothesize that self-organization of decision and spatial structures can emerge and evolve in the spatial garbage-can model, or in other words, these structures are adaptive. This is based on the concept of "adaptive efficiency" explained by North (1998). It implies that different rules evolve over time with respect to two basic abilities of an organization: the ability to innovate and learn. In the present simulation, the rules for adaption are not given, but evolve in the decision-making process as follows:

1. If the total net energy of the five types of agents at one cell is positive (resolution), the corresponding values of structural constraints will be assigned a value of or remain to be 1. It means that after a resolution, the agents of decision-makers and locations will have a greater probability of meeting choice opportunities in which resolution decisions are likely to be made.
2. If an oversight has been made, or if the total net energy of the five types of agents at a particular cell is negative, the corresponding values of the structural constraints will be assigned to a value of or remain to be 0. It means that an inefficient decision has been made during that process. Therefore, when the decision-makers or locations meet the same choice opportunities in the future in which a resolution decision has been not made, they will choose not to participate in the decision-making in order to increase the efficiency.

In essence, the more decisions that decision-makers and locations participate in, the more knowledge or capability they can acquire to make more efficient decisions in future.

3.4 Data Recording and Interface

The total net energy of the system, the entropy of the decision structure, the entropy of the spatial structure, and the numbers of oversight and resolution decisions are recorded in the simulation. We used the entropies to measure the degree of order in decision and spatial structures. Following Shannon (1948), entropy is calculated through the following formula:

$$H(X) = -\sum_{i=1}^{n} P(x_i) \log_b P(x_i) \qquad (1)$$

where b is set to be 2, H is the entropy for x_i which is a random variable of row I in the structure; P is the probability that x_i occurs.

In each of the initial arrays of decision and spatial structures, there are 50% of 0s and 1s, respectively. With the unfolding of the simulation over time, the proportions of 0s and 1s change over time. The greater the entropies are, the more chaotic the system tends to be. We can regard the system as self-organizing and evolving toward order if the entropies of both the decision structure and the spatial structure decrease.

In the present study, we aim at examining: (1) whether order would emerge within the decision structure and the spatial structure over time, and (2) whether the decision structure and the spatial structure could have significant influence on the total net energy of the system.

The fluctuations of the entropies are recorded dynamically in the plots. Through the plots, we can visualize the trends and patterns for the evolution of entropies so as to judge whether the structural constraints are stable or not.

Of the four types of structural constraints in this simulation, the access and solution structures are fixed at unsegmented, hierarchical, or specialized patterns, while the decision and spatial structures can be either adaptive or non-adaptive, with no pre-specified patterns. There are altogether 3×3×2×2 = 36 combinations of the four types of structural constraints. According to a preliminary analysis that showed no significant difference between the impacts of decision and spatial structures on the system, we define a combination of the four types of agents as restrictive constraint when both access and solution structures are unsegmented or hierarchical, and loose constraint when either access or solution structure is specialized. Therefore, all the 36 combinations of four types of structural constraints can be classified into two groups: 16 combinations as loose constraint and 20 as restrictive constraint (Table 4.1). Note that decision structure specifies which problem could be associated with which choice opportunity and can be regarded as the institutional constraint, while spatial structure depicts which choice opportunity could appear in which location and can be considered as spatial constraint.

Table 4.1 Classification of structural constraints

Access structure	Solution structure	Decision structure	Spatial structure	Group
Unsegmented	Unsegmented	Non-adaptive	Non-adaptive	Group 1
Hierarchical	Hierarchical	Adaptive	Adaptive	(Loose)
Unsegmented	Specialized	Non-adaptive	Non-adaptive	Group 2
Hierarchical		Adaptive	Adaptive	(Restrictive)
Specialized	Unsegmented Hierarchical Specialized	Non-adaptive Adaptive	Non-adaptive Adaptive	

The computer experiment was implemented on the NetLogo 4.0.3 platform on a personal computer. Figure 4.4 shows a snapshot of the simulation where different shapes of objects represent different elements of the SGCM.

Approach to Comparing Institutional and Spatial Changes 71

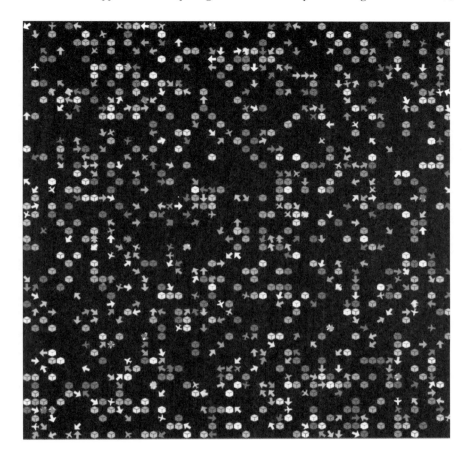

Figure 4.4 A snapshot of the simulation

4 Results

4.1 Entropies of Decision and Spatial Structures

The result of simulation showed that the entropy decreased when decision and spatial structures were both adaptive, regardless of the pre-specified patterns of access or solution structure. In the first 500 time steps, the entropy decreased dramatically. That was mainly because choice opportunities had entered continuously into the system during that time. After the 500th time step, the entropies of both decision and spatial structures decreased slowly over time, showing that the system was self-organizing itself. Figures 4.5 and 4.6 show the trajectories of entropy (vertical axis) over time (horizontal axis) for decision and spatial structures, respectively, given four combinations of decision and spatial structures when access and solution structures were both unsegmented. For both figures, the combinations of decision structure/access structure were non-adaptive/non-adaptive (the up-left plot), non-adaptive/adaptive (the up-right plot), adaptive/non-adaptive (the down-left plot), adaptive/adaptive (the down-right plot).

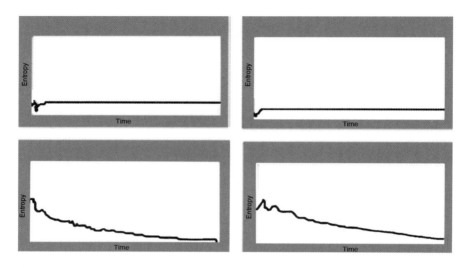

Figure 4.5   Trajectories of entropy for decision structure

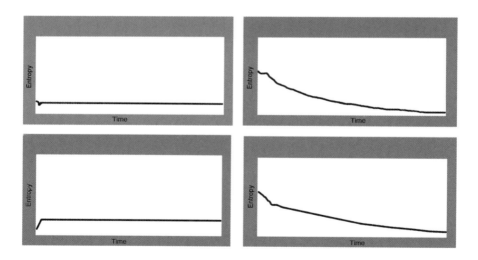

Figure 4.6   Trajectories of entropy for spatial structure

4.2 Problem-solving Efficiency of Decision and Spatial Structures

Regardless of the combinations of access and solution structures, there were more resolution decisions in the combination of adaptive decision structure/non-adaptive spatial structure than in that of non-adaptive decision structure/adaptive spatial structure (in almost all cases in Table 4.2). This suggests that the efficiency of institutional design, when left adaptive in resolving problems, was more significant than that of spatial design.

Table 4.2 Numbers of resolution in the decision structure and spatial structure

Access structure	Solution structure	Decision structure	Spatial structure	Numbers of resolution
Unsegmented	Unsegmented	Non-adaptive	Adaptive	387
Unsegmented	Unsegmented	Adaptive	Non-adaptive	394
Unsegmented	Hierarchical	Non-adaptive	Adaptive	346
Unsegmented	Hierarchical	Adaptive	Non-adaptive	354
Unsegmented	Specialized	Non-adaptive	Adaptive	15
Unsegmented	Specialized	Adaptive	Non-adaptive	15
Hierarchical	Unsegmented	Non-adaptive	Adaptive	361
Hierarchical	Unsegmented	Adaptive	Non-adaptive	367
Hierarchical	Hierarchical	Non-adaptive	Adaptive	271
Hierarchical	Hierarchical	Adaptive	Non-adaptive	282
Hierarchical	Specialized	Non-adaptive	Adaptive	5
Hierarchical	Specialized	Adaptive	Non-adaptive	11
Specialized	Unsegmented	Non-adaptive	Adaptive	7
Specialized	Unsegmented	Adaptive	Non-adaptive	15
Specialized	Hierarchical	Non-adaptive	Adaptive	8
Specialized	Hierarchical	Adaptive	Non-adaptive	7
Specialized	Specialized	Non-adaptive	Adaptive	0
Specialized	Specialized	Adaptive	Non-adaptive	0

4.3 Influence of Decision and Spatial Structures on the Total Net Energy

The tests of between-subjects effects for group 1 suggest that neither decision structure nor spatial structure had significant impact on the total net energy of the system (Table 4.3). Considering that decisions were more difficult to make in the last combination (access and solution structures were both specialized), where the rule for the movement of agents was too restrictive, we excluded this combination in the tests of between-subjects effects for group 2. The result showed a result similar to that for group 1 (Table 4.4). That is, neither decision nor spatial structure had significant impact on the total net energy of the system. However, the interaction of the two structures was significant (at the level of 0.05).

Table 4.3   Tests of between-subjects effects for group 1

Dependent: total net energy					
Model	Sum of squares	df	Mean square	F	Sig.
Decision	4.564	1	4.564	.000	.992
Space	119.697	1	119.697	.003	.959
Decision Space	127.689	1	127.689	.003	.958
Error	708502.062	16	44281.379		
Total	1.384 E7	20			

Table 4.4   Tests of between-subjects effects for group 2

Dependent: total energy					
Model	Sum of squares	df	Mean square	F	Sig.
Decision	2.184	1	2.184	.119	.736
Space	1.820	1	1.820	.099	.758
Decision x Space	200.946	1	200.946	10.961	.006*
Error	219.993	12	18.333		
Total	8209042.514	16			

Consequently, we made a closer examination of the effects of decision and spatial structures for group 2. The result shows that when decision structure was non-adaptive, spatial structure was significant in relation to the total net energy of the system. When spatial structure was non-adaptive, decision structure was almost significant in relation to the total net energy of the system. At the same time, when either decision or spatial structure was adaptive, the other structure was insignificant in relation to the total net energy of the system (Table 4.5).

Table 4.5 ANOVA for decision and spatial structures in group 2

	Sum of squares	df	Mean square	F	Sig.
Test for spatial structure when the decision structure is non-adaptive					
Between groups	120.509	1	120.509	11.596	.014[†]
Within groups	62.353	6	10.392		
Total	182.862	7			
Test for decision structure when the spatial structure is non-adaptive					
Between groups	122.516	1	122.516	5.745	.054
Within groups	127.963	6	21.327		
Total	250.479	7			
Test for spatial structure when the decision structure is adaptive					
Between groups	82.257	1	82.257	3.131	.127
Within groups	157.640	6	26.273		
Total	239.898	7			
Test for decision structure when the spatial structure is adaptive					
Between groups	80.614	1	80.614	5.256	.062
Within groups	92.031	6	15.338		
Total	172.645	7			

Note: [†]Indicates significance at 0.05 level.

5 Conclusions

The evidence derived from the present computer experiment seems to imply that the city is a self-organizing system. Its order emerges from some intrinsic rules and is shown in many aspects, such as the spatial structure of land uses and the spatial distribution of its population. Different from most previous studies which pay more attention to the driving forces for urban development, this research explores the influence of different structural constraints on urban development.

By integrating the concept of adaptability and modifying the spatial garbage-can model into an ABS framework, we find that:

1. The entropy of the structural constraints, at least for decision and spatial structures, in the system decreases over time, indicating that the system tends to self-organize itself.
2. The adaptive decision structure has higher efficiency in problem-solving than the adaptive spatial structure, showing that institutional design is no less efficient than spatial design in improving urban development.
3. There is strong interaction between decision and spatial structures, together influencing the total net energy of the system. The extents to which the two structures influence on the total net energy of the system are almost the same. This shows that institution and space might have effects to the same extent on urban development. The implication is that we need to consider both institutional and spatial designs in improving urban development.

The ABM approach to urban socio-spatial processes in general, and to the SGCM in particular, provides a novel way of looking at and understanding cities. The approach is rich enough in order to gain insights into how cities work and what we can do about it. The computer experiment reported here in no way conveys a complete picture of urban socio-spatial processes. It provides, however, a continuing endeavour toward a better understanding of how cities work. Much remains to be done.

References

Batty, M. 2003. "Agent, cells and cities: New representational modelings for simulating multi-scale urban dynamics." Centre for Advanced Spatial Analysis Working Paper Series, 65.

Benenson, I. 1998. "Multi-agent simulations of residential dynamics in the city, Computers." *Environment and Urban Systems* 22(1): 25–42.

Benenson, I., I. Omer, and E. Hatna. 2002. "Entity-based modeling of urban residential dynamics: the case of Yaffo, Tel Aviv." *Environment and Planning B: Planning and Design* 29(4): 491–512.

Cohen, M.D., J.G. March, and J.P. Olsen. 1972. "A garbage can modeling of organizational choice." *Administrative Science Quarterly* 17(1): 1–25.

Conway, J. 1970. "The game of life." Scientific American.

Fioretti, G. and A. Lomi. 2008. "Agent-based representation of the garbage can modeling of organizational choice." *Journal of Artificial Societies and Social Simulation* 11(1), at http://jasss.soc.surrey.ac.uk/11/1/1.html.

Hanley, P.F., and L.D. Hopkins. 2007. "Do sewer extension plans affect urban development? A multiagent simulation." *Environment and Planning B: Planning and Design* 34(1): 6–27.

Lai, S-K. 2006. "A spatial garbage-can modeling." *Environment and Planning B: Planning and Design* 33(1): 379–89.

Lai, S-K., and H. Han. 2009. *Complexity: The New Perspectives of Urban Planning*. Beijing: China Building Industry Press (in Chinese).

Li, X., G.O. Yeh, and X. Liu. 2007. *Geographic Simulation System: Cellular Automata and Multi-Agent System*. Beijing: The Science Press (in Chinese).

Ligtenberg, A., A.K. Bregt, and R. van Lammeren. 2001. "Multi-actor-based land use modelling: spatial planning using agents." *Landscape and Urban Planning* 56(1, 2): 21–33.

von Neumann, J. 1966. Theory of Self-reproducing Automata (edited and completed by Arthur Burks), Champaign, Illinois: University of Illinois Press.

North, D.C. 1998. "Institutions, ideology, and economic performance." In J.A. Dorn, S.H. Hanke, and A.A. Walters eds. *The Revolution in Development Economics*. Washington: Cato Institute.

Saarloos, D.J.M., T.A. Arentze, A.W.J. Borgers, and H.J.P. Semboloni, F., J. Assfalg, S.I. Armeni, R. Gianassi, and F. Marson. 2004. CityDev, "An interactive multi-agents urban model on the web." *Computers, Environment and Urban Systems* 28(1–2): 45–64.

Shannon, Claude E. (July and October) 1948. "A mathematical theory of communication." *Bell System Technical Journal* 27: 379–423 and 623–56.

Timmermans. 2008. "A multi-agent paradigm as structuring principle for planning support systems." *Computers, Environment and Urban Systems* 32(1): 29–40.

Chapter 5

On Traction Rules of Complex Structures in One-dimensional Cellular Automata: Some Implications for Urban Change[1]

1 Introduction

The book investigates explanations of the local-global interaction of urban spatial systems, with a focus on one-dimensional cellular automata representing hypothetical, linear cities as an analytical tool for urban change. It is grounded on the hypothesis that the global characteristics of complex spatial systems, such as cities, emerge from the local interaction among the elements consisting of these systems, such as individual agents in an economy (e.g., Holland, 1995, pp.1, 41–2; Krugman, 1996, p.21; Simon, 1998, p.33–4). Though it is arguably true that using one-dimensional cellular automata may render the analytical frames and results unrealistic or too simplistic, analyzing 'long, narrow' cities has been a long tradition in urban economic theory (Krugman, 1996, p.22). I follow that tradition here, by focusing on interaction among local agents, hoping that this new approach would yield useful insights into our understanding of how urban systems evolve. The physical environment of a city is the outcome of interacting local development decisions. Models on urban evolution based on the top-down approach but ignoring the local interaction imply that planning can be carried out in a similar way, for example, vertical, centralized organizations, comprehensive process, and generic policies for land development. With such a conception distinct from the fundamental characteristics of spatial evolution, urban change is thus difficult to be tamed in reality by traditional planning techniques because of the complexity of relatedness among spatial decisions (Batty, 1995). Insight into effective planning techniques may be gained through the bottom-up approach to urban change, that is, understanding how the local interaction among the development decisions affects the overall trend in the urban physical change. Therefore, I tend to explore into such possibility by focusing on the local-global interaction at the most fundamental, abstract level. I thus set aside the substantive interpretation of or elaboration on the abstract structure as future work. Obviously, the price of abstractness is the deviation from realism, but if interpreted appropriately, we can still gain useful insight from the abstract construct. A similar example

---

1 This chapter has been published in *The Annals of Regional Science* (2003) 37:337–52.

following this line of research is conducted by Hillier (1996), but he did not focus on the formalization of the conceptual models of spatial organization, which I set as our long-term objective. Thus the book serves as a starting point toward that end. I have, however, conducted concrete computer experiments, searching for the order out of chaotic evolution of complex spatial systems and reported our findings elsewhere (Lai, 1999). Different from most current two-dimensional cellular automata spatial simulations, the present book explores deductively into the mechanisms underlying the emergence of complex structures using one-dimensional cellular automata representing hypothetical, linear cities.

There is a shift recently in paradigm on urban spatial modeling approaches from the top-down approach, that views the aggregate pattern of urban change as equilibrium seeking, to the bottom-up approach, that considers the seemingly stable pattern as emerging from the dynamics and interaction among local actions (Batty, 196). This perspective of understanding urban change is in part influenced by a new orientation in science that concerns the behavior of complex systems: complexity.

Most planning behavior takes place in complex settings. The elements in these settings interact with each other not only forming a complex network of information flow, but also resulting in uncertainty or incomplete information faced by planners. Understanding the nature of the complex system is helpful in developing a prescriptive theory of planning to aid planners to cope with uncertainty. Recent development in such understanding leads to a set of related new fields, including artificial life (e.g., Emmeche, 1994) and complexity theory (e.g., Gell-Mann, 1994).

The central idea of artificial life is that simple rules result in complex behavior of a system. Artificial life researchers conduct their experiments on computers by assuming that life can emerge from very simple rules and creating their own universes or games of life on computers. The validity of these computer experiments is being debated, but they may be efficient tools for discovering the simple rules of nature, which can possibly be replicated in the real experiments. The ultimate objective of the artificial life research is to search for the plausible laws of nature for further mathematical proof. The computer experiment approach used in the artificial life research is quite promising for developing ill-understood theories.

An even more powerful, ambitious theory encompassing a wider range of phenomena is complexity theory (Gell-Mann, 1994). It is an attempt of a crude integration of the current state of knowledge scattered across various disciplines, including theoretical physics, psychology, computer science, political science, and economics. The objective of the theory is to discover complex adaptive systems in nature and explain their behavior. It is distinct from the traditional systems approach in that complexity theory can, to some extent, be thought of as a bottom-up approach, whereas the traditional systems approach is a top-down one. Many urban dynamical and spatial models are based on the latter approach (e.g., Forrester's urban system dynamics model, 1973). Complexity theory seeks the fundamental laws of how a system adapts to interference, exogenous or endogenous. Information is an important measure of describing the system's behavior. The system approach tends to divide the whole system into functional components. The relationship among these components is subject to rigorous tests to verify the model. No fundamental laws are required in building that model. Complexity theory provides a powerful perspective of interpreting observed social and natural phenomena, but its development is still in an early stage.

There are other earlier works on complexity, most notably Simon (1998) and Alexander (1965), which are more pertinent to our discussion of land-use change in cities. Simon considered the complex structures emerging in nature as "nearly decomposable systems," meaning the elements in these systems are organized in an almost hierarchical form of structures. But unlike pure hierarchies where the elements are related only from the top down, the elements at the same level in these complex structures are interrelated among each other. Such structures have the advantage of growing fast, thus resulting in higher probabilities of being existent. In an attempt to search for the organizational principles of how natural cities grow, Alexander proposed a generic structural principle called "semi-lattice," similar to Simon's idea about complexity for spatial organization. In contrast to a tree, in this principle the relationship among elements of a system is similar to that in what Simon called nearly decomposable system, in that if any two elements have common subsets of the system, then these subsets also belong to the system. A tree structure where the relationship among elements is based on which belongs to which is thus by definition a semi-lattice structure. The relationship underlying most semi-lattice structure is much more complex and richer than that in a simple tree structure. Alexander (1965) argued that cities grow following the semi-lattice principle, and planners should recognize such a principle and provide appropriate spatial structures accordingly.

Cellular automata, as a metaphor of urban change in linear cities used here, are a branch of complexity theory. They are the simplest models of investigating the local-global interaction in complex systems. The research on cellular automata was pioneered by von Neumann (1966) and thoroughly investigated by Wolfram (1994c, 2002). The behavior of cellular automata has not been fully understood, but researchers have gained enough experience in order to formalize its dynamics (e.g., Urias et al., 1996).There are at least two approaches to understand the cellular automata behavior: computer experiments (e.g., Wuensche and Lesser, 1992; Wolfram, 2002) and mathematical deduction (e.g., Urias et al., 1996; Wolfram, 1994a and 1994b). Distinct from computer simulations using two-dimensional cellular, I intend to explore urban change, metaphorically based on the mathematical deduction approach. General structural transition rules of how spatial agents interact that characterize complex spatial systems can be derived from the deduction, as will be depicted shortly. A promising research agendum would be to incorporate a set of hypothetical structural considerations, such as Alexander's semi-lattice structure, into the cellular automata model by designing or discovering evolution rules according to the logic of that structure.

Through deductive reasoning based on automata theory and mathematical logic (e.g., Hopcroft and Ullman, 1979; Mendelson, 1987), we could then look into the trajectories of the system to generalize how each of such rules affects the evolutionary outcomes. Finally, we would evaluate how well each rule thus selected in the cellular automata model maps the real urban dynamics on the empirical urban growth indices, such as population and morphology of urban boundaries.

Therefore, the main construct underlying our exploration is cellular automata, in particular those of one dimension, that have been used to investigate evolution of complex systems (e.g., Wolfram, 1994c, 2002). They are recently being applied in the explanation of or experimentation on urban development (e.g., Couclelis, 1985; Cecchini, 1996). Instead of modeling the reality of urban change based on cellular automata as most such work seems to imply, I use one-dimensional cellular automata here as an analytic tool representing hypothetical, linear cities to examine how complex spatial structures emerge. That is, I view cities as complex spatial system reminiscent of those emerging from cellular automata and search for possible rules that govern their evolution.

Section 2 introduces briefly the one-dimensional cellular automata model and distinguishes between a tree and semi-lattice rules based on the state transition graphs. Section 3 classifies the 256 transition rules for the model where k (number of cell values or states) and r (number of interacting neighbors) are equal to 2 and 1, respectively, in terms of rule types and Wolfram's four-class categories (1994b). In particular, a characteristic transition rule is derived from the eight rules that are classified as semi-lattices and exhibit complex structures. Section 4 provides implications for urban change based on the characteristic transition rule found in Section 3 and discusses some spatial issues and possible future extension of the model.

2 The Model

Consider a linear city of a finite set of spatial agents or blocks represented by a one-dimensional cellular automaton. Assume each block can be of one of two types of land use, retail with a value of one or residential of zero. There can be many ways in which the linear city could evolve in space and time. Grounded on the assumption that cities are complex structures in the form of semi-lattices, the question is: are there underlying mechanisms of the interaction of these blocks in the linear city that give rise to semi-lattice structures? There are at least three ways of defining the semi-lattice form of one-dimensional cellular automata models: 1) direct specification of transition rules (i.e., how blocks affect each other in land use); 2) pattern recognition of configurations through time in the space-time plots; and 3) pattern recognition of configurations of space at each time step. The common framework on which the three definitions are based to identify the semi-lattice form of cellular automata models is automata theory and formal languages. Since there is no easy way to define the semi-lattice form through pattern recognition for the one-dimensional cellular automata, I focus here on the first approach to defining semi-lattices. The evolution of a one-dimensional cellular automaton can be viewed as a set of languages generated by a finite automaton. Following Wolfram (1994a), let the value (land-use type) of site (block) i at time step t be denoted as ai(t) and be a symbol selected from the alphabet:

$$S=\{0,1,\ldots,k-1\} \tag{1}$$

All possible sequences of these symbols form the set Σ of cellular automaton configurations $A^{(t)}$. At each time step, each site value is updated according to the values of a neighborhood of $2r+1$ sites around it by a local (or transition) rule (determining how the blocks interact):

$$\psi: S^{2r+1} \to S \tag{2}$$

of the form:

$$a_i^{(t)} = \Psi\left[a_{i-r}^{(t-1)}, a_{i-r+1}^{(t-1)}, \ldots, a_{i+r}^{(t-1)}\right] \tag{3}$$

This transition rule leads to a global mapping:

$$\Phi: \Sigma \to \Sigma. \tag{4}$$

on the complete cellular automaton configurations. Let $\Omega^{(t)}$ denote the set of configurations generated after t iterated applications of Φ on Σ, i.e.:

$$\Omega^{(t)} = \Phi^t \Sigma. \tag{5}$$

There is an economic way of representing all possible configurations generated by Φ over t time steps on Σ based on a so-called state transition graph for the non-deterministic finite automaton (NDFA) corresponding to Φ (c. f., Appendix A). Take rule 76 as defined by Wolfram (1994a) (cf., Appendix B). Figure 5.1 shows the corresponding NDFA of the rule.

Each node represents a state of the automaton. Each arc with a symbol (0 or 1) is the mapping from a subset of three neighbors at the previous time step to a symbol for the central site of the subset at current time step. For example the arc from node 11 to 10 with the symbol of 1 represents the mapping from 110 to 1. The finite automaton is non-deterministic because there are same symbol emanating from a particular set of nodes. This means that transformations from these nodes cannot be determined definitely. For example, node 00 has two arcs labeled 0 emanating from it to node 01 and itself. Thus the finite automaton transition graph for rule 76 in Figure 5.1 is non-deterministic. For each non-deterministic finite automaton, there exists at least a corresponding deterministic finite automaton

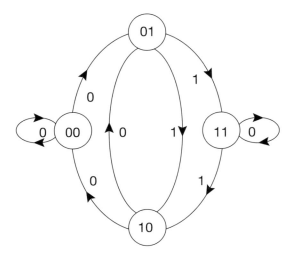

Figure 5.1 The NDFA corresponding to rule 76

(DFA) generating the same language based on subset construction (Hopcroft and Ullman, 1979). Take rule 76 again. The state transition graph for one such corresponding deterministic finite automaton is shown in Figure 5.2. Since there can be more than one DFA corresponding to an NDFA, for my classification purpose I developed an algorithm to derive the minimal DFA for each transition rule, that is, uniquely associated with the NDFA for that rule (cf. Appendix A).

As depicted earlier, Alexander's notion of semi-lattice is the original idea concerning spatial overlaps of categories (1965), whereas I use one-dimensional cellular automata here as the simplest discrete dynamic system mimicking evolution of the linear urban system. Even though the relationship between the semi-lattice in the spatial context of urban systems and those in the cellular automata rules is difficult to pin down analytically, they are at least topologically equivalent. Alexander's original idea of spatial overlaps is based on set theory and topology, which is also the theoretical foundation of my approach to the typology of the one-dimensional cellular automata rules. There might be links between the two, but they fall outside the scope of the present book. Since both Alexander's and my expositions are based on the same theoretical foundation, at a higher level, the notion of semi-lattice can be used here to examine its relation to urban change. Based on Alexander's distinction between trees and semi-lattice (1965), we can define two types of transition rules according to the concept of deterministic finite automata.

Definition 1 The Tree Rule: A transition rule is called a tree rule if, and only if, when one node is a subset of another in the state transition graph corresponding to the minimal DFA obtained from the NDFA, and there exists at least one arc connecting the two nodes.

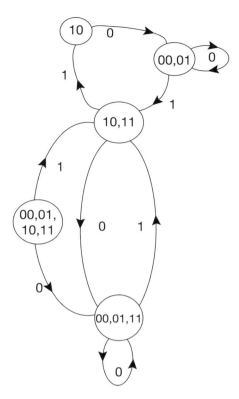

Figure 5.2 A DFA corresponding to the NDFA for rule 76

Definition 2 The Semi-lattice Rule: A transition rule is called a semi-lattice rule if, and only if, when two nodes in the state transition graph corresponding to the minimal DFA obtained from the NDFA have common elements (or subsets of the nodes in the NDFA), and there exists at least one arc connecting the nodes. If a transition rule includes both the tree and semi-lattice cases, it is classified as a semi-lattice rule.

According to these definitions, the DFA for rule 76 as shown in Figure 5.2 belongs to the semi-lattice structure. Appendix A depicts how the DFA is constructed. In order to determine the DFAs uniquely for the purpose of rule classification, I graphed the minimal ones with the smallest numbers of arcs and nodes. The minimal DFAs thus obtained should be unique (cf. Appendix A). It turns out that rule 76 indeed belongs to semi-lattices. By searching out all such rules in a given one-dimensional cellular automaton, we can find their general characteristics of its evolution and analyze their behavior as will be shown on the following sections.

3 Simulation Design and General Observations

According to the patterns of evolution in the space-time configurations, one-dimensional cellular automata can be classified into four categories (Wolfram, 1994b).[2] The four general classes are:

>Class 1: A fixed, homogeneous state is eventually reached;
>Class 2: A pattern consisting of separated periodic regions is produced;
>Class 3: A chaotic, aperiodic pattern is produced; and
>Class 4: Complex, localized structure are generated.

Class 4 structures are of particular interest because theoretically they are capable of universal computation and reminiscent of Game of Life (Wolfram, 1994; Berlekamp et al., 1985). I argue that if the spatial evolution of cities can be viewed as governed by the interaction rules yet to be found similar to those in cellular automata, the changing spatial configuration of cities suggest that the Class 4 structures would most likely, at least in the simplest case of a linear city, represent such evolution. Buildings are being constructed and torn down; factories and stores being opened and closed; houses being built and abandoned; population concentrations prospering and declining; and commercial and residential areas moving from one place to another. Behind all these dynamics might lie the fundamental rules according to which individual agents interact spatially. With the two structural assumptions on the spatial evolution of cities depicted earlier (i.e., semi-lattice rules and complex structures) and imposed on the one-dimensional cellular automaton, we can search out these transition rules conforming to the assumptions from which insight into the origin of urban spatial evolution might be gained.

Using the one-dimensional cellular automaton with $k = 2$ (two uses of land) and $r = 1$ (number of blocks affecting each other), I first grouped the 256 rules into the semi-lattice, tree, and the remaining rules as defined earlier. I then further classified each group of rules according to Wolfram's four-class categories. The following table shows the result. The detailed classification of the transition rules is given in Appendix B.

---

2 Though Wolfram claimed that "approximately" there are no Class 4 structures in one-dimensional cellular automaton with $k = 2$ and $r = 1$ (1994b), the observation seems inconclusive because it is only an "approximate" estimation. In the book, I summarized all the 256 rules in terms of the four classes by running the program provided by Wuensche and Lesser (1992). The number of the rules yielding the Class 4 structure was indeed small (only 8 out of 256), which, I think, is consistent with Wolfram's findings. Evan though these structures are much simpler than the Class 4 structures found in other one-dimensional cellular automata with greater ks and rs, they cannot be apparently classified into any of the rest of the three classes. The simplicity of the structure might be caused by the simplicity of the rules with $k = 2$ and $r = 1$, but we cannot thus conclude that there are no Class 4 structures in this model.

Table 5.1 Classification of transition rules for one-dimensional cellular automata with $k=2$ and $r=1$ by types of rules and classes of structures

	Semi-lattice rules	Tree rules	Others	Total
Class 1 Structures	58	24	2	84
Class 2 Structures	87	32	4	123
Class 3 Structures	25	4	12	41
Class 4 Structures	8	0	0	8
Total	178	60	18	256

It can be found from Table 5.1 that almost all transition rules are semi-lattices or trees. Among these rules, 70.0% of the total are semi-lattices. The number and percentage of transition rules that result in the Class 4 structure (8 rules and 4.5%) are relatively greater for the semi-lattice rules than those for the tree rules (0 rules and 0.0%). The proportion of the transition rules yielding the Class 4 structure is significantly low among all transition rules (3.1%). Note that the transition rules resulting in the Class 4 structure are all semi-lattices. A closer examination of the transition rules that are semi-lattices and yield the Class 4 structure can be used to generalize the characteristics of such rules. Table 5.2 shows the 8 rules within this category.

Table 5.2 The eight transition rules that are semi-lattices and result in class 4 structures

Rule Number	111	110	101	100	011	010	001	000
9	0	0	0	0	1	0	0	1
41	0	0	1	0	1	0	0	1
65	0	1	0	0	0	0	0	1
97	0	1	1	0	0	0	0	1
107	0	1	1	0	1	0	1	1
111	0	1	1	0	1	1	1	1
121	0	1	1	1	1	0	0	1
125	0	1	1	1	1	1	0	1

The general characteristics of the eight rules can be summarized as below (see Table 5.3):

1. If the central cell (block) has the same value (type of land uses) as that of the two neighbors at time t (000 and 111), its value will change at time t+1.

2. If the central cell has the value of 0 at time t with its two neighbors having different values (001 and 100), there is a probability of 3/4 that the value of that cell remain the same, while 1/4 that the value will change at time t +1.
3. If the central cell has the value of 0 at time t with its two neighbors having the values of 1 (101), there is a probability of 3/4 that the value of that cell will change, while 1/4 that the value will remain the same at time t +1.
4. If the central cell has the value of 1 at time t with its two neighbors having the values of 0 (010), there is a probability of 3/4 that the value of that cell will change, while 1/4 that the value will remain the same at time t +1.
5. (5) If the central cell has the value of 1 at time t with its two neighbors having different values (110 and 011), there is a probability of 1/4 that the value of that cell will change, while 3/4 that value will remain the same at time t +1.

Table 5.3 The characteristic transition rule for semi-lattices with complex structures

State of surrounding	State of cell under consideration	
	Live cell (1)	Dead cell (0)
Two Live Cells	Dead	¼ Chances of Being Dead
One Live and One Dead Cells	¾ Chances of Being Live	¾ Chances of Being Dead
Two Dead Cells	¼ Chances of Being Live	Live

4 Implications and Discussion

The characteristic transition rule found here may shed some promising light on understanding the origin of urban change. Firstly, viewing the values or states of cells as different land uses, we can observe how these land uses interact spatially. Consider, for example, retail and residential uses as live (whose value is 1) and dead (whose value is 0) cells, respectively. The characteristic transition rule shows that when there are only retail uses in a neighborhood with no residential uses, the central site will change from the retail to residential use, whereas when there are only residential uses in that neighborhood with no retail uses, the central site will change from residential to retail use. This is intuitively plausible because the residential uses form the market for the retail uses, and without the market, the retail uses cannot survive. Secondly, the characteristic transition rule is stochastic, implying that determinism at one level can give rise to stochasticity at another level. The seemingly probabilistic processes of urban evolution might indeed be governed by a few deterministic interaction rules.

The proportion of the 256 rules in terms of rule types and classes in Table 5.1 imply that a tree rule may lead to a structure different from a semi-lattice rule. The crux is, however, that the eight rules found resulting in the Class 4 structure are all semi-lattices. This means that the transition rules embedded in the complex structure are themselves semi-lattices. More realistically, urban systems may be viewed as two-dimensional cellular automata. It is very likely that these systems are also the Class 4 structure in the space-time plots because two-dimensional cellular automata also appear to exhibit the four classes of structures identical to those in one-dimensional cellular automata (Wolfram, 1994b). The implication is that the deterministic transition rules that govern the evolution of urban systems are semi-lattices. Put differently, though Alexander's definition of semi-lattices is concerned with spatial overlaps in a city and there is no simple mapping between the semi-lattices in the spatial context of urban systems and those in automata theory, it is likely, as my findings seem to imply, that the two definitions might be closely related. The spatial overlaps in terms of semi-lattices might imply that the dynamic representation of these overlaps, for example, the minimal DFAs in the one-dimension cellular automaton, is also a semi-lattice. That is, they are at least topologically equivalent.

It is too simple minded at present to argue that urban spatial evolution indeed follows the analysis suggested here. As put earlier, I use the one-dimensional cellular automata model only as a representation of a hypothetical, linear city to understand the origin of urban change, setting aside the substantive meanings of the dynamics for future work. I have, however, conducted computer experiments based on a two-dimensional cellular automaton where the transition rules could evolve and land developers could learn these rules over time (Lai, 1999). Preliminary findings showed that the complex spatial system tended to self-organize itself toward a critical state (Bak and Chen, 1991).

The implication is that the complex structure in the two-dimensional cellular automaton and the self-organizing process might be closely related.

To render the findings useful in planning, the immediate future work is to determine whether urban spatial models built on the rules similar to the characteristic transition rule can map the real data of urban change. Based on the hypothesis that the dynamics of cities have common characteristics across all scales, we need first to search for a general, scale free principle governing the dynamics based on which to evaluate the alternative models using the real data, such as the growth of populations. One possible alternative of such principle is Stanley et al.'s (1996) work on scaling behavior in the growth of companies. Based on the data on growth rates of sales of all US manufacturing publicity traded companies, Stanley et al. (1996) found the growth rates could be all scaled according to an exponential distribution function and collapsed across all scales of sales into a single distribution given the scaling functions of parameters in the exponential distribution. Stanley et al. thus concluded that "these findings are reminiscent of the concept of university found in statistical physics, where different systems can be characterized by the same fundamental laws, independent of 'microscopic' details". Extending Stanley et al.'s models on growth rates of companies, we can search for a similar principle that governs growth rates of cities based on the real data on populations for all scales of cities. The cellular automata models on urban change derived from the characteristic transition rule are then evaluated according to the principle. The most effective model should yield the prediction of the population growth across all scales of cities closest to the reality.

5 Conclusions

Grounded on the hypothesis that the spatial evolution of urban systems can be characterized by the local interaction of individual agents, I expect to gain progress ultimately in understanding the origin of urban change from the new, bottom-up perspective that has arisen in recent years. In the present book, I have found, at least for a hypothetical, linear city of one-dimensional cellular automata, that the complex structure is derived from a set of transition rules whose dynamic representations are semi-lattices, not trees. These deterministic transition rules can be further grouped into a stochastic transition rule that gives rise to the Class 4 structure. The implication is that the evolution of urban systems, when viewed as cellular automata, might be governed by a few deterministic transition rules which are semi-lattices in the dynamic representation. A few deterministic rules might indeed be embedded in the seemingly stochastic processes of urban evolution.

Acknowledgements

The original version of the book was presented at the International Conference on Computers in Urban Planning and Urban Management 1997 (CUPUM97) held in Bombay, India. The author is grateful for the analytic assistance by Lee-Guo Wang, in particular in developing the minimization algorithm of transforming NDFAs to DFAs. The author also thanks the anonymous reviewer for the useful comments on an earlier version of book.

References

Alexander, C. 1965. A city is not a tree. *Architectural Forum* 122 (1, 2): 58–61.
Bak, P., and K. Chen. 1991. Self-organized criticality. *Scientific American* 1: 26–33.
Batty, M. 1995. New ways of looking at cities. *Nature* 377 (19): 574.
Batty, M. 1996. Urban change. *Environment and Planning B* 23: 513–4.
Berlekamp, E.R., J.H. Conway, and R.K. Guy. 1985. *Winning Ways for Your Mathematical Plays, Volume 2: Games in Particular.* New York: Academic Press.
Cecchini, A. 1996. Urban modeling by means of cellular automata: generalised urban automata with the help on-line (AUGH) model. *Environment and Planning B* 23: 721–32.
Couclelis, H. 1985. Cellular worlds: a framework for modeling micro-macro dynamics. *Environment and Planning A* 17: 585–96.
Emmeche, C. 1994. *The Garden in the Machine: The Emerging Science of Artificial Life.* Princeton, New Jersey: Princeton University Press.
Forrester, J. 1973. *Principles of Systems.* Cambridge, MA: MIT Press.
Gell-Mann, M. 1994. *The Quark and the Jaguar.* New York: W.H. Freeman.

Hillier, B. 1996. *Space Is the Machine*. Cambridge, UK: Cambridge University Press.
Holland, J.H. 1995 *Hidden Order: How Adaptation Builds Complexity*. Reading. Massachusetts: Preseus Books.
Hopcroft, J.E., and J.D. Ullman. 1979. *Introduction to Automata theory, Languages, and Computation*. London: Addison-Wesley.
Krugman, P. 1996. *The Self-Organizing Economy*. Cambridge, Massachusetts: Blackwell Publishers.
Lai, S-K. 1999. Self-organized criticality in urban spatial evolution: two empirical studies. *Proceedings of the International Conference on Computers in Urban Planning and Urban Management*. Venice, Italy: DAEST.
Mendelson, E. 1987. *Introduction to Mathematical Logic*. Monterey: Wadsworth & Brooks/Cole Advanced Books & Software.
von Neumann, J. 1966. "Thoery of self-reproducing automata." In A.W. Burks (ed.) *1949 Univ. of Illinois Lectures on the Theory and Organization of Complicated Automata*. Urbana, Illinois: University of Illinois Press.
Simon, H. 1998. *The Sciences of the Artificial: Third Edition*. Cambridge, Massachusetts: the MIT Press.
Stanley, M.H.R., L. Amaral, S.V. Buldyrev, S. Havlin, H. Leschhorn, P. Maass, M.A. Salinger, and H.E. Stanley. 1996. Scaling behaviour in the growth of companies. *Nature* 179 (29): 804–806.
Urias, J., G. Salazar-Anaya, E. Ugalde, and A. Enciso. 1996. Traveling patterns in cellular automata. *Chaos* 6 (3): 493–503.
Wolfram, S. 1994a. "Computation theory of cellular automata." In S. Wolfram, *Cellular Automata and Complexity*. New York: Addison-Wesley.
Wolfram, S. 1994b. "Universality and complexity in cellular automata." In S. Wolfram, *Cellular Automata and Complexity*. New York: Addison-Wesley.
Wolfram, S. 1994c. *Cellular automata and Complexity*. New York: Addison-Wesley.
Wolfram, S. 2002. *A New Kind of Science*. Champaign, Ill.: Wolfram Media, Inc.
Wuensche, A., and M. Lesser. 1992. *The Global Dynamics of Cellular Automata*. New York: Addison-Wesley.

92   Urban Complexity and Planning

Appendix A

The Minimization Algorithm of Transforming NDFAs to DFAs

Since an NDFA for a rule corresponds to more than one DFA for the same rule, it is necessary to find a unique representation of the DFA for that rule in order to determine whether the rule is a tree or semi-lattice. One way to accomplish this is to transform the NDFA to the unique DFA by the minimization algorithm given by Wolfram (1994a) and Hopcroft and Ullman (1979). Using rule 76 as an example, I propose here a three-step operational version of the algorithm based on which the 256 rules are classified.

Step 1: Initiate the Binary Relations from the NDFA

Denote nodes 00, 01, 10, and 11 by u_0, u_1, u_2, and u_3 respectively. The NDFA for rule 76 as shown in Figure 5.1 can be represented by the following binary relations:

$$u_0 \to 0u_0,\ u_0 \to 0u_1,\ u_1 \to 1u_3,\ u_1 \to 1u_3,\ u_1 \to 1u_2,\ u_2 \to 0u_1,\ u_2 \to 0u_0,\ u_3 \to 0u_3,\ \text{and}$$
$$u_3 \to 1u_2 \tag{6}$$

where the left-hand side in a relation is the current state (node), while the right-hand side the next state, and the number is the output of the transition.

Step 2: Construct a DFA Based on Sequential Subset Construction

Let σ be the set of all possible subsets of nodes u_i, for $i = 0, 1, 2,$ and 3. There, exit totally 2^4 or 16 possible subsets. Each subset is a candidate for the nodes in a corresponding DFA, and the starting node for the DFA is defined as the subset $\sigma \cdot = \{u_0, u_1, u_2, u_3\}$. Consider the set of relations in (6) and proceed from the starting node. Given the output value, that is, the number on the right-hand side, as 0, the elements in the starting node, that is, $u_0, u_1, u_2,$ and u_3 are transformed, if any, into the elements in the subset $\{u_0, u_1, u_3\}$, which is represented by an extended relation $\{u_0, u_1, u_2, u_3\} \to 0 \{u_0, u_1, u_3\}$. Similarly, given the output value as unity, we can obtain another extended relation $\{u_0, u_1, u_2, u_3\} \to 1 \{u_2, u_3\}$. Apply the same logic to the resulting subsets on the right-hand side in the above relations sequentially until no new subsets are enumerated, and we can construct the extended relations in the DFA as shown below. Note that not all the 16 subsets are included in the set of extended relations.

$$\{u_0, u_1, u_2, u_3\} \to 0 \{u_0, u_1, u_3\},\ \{u_0, u_1, u_2, u_3\} \to 1 \{u_2, u_3\},\ \{u_0, u_1, u_3\} \to 0 \{u_0, u_1, u_3\},\ \{u_0, u_1, u_3\} \to 1 \{u_2, u_3\},\ \{u_2, u_3\} \to 0 \{u_0, u_1, u_3\},\ \{u_2, u_3\} \to 1 \{u_2\},\ \{u_2\} \to 0 \{u_0, u_1\},\ \{u_2\} \to 0 \{\},\ \{u_0, u_1\} \to 0 \{u_0, u_1\},\ \text{and}\ \{u_0, u_1\} \to 1 \{u_2, u_3\} \tag{7}$$

where {} represents the empty set.
Given the extended relation set (7), we can easily construct the DFA for rule 76 as shown in Figure 5.2.

Step 3: Minimize the DFA to Obtain the Unique Representation

The DFA obtained from Steps 1 and 2 may not be unique because some nodes can be further combined in light of these extended relations in order to reduce the size of the DFA. The minimization step is to find pairs of nodes where the arcs with the same values are directed to the same nodes, and then combine these pairs of nodes into single ones. Consider the extended relation set in (7) and the DFA shown in Figure 5.2 for rule 76. The nodes $\{u_0, u_1, u_3\}$ and $\{u_0, u_1\}$ are directed to themselves given the output value as 0, while to $\{u_2, u_3\}$ given the output value as unity. The two nodes can thus be combined into $\{u_0, u_1, u_3\}$ with other extended relations remaining the same. A closer examination cannot find further combinations, and the resulting DFA as shown in Figure 5.3 is the minimal representation of the DFA for rule 76, which is also unique.

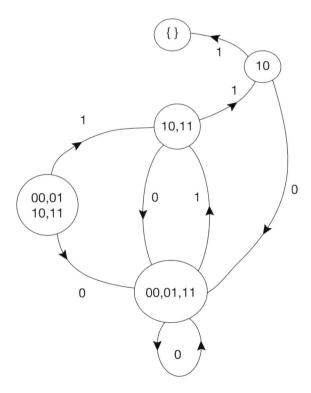

Figure 5.3 **The minimal representation of the DFA for rule 76**

Appendix B

Classification of Transition Rules into Semi-lattices and Trees

The 256 transition rules of the one-dimensional cellular automata with two neighbors ($r = 1$) and two cell values ($k=0$ or 1) are classified into 12 categories according to rule types (trees, semi-lattices, or other) and structure classes (Classes 1 through 4): S1 stands for semi-lattice, Class 1 rules; S2 semi-lattice, Class 2; S3 semi-lattice, Class3; S4 semi-lattice, Class 4; T1 tree, Class1; T2 tree, Class2; T3 tree, Class 3; T4 tree, Class 4; O1 other, Class1; O2 other, Class 2; O3 other, Class3; and O4 other, Class 4. The determination of the semi-lattice, tree, or other structural rules is based on the definition given in Section 3, according to the minimization algorithm as illustrated in Appendix A. The resulting classification is shown in Table 5.4.

Table 5.4 Classification of transition rules into semi-lattices and trees

Rule number	Binary code	Classification	Rule number	Binary code	Classification
0	00000000	O1	128	10000000	T1
1	00000001	T2	129	10000001	T3
2	00000010	T2	130	10000010	S2
3	00000011	T2	131	10000011	S1
4	00000100	S2	132	10000100	S2
5	00000101	S2	133	10000101	S1
6	00000110	S2	134	10000110	S2
7	00000111	S1	135	10000111	O3
8	00001000	T1	136	10001000	S1
9	00001001	S4	137	10001001	S3
10	00001010	S2	138	10001010	S2
11	00001011	S2	139	10001011	S2
12	00001100	T2	140	10001100	S2
13	00001101	T1	141	10001101	S1
14	00001110	T2	142	10001110	S2
15	00001111	O2	143	10001111	T2
16	00010000	T2	144	10010000	S2
17	00010001	T2	145	10010001	S1
18	00010010	S3	146	10010010	S3
19	00010011	T1	147	10010011	S3
20	00010100	S2	148	10010100	S2
21	00010101	S1	149	10010101	S3
22	00010110	S3	150	10010110	O3
23	00010111	S1	151	10010111	S1
24	00011000	T2	152	10011000	S2

Table 5.4 *Continued*

Rule number	Binary code	Classification	Rule number	Binary code	Classification
25	00011001	S2	153	10011001	T3
26	00011010	S3	154	10011010	S3
27	00011011	S2	155	10011011	S2
28	00011100	S1	156	10011100	S1
29	00011101	S2	157	10011101	S1
30	00011110	O3	158	10011110	S2
31	00011111	S1	159	10011111	S1
32	00100000	T1	160	10100000	S1
33	00100001	S2	161	10100001	S3
34	00100010	T2	162	10100010	S2
35	00100011	S2	163	10100011	S1
36	00100100	T2	164	10100100	S2
37	00100101	S2	165	10100101	O3
38	00100110	S2	166	10100110	S2
39	00100111	S2	167	10100111	S3
40	00101000	S1	168	10101000	S1
41	00101001	S4	169	10101001	S3
42	00101010	S2	170	10101010	T2
43	00101011	S2	171	10101011	S2
44	00101100	S2	172	10101100	S2
45	00101101	O3	173	10101101	S2
46	00101110	S2	174	10101110	S2
47	00101111	S2	175	10101111	S2
48	00110000	T2	176	10110000	T2
49	00110001	S2	177	10110001	S1
50	00110010	S1	178	10110010	S1
51	00110011	T2	179	10110011	S1
52	00110100	S2	180	10110100	O2
53	00110101	S2	181	10110101	S3
54	00110110	S3	182	10110110	S3
55	00110111	T1	183	10110111	S1
56	00111000	T2	184	10111000	S2
57	00111001	S1	185	10111001	S2
58	00111010	S1	186	10111010	S1
59	00111011	S2	187	10111011	T2
60	00111100	O3	188	10111100	S2
61	00111101	T2	189	10111101	T2
62	00111110	S1	190	10111110	S2
63	00111111	T1	191	10111111	T1
64	01000000	T1	192	11000000	T1
65	01000001	S4	193	11000001	S3

Table 5.4 *Continued*

Rule number	Binary code	Classification	Rule number	Binary code	Classification
66	01000010	T2	194	11000010	T2
67	01000011	S2	195	11000011	O3
68	01000100	T2	196	11000100	S2
69	01000101	S1	197	11000101	S1
70	01000110	S1	198	11000110	S1
71	01000111	S2	199	11000111	S1
72	01001000	S1	200	11001000	T1
73	01001001	S3	201	11001001	T1
74	01001010	S2	202	11001010	S2
75	01001011	O3	203	11001011	S2
76	01001100	S2	204	11001100	S2
77	01001101	S1	205	11001101	T2
78	01001110	S1	206	11001110	S1
79	01001111	T1	207	11001111	T2
80	01010000	S2	208	11010000	S2
81	01010001	S2	209	11010001	S2
82	01010010	S3	210	11010010	O3
83	01010011	S2	211	11010011	S2
84	01010100	S2	212	11010100	S2
85	01010101	T2	213	11010101	S2
86	01010110	S3	214	11010110	S2
87	01010111	S1	215	11010111	S1
88	01011000	S2	216	11011000	S2
89	01011001	S3	217	11011001	S2
90	01011010	O3	218	11011010	S3
91	01011011	S2	219	11011011	T2
92	01011100	S1	220	11011100	S1
93	01011101	S1	221	11011101	T2
94	01011110	S1	222	11011110	S1
95	01011111	S1	223	11011111	T1
96	01100000	S1	224	11100000	S1
97	01100001	S4	225	11100001	O3
98	01100010	S2	226	11100010	S2
99	01100011	S1	227	11100011	S2
100	01100100	S2	228	11100100	S2
101	01100101	S3	229	11100101	S2
102	01100110	T3	230	11100110	S2
103	01100111	S2	231	11100111	T2
104	01101000	S1	232	11101000	S1
105	01101001	O3	233	11101001	S1
106	01101010	S3	234	11101010	S2

Table 5.4 *Concluded*

Rule number	Binary code	Classification	Rule number	Binary code	Classification
107	01101011	S4	235	11101011	S1
108	01101100	S2	236	11101100	T2
109	01101101	S3	237	11101101	S1
110	01101110	S3	238	11101110	T1
111	01101111	S4	239	11101111	T1
112	01110000	T2	240	11110000	O2
113	01110001	S2	241	11110001	T2
114	01110010	S1	242	11110010	T1
115	01110011	S2	243	11110011	T2
116	01110100	S2	244	11100100	S2
117	01110101	S2	245	11110101	S2
118	01110110	S1	246	11110110	S1
119	01110111	T1	247	11110111	T1
120	01111000	O2	248	11111000	S1
121	01111001	S4	249	11111001	S1
122	01111010	S1	250	11111010	S1
123	01111011	S2	251	11111011	S1
124	01111100	S3	252	11111100	T1
125	01111101	S4	253	11111101	T1
126	01111110	T3	254	11111110	T1
127	01111111	T1	255	11111111	O1

Chapter 6
Applying Cellular Automata to Simulate Spatial Game Interactions to Investigate Effects of Planning

1 Introduction

A city is a complex system. Cities are formed through the accumulation of many development decisions and the interaction of these decisions across time and space. Our limited comprehension of the characteristics of complex systems could be improved by utilizing computer simulation rather than mathematical models (Casti, 1997). The main reason is that traditional mathematics is limited in describing complex natural and social phenomena. After analyzing in detail the shortcomings of traditional mathematical methods in describing complex systems, Wolfram (2002) argued that many complex phenomena, such as fluid dynamics, are beyond the description of traditional mathematics and should be simulated by simple computer programs like one-dimensional cellular automata. In this research, we hold the same opinion, believing that many complex phenomena, including the evolution of cities, cannot be described adequately with mathematical models, despite their many merits. We also believe that rational computer simulation enables one to better understand the basic causes of urban spatial development. Only limited research has previously been conducted on the impact of planning on urban space evolution (Hopkins, 2001). The basic reason is that it has been difficult to collect data and define the causes and effects of the process. In this research, we applied a simple computer simulation model, one-dimensional cellular automata, as the basis with which to describe and explain the evolution of urban space and examine the influence of plans on urban spatial development. The term "plan" was narrowly defined in this research as the optimum strategy for collecting information and minimizing uncertainty.

Because many traditional urban spatial structure models have been constructed using very abstract mathematical language (Anas et al., 1998), we started from a simple and abstract model, capable of explaining the basic characteristics of the phenomena. This model is based on one-dimensional cellular automata. Although there appears to be only a limited relationship between one-dimensional cellular automata and urban physical or spatial structures, the model has already been applied to explain many complex phenomena in both natural and human environments, including the fluctuation of stock markets, natural evolution, and the theory of relativity (Wolfram, 2002). Some one-dimensional cellular automata are even capable of universal computation and the simulation of any complex process. Therefore, if we regard the spatial evolution of a city as a complex process, we can simulate it using one-dimensional cellular automata, even though it has not yet been developed using an iconic approach. In fact, we used one-dimensional cellular automata to develop a common program rather than a common iconic model, despite the fact that many scholars have adopted the latter in their research of CA in recent years. We believe that even with the iconic approaches to comparing simulation results with actual urban space evolution, the original meaning of CA is lost. CA is essentially a simplified pattern language for explaining complex phenomena; therefore, it is not necessarily appropriate for a direct comparison of simulated images with concrete ones.

Driven by the pursuit of reductionism, modern science has for a long time explored the basic causes of complex events and achieved a great deal. With the tools provided by mathematics, traditional science has successfully explained many natural phenomena and has revealed many important natural laws. However, the limitations of mathematical models have become apparent in many fields. For example, the movement of more than three particles in physics still cannot be explained by mathematical models. In this research, we refer to Wolfram's findings and believe that the number of systems that can be explained by mathematics is very limited and these are mostly simple. The evolution of urban space is diverse; however, we believe that simple rules govern these complex urban systems. The one-dimensional cellular automata developed by Wolfram can be applied as an effective tool to analyze the factors that drive the evolution of cities.

Planning is a common phenomenon. All decision-makers make plans for their actions when facing complex tasks. Urban development requires planning because the basic characteristics of urban development do not accord with the assumption of equilibrium in neoclassical economics (Hopkins, 2001). Although the definition of plans and the description of planning (the process of making plans) have been debated, information economics has proven to be a persuasive explanation. Similar to making good decisions, making plans relies on correct and useful information. Therefore, although the definitions of planning are diverse, the concept of "information collection," which was developed from information manipulation, can be provided as an important definition. Hopkins (1981, 2001) defined planning as "the collection of information to minimize uncertainty." Schaeffer and Hopkins (1987) described planning in land development based on a systematic framework and defined planning as "a process of collecting and producing information." They regarded information as an input variable that reduces uncertainty in decision-making. "Information collection to reduce uncertainty" has been a key concept in planning behavioral theory. Based on the concept of information economics, Lai (2002) also proved that the basic principles involved in the collection of information are precision and payoff dependence. Planning usually occurs in a complex environment with a certain degree of uncertainty. This uncertainty is the result of imperfect information due to the complexity of the environment. Information collected by decision-makers usually varies according to the environment; thus, information collection is limited by space. Nonetheless, in most previous studies on planning behaviors, spatial factors could not be directly defined as decision variables (e.g., Hopkins, 1981, 2001; Knaap et al., 1999; Lai and Tseng, 1996; Lai, 1998). Thus, there is an urgent need to integrate spatial categories into information collection in the research of planning behaviors in order to observe the structural characteristics of the interactive evolution of decision-makers in spatial systems. In this research, we adopted the narrow explanation of planning as information manipulation rather than using a more general explanation.

Traditional mathematical models are limited in their ability to describe the development of urban space primarily because mathematical language is incapable of describing complex phenomena. Computer simulation can reproduce the dynamics of many complex systems that mathematical models cannot construct, such as those associated with urban and regional systems. Nonetheless, computer simulation cannot replace mathematical modeling; rather, the two methods can supplement each other. Based on a simple but explanatory computer simulation model, this research explored the impact of the change in the scope of information collection on spatial evolution. The urban space evolution theory has been discussed in many fields, such as ecology, sociology, economics and political economy (Kaiser et al., 1995). Game theory, which considers interactions among different developers, appears to be more appropriate when describing the formation of development schemes that maximize the interests of developers (Rudel, 1989). The well-known prisoner's dilemma (based on game theory) clearly illustrates the interaction mechanism of decision-makers based partially on real world situations. It also suggests the best strategy for each decision-maker based on the information acquired from the continual accumulation of experience and ongoing study (Axelrod, 1984, 1997). This research primarily explored how the scope of information collection influences urban development instead of the evolution of strategies in the form of games. Thus, we did not discuss game theory in detail. By adopting the prisoner's dilemma as the basic mechanism of urban development, this research was able to capture an aspect of real interaction in land development, such as the strategy of owners of adjacent land parcels in deciding whether they should redevelop their land together to improve their living environment. To simplify the simulation, we defined the purpose of information collection by developers as a means to mimic rather than predict the decision schemes and actions of the optimum decision-maker in his surroundings. Consequently, in this research, information collection can be defined as planning – an activity that reduces uncertainty related to the environment.

Axelrod (1984, 1997) developed in-depth research on human activities in the context of the prisoner's dilemma game and particularly analyzed the circumstances in which cooperation usually occurs. In this research, we explored the impact of the changes in planning effects on urban space evolution based on the framework of the prisoner's dilemma game. We included CA (cellular automata) to provide a model by which to consider spatial factors as a supplement to the original prisoner's dilemma game which was proposed by Nowak and May (1993). This research only explored the interaction model based on one-dimensional cellular automata, the simplest CA (all cells are arrayed in one-dimensional or linear space), which has already been analyzed in detail in previous studies (e.g., by Wolfram, 1994, 2002; Wuensche and Lesser, 1992). Based on one-dimensional CA, we established the rules of evolution for the prisoner's dilemma model and the effects of plans, exploring the interactive evolution of the strategies and behaviors of decision-makers who view information collection differently. Through the results of computer simulation in the simple spatial interaction model, we were able to understand the impact of information collection on the evolution of urban space, and consequently explore the possibilities of using this model to explain planning issues in the real world. Section 2 explains the framework of the one-dimensional CA and the prisoner's dilemma game. Section 3 introduces the research design of the computer simulation, including the rules of CA. Section 4 provides the results of the simulation. Section 5 discusses the results, and Section 6 presents the conclusions.

2 Cellular Automata and the Prisoner's Dilemma Game

The concept of CA originated from the self-reproducing automata conceived by von Neumann and Morgenstern (1966). Based on that concept, Conway et al. (1985) created the "game of life" as an analytical means to explore complex phenomena. CA has subsequently been improved (Nowak and May, 1993) and applied in urban planning (e.g., Environment and Planning B: Planning and Design published its special issue on CA in 1997). It has also been widely adopted in ecology (Nowak and May, 1992), economics (Chen and Cheng, 1995) and cities (Batty and Xie, 1994) as well as in many other fields. Complex phenomena can emerge from the simple rules of CA. The principal concept is that a cell is only influenced by a limited number of its neighboring cells within a large space. The value of a cell in the next moment is determined by its neighboring cells within the radius r. For example, suppose there are $2r+1$ one-dimensional CA denoted as:

$a_{i-r}, a_{i-r+1}, \ldots, a_i, \ldots, a_{i+r-1}, a_{i+r}$

The dynamic equation is a discrete function of time:

$$a_i^{(t)} = F[a_{i-r}^{(t-1)}, a_{i-r+1}^{(t-1)}, \ldots, a_i^{(t-1)}, \ldots, a_{i+r-1}^{(t-1)}, a_{i+r}^{(t-1)}] \tag{1}$$

in which:

a_i = the *i-th* cell

t = time, and

r = radius of interaction.

Suppose F takes the integer value of 1 or 0, namely {1,0}, then F can be defined as:

$$F : \{1,0\}^{(2r+1)} \to \{1,0\} \tag{2}$$

F has a limited number of possibilities: $k^{k^{(2r+1)}}$, where k denotes the number of possible values for each cell. For example, when $r = 1$ and $k = 2$, there are a total of 8 possibilities for a middle cell in 3 ($2r + 1 = 3$) consecutive neighboring cells—111, 110, 101, 100, 011, 010, 001, and 000. Because each cell may have one of two possible values, 0 or 1, the value of k is 2. Therefore, there would be $2^8 = 256$ possible values for the function F. This demonstrates that a very simple function can lead to highly complex results. The interaction of a cell in CA is confined to "$2r+1$" cells (considering the spatial scope of interactions); however, the associated propagation rule implies that each cell has a holistic influence on the system.

Although the 256 rules for one-dimensional CA in Wolfram's research appear simple, the implications are profound. By considering the 256 rules as the universal set of basic rules or natural laws for complex systems (including cities), the model is capable of explaining all complex phenomena including urban evolution. For instance, Wolfram classified those 256 rules into four categories (which will be elaborated upon later). One category is called complex structures, the evolution pattern of which is diverse and unpredictable. Urban spatial evolution has such characteristics. Those basic rules form stochastic evolution rules, making the evolution of cities full of uncertainty (Lai, 2003).

Nowak and May (1992) analyzed how complex structures emerge from simple rules by integrating the prisoner's dilemma with CA in computer simulation. They first simplified the prisoner's dilemma (as shown in Figure 6.1) by reducing the four categories in the original prisoner's dilemma to two. They denoted the payoff for the CC (cooperate-cooperate, meaning to choose the strategy of cooperation when the opposite side is known to have chosen the strategy of cooperation) strategy as 1 and that for the DC (defect-cooperate) strategy as b. The payoffs for the other two strategies (DD: defect-defect, and CD: cooperate-defect) were both 0. Therefore, the behavior dynamics in the system depends entirely on the value of b. Thus, the prisoner's dilemma was simplified to a single variable. Although such a simplified structure differed somewhat from the original prisoner's dilemma, its basic logic is identical to the original. For example, when *b* is larger than 1, the predominant strategy for both players is to defect, the same as in the original prisoner's dilemma game. The operation of the CA model was based on the interaction of a cell with its neighboring cells within a fixed spatial scope. The results of the interaction were denoted as payoffs. The sum of the payoffs of the middle cell and its neighbors within the scope of interaction are calculated. The strategy of the middle cell at the next time frame is to copy the cell with the highest sum payoff within the scope of interaction. This simulates the strategy of imitating winners. Based on this rule, cells can also interact in the two-dimensional CA, and results can be obtained by adjusting the scope and value of *b*. The simplified prisoner's dilemma can describe many urban planning events, such as the provision of public property rights, the construction of neighborhood facilities, and the decision-making of reconstruction. Taking the redevelopment of two neighboring land parcels as an example, the payoffs of both land owners are 0 if neither chooses to redevelop his land and 1 if both of them choose to redevelop. If one developer chooses to redevelop and the other chooses not to redevelop, the payoff of the latter will be *b*, which is higher than that of the former, which is 0. This result is in agreement with the logic of the original prisoner's dilemma.

	C	D
C	1	0
D	*b*	0

C: cooperate, D: defect, *b*: variable in the (D,C) game

Figure 6.1 Payoff matrix in the simplified prisoner's dilemma game

3   Research Design for the Computer Simulation

The design of computer simulation in this research is based on the integration of the prisoner's dilemma game and one-dimensional CA; that is, the application of the concept of Nowak and May (1992) to one-dimensional CA. The primary aim was to explore the influence of planning (as a controlled variable) on the structure of space evolution. According to the rules of the one-dimensional CA presented in the previous section, the value or strategy of a cell in the next time frame depends on the interaction between the cell and its neighboring cells in the current time frame. The spatial scope of interaction has two directions in only one dimension. The controlled variables of the one-dimensional CA model in this research are elaborated upon below.

(1) The Value of k in Each Cell

In this research, k denotes the number of possible values a cell can take, and in this study this was equal to 2 because each cell has two basic strategies: to cooperate or to defect. We assigned 1 as the value for the strategy of defection and 0 as that for the strategy of cooperation:

$a_i \in \{1,0\}$, in which:

1 = (D), denotes the strategy of defection

0 = (C), denotes the strategy of cooperation

k is a constant with the value of 2 in the simulation in this research.

(2) Scope of Interaction r and Scope of Comparative Strategies n

The scope of interaction r represents the distance of the interactive neighboring cells. The scope of comparative strategies n represents the number of cells with comparative strategies. It should be noted that Nowak and May (1993) did not consider the relationship between r and n, nor how many cells were within the scope of its comparative strategies. In Nowak and May's (1993) research, a cell was designed to interact only with its four immediately adjacent cells in four directions. Therefore, the scope of interaction r is a constant with the value 1 and the scope of comparative strategies n is 4. In the present research, r and n were both considered. The value of n can be regarded as the scope of information collection or the effects of planning; while the value of r is viewed as the scope of interaction for each cell in the prisoner's dilemma game or the scope of influence of the decision interaction. Suppose $r = 1$ and $n = 3$. "$r = 1$" indicates that a cell interacts with its two neighbors, one on the left and one on the right. The result of the interaction is denoted as the payoffs in the prisoner's dilemma (see the payoff matrix in Figure 6.1). "$n = 3$" indicates that, based on the above pattern of interaction, the sum of the payoffs of the 3 cells, the middle cell and its two neighbors, are respectively calculated and compared. The strategy of the middle cell in the next time frame is to adopt that of the cell with the highest payoff.

(3) Effects of Planning

In this research, we added the influence of planning in information collection into the rules of CA by strengthening the capability of each cell to collect information. In the CA model, this was achieved by increasing the value of n. In practice, planning changes decisions according to the information acquired from sampling or experiments. The influence of planning in information manipulation becomes apparent when the results of sampling or experiments change the decision-making strategies. In cities, sampling is shown as the data collection of the site and experiments as mathematical modeling, both of which can be applied to predict the impact of urban policies and to choose or change them. As previously discussed, the scope of planning did not consider strategic actions, which means selecting one's strategy according to the possible actions of the opposite side. Therefore, the purpose of information collection is to be aware of the actions of one's surrounding decision-makers and choose or simulate the optimum or most profitable strategy. That can be explained as the information collection of the decision scenario. In addition to the two previously discussed scenarios where $r = 1$, $n = 3$ or $r = 2$, $n = 3$, the intensification of the effect of planning can create two additional scenarios: $r = 1$, $n = 5$ or $r = 2$, $n = 5$. In the four possible scenarios (Table 6.1), many different rules were created by adjusting the payoff variable b in the prisoner's dilemma game.

Table 6.1 Simulation scenarios

Scope of comparative strategy Scope of interaction	n = 3	n = 5
$r = 1$	$r = 1 、 n = 3$	$r = 1 、 n = 5$
$r = 2$	$r = 2 、 n = 3$	$r = 2 、 n = 5$

Based on Wolfram's (1994) design, we established two patterns for the original structure of the simulation: "seed" and "random." In "seed," D only exists in the middle cell, and all the other cells choose C. In "random," C and D are designated randomly. Those two patterns were simulated in each of the four situations, which provide a total of eight scenarios, as shown in Table 6.2.

Table 6.2 Simulation design

	Seed	Random
Simulation scenarios	$r=1 、 n=3$	$r=1 、 n=3$
	$r=2 、 n=3$	$r=2 、 n=3$
	$r=1 、 n=5$	$r=1 、 n=5$
	$r=2 、 n=5$	$r=2 、 n=5$

Based on Nowak and May's (1992) research, we modified the transformation rules of the original one-dimensional CA. Take the scenario of $r = 1$ and $n = 3$ as an example. There are five cells in the scope of interaction because each of the three adjacent cells interacts with its neighbors within the distance of 1 ($r = 1$); including the original three cells ($n = 3$), the central cell plus one to the left and one to the right. The values of the latter two new cells were unknown. The sum interaction payoff of each cell was calculated. The strategy of the cell with the highest sum payoff was adopted by the middle cell in the next time frame. If the values of the three adjacent cells were 101, there would be a total of four possibilities for the five cells: 01010, 01011, 11010, and 11011. For each of the three cells, the sum of the payoffs of all four possibilities was calculated. The sum of the payoffs of the three cells was then compared. This enabled us to determine the value of the middle cell. If it had the highest payoff, its value would remain as 0 in the next time frame. If either of its adjacent cells (with the value of 1) had the highest payoff, its value would change from 0 to 1 in the next time frame. If the payoffs of the three cells were the same, its value would remain as 0 in the next time frame. This method provided a total of 40 rules, as shown in Table 6.3, and elaborated upon in the appendix.

Table 6.3　Distribution of rules

Variable	Number of rules
$r=1 \cdot n=3$	5
$r=2 \cdot n=3$	3
$r=1 \cdot n=5$	14
$r=2 \cdot n=5$	18

4　Results

Based on Wolfram's (1994) classification, we classified the simulation results by considering the two patterns in the original structure of the simulation: "seed" and "random." We then discussed the impact of the variation in the scope of interaction and the scope of comparative strategies in the operation of CA. We also described how the agglomeration of C and D evolved. The simulation was performed using a one-dimensional CA program, based on a similar program developed by Wuensche and Lesser (1994). The number of neighboring cells was limited to 3 or 5 in this simulation ($n=3$ or $n=5$).

(1) Classification of the Simulation Results by CA

The evolution of CA is complex and diverse. However, according to Wolfram's (1994) study on the evolution of one-dimensional CA, all CAs can be assorted into four universality classes as shown below. We adopted Wolfram's (1994) totalistic codes for this research.

Class 1   In Class 1, the behavior is very simple, and nearly all initial conditions lead to precisely the same uniform final state.

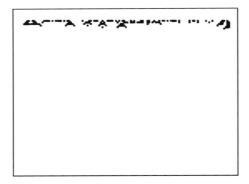

Figure 6.2   Evolution pattern of the CA in class 1

Class 2   Class 2 provides many different possible final states; however, all of them comprise only a specific set of simple structures that either remain the same forever or repeat every few steps.

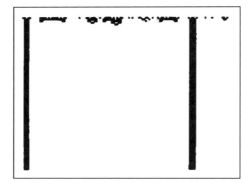

Figure 6.3   Evolution pattern of the CA in class 2

Class 3   In Class 3, the behavior is more complex, and appears in many respects random; however, triangles and other small-scale structures always remain visible at some level.

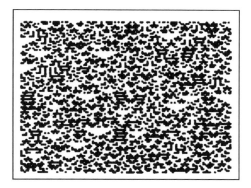

Figure 6.4 Evolution pattern of the CA in class 3

Class 4 Class 4 involves a mixture of order and randomness: localized structures are produced, which on their own are fairly simple, but these structures move around and interact with each other in very complex ways. Wolfram (1994) found that the CA in this class is seldom observed when $k=2$ and $r=1$, and becomes more popular as r increases.

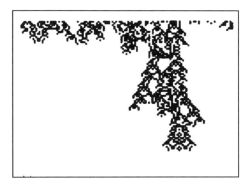

Figure 6.5 Evolution pattern of the CA in class 4

The classification of the CA in this research was based on the four classes discussed above. However, the patterns of CA in classes 3 and 4 are so complicated that we had to use entropy as an indicator in the measurement (Wofram, 1984). This research identified CA in the first two classes but not in classes 3 or 4.

Using Wolfram's classification, we found that most of the rules evolved to class 1 and class 2, and only one rule evolved to class 3 or 4 (when $r=2$, $n=5$, $9/7<b<4/3$) (Table 6.4). This shows that most of the systems can evolve to a fixed, homogeneous, and stable structure and it is difficult to reach a complex structure like class 4. The explanation for the evolution of rules is elaborated upon in the appendix.

Table 6.4 Classification and numbers of the simulation results

Class Variable	Class 1	Class 2	Class 3 or 4
r=1、n=3	3	2	0
r=2、n=3	2	1	0
r=1、n=5	9	5	0
r=2、n=5	10	7	1

(2) Situations of Interaction (n is Fixed, r is Adjustable)

As shown in Table 6.5, as the scope of interaction increases (the value of r increases from 1 to 2), the scope of b reduces. In this research, we used the parameter of "relative sensitivity" to illustrate the average variation in b. Relative sensitivity was defined as the scope of b divided by the number of rules. A high degree of relative sensitivity means that the variation in b was relatively small, and a slight change in the value of b would result in a change in the entire rule. This implies that the variation in b diversified the transformation rules in the system. The evolution of the system became unstable as the scope of interaction increased. When $n = 3$, the number of rules decreased as the scope of interaction increased. However, when $n = 5$, the number of rules increased as the scope of interaction increased. In addition, the system evolved to Class 1 when b was located at the two ends of the scope, and to other more complicated classes when b was located in the middle of the scope. This indicates that the system tended to evolve toward homogeneous patterns when the value of b in (D, C) was overly large or overly small compared with the value of 1 in (C, C). The implication is that the underlying mechanism associated with the evolution of cities may change with variations in the value of b, resulting from the influence of policy or environment.

Table 6.5 Characteristics of evolution of CA with the interaction of different ranges and neighboring cells

Class variable	Scope of b	Range	Number of rules	Relative sensitivity	Classes of evolution			
					Class 1	Class 2	Class 3
r=1, n=3	$2/3 \leq b \leq 5/3$	1	5	0.20	3	2	0
r=2, n=3	1	0	3	0.00	2	1	0
r=1, n=5	$1/2 \leq b \leq 3$	2.5	14	0.18	9	5	0
r=2, n=5	$1/2 \leq b \leq 8/5$	1.1	18	0.06	10	7	1

(3) Effects of Planning (n is Adjustable, r is Fixed)

According to Table 6.5, the increase in the effects of planning was manifested as an increase in the scope of information collection or an increase in the value of n. By observing the relative sensitivity, we found that as the effects of planning increased which is manifested by the increase of the value of n, the CA was highly sensitive to the value of b when $r = 1$, and not sensitive when $r = 2$, although the reason for this difference remains to be explored. In addition, as the effects of planning increased, the number of rules increased for both $r = 1$ and $r = 2$, and the patterns of evolution diversified. This implies that the effects of planning can change the mechanism underlying the evolution of cities and the sensitivity of the interaction payoff b.

(4) Increases and Decreases in C and D

The simulation results suggest that the agglomeration of C and D changed with the variation in the scope of b. We elaborate on these results below with respect to "seed" and "random," the two patterns of the original structure of the simulation in the four scenarios: $r = 1, n = 3; r = 2, n = 3; r = 1, n = 5$ and $r = 2, n = 5$.

The Final Evolution Results were not Influenced by the Original Structure

In the "seed" pattern of the original structure of the simulation, the system evolved toward a well-ordered fixed structure. This was very similar to the result in the "random" pattern. The final results in both patterns were the same with only one exception, when $r = 2$, $n = 5$ and $9/7<b<4/3$. Moreover, in the "random" pattern, the evolution to the final structure took slightly longer than in the "seed" pattern. We can conclude that the final evolution result was not influenced by the original structure.

The Agglomeration of C was Superior to that of D

The results of the simulation suggest that the agglomeration of C was superior to that of D. This means that when cells with the strategy of C agglomerated (the cells bordered next to each other), D was unable to invade. As was shown in the simplified payoff matrix in Figure 6.1, when $b>1$, both cells choose D (the strategy of defection). However, C (the strategy of cooperation) continues to survive when it is capable of gaining an advantage from the agglomeration of C. The agglomeration of C can only be broken by a set increase in the value of b. The advantage of agglomeration arises mainly from the asymmetry of the structure of the payoff matrix (Figure 6.1) since the payoff of (C, C) was 1, which is noticeably larger than 0, the payoff (D, D). In comparison, D did not have the advantage of agglomeration and disappeared when $b<1$. Even when b was slightly larger than 1, the agglomeration of C could still not be broken. Table 6.6 clearly illustrates this situation: when b was close to or smaller than 1, the agglomeration of C rapidly dominated; when b was slightly larger than 1, the advantage of the agglomeration of C made the invasion of D difficult; only when b increased to a relatively high value, could D successfully invade the agglomeration of C. This may be the result of the structure and spatial characteristics of the payoff matrix associated with the prisoner's dilemma. Another possible explanation is that in the iterative prisoner's dilemma game, each side attempts to prevent the future revenge of the opposite side, and tends to choose the strategy of cooperation. This is also in accordance with Axelrod's (1984) finding and implies that such a strategic framework is suitable for explaining the development of urban regions, such as a fully developed metropolitan area, where there is high possibility of an iterative encountering.

Table 6.6 Evolution of the homogeneous agglomeration of C or D and the scopes of b

Class variable	All cells dominated by C	All cells dominated by D
$r = 1 、 n = 3$	$b < 3/4$	$b > 5/3$
$r = 2 、 n = 3$	$b < 1$	$b > 1$
$r = 1 、 n = 5$	$b < 5/4$	$b > 2$
$r = 2 、 n = 5$	$b < 7/8$	$b \geq 4/3$

5 Discussion

This research integrated the prisoner's dilemma game and the effects of plans into the rules of one-dimensional CA and applied the designed rules in computer simulation. Although the simulation and analysis in this research were highly abstract, the characteristics of the simulated system could be used to explain land development behaviors in the real world. Wolfram (2002) demonstrated the ability of the one-dimensional CA to explain many complex physical and non-physical phenomena, including the complex characteristics of urban spatial evolution. The values of 1 or 2 for the scope of interaction variable r and the values of 3 or 5 for the planning effect variable n do not represent the absolute values of those two variables, but represent a relatively small scope of interaction ($r=1$), a relatively large scope of interaction ($r=2$), a relatively small information collection effect ($n=3$), or a relatively large information collection effect ($n=5$). Similarly, variable b in the payoff matrix denotes an overall extrinsic impact factor, which may include taxes, revenues, or expenses associated with the development of land, and even uncertainties regarding the evolution of the environment. The implications of the simulation results for land-use planning were explained from the perspectives of the scope of information collection and the scope of interaction, as shown below.

(1) Planning Effect n

According to the above definition of n, an increase in the scope of comparative strategies can be regarded as an increase in the scope of information collection. As the scope of information increases, the number of rules increases, and more evolution results emerge. This indicates that the system becomes increasingly diverse and complex when the effects of individual cells increase. It refutes the argument that the market can efficiently allocate resources without the interference of planning. Planning, according to its narrow definition in this research, can influence the evolution of spatial systems.

(2) Scope of Interaction r

In the present research, payoffs were calculated from the interaction of cells in the prisoner's dilemma game. This interaction represents the spatial relationships among various decision-makers in the real world (the decision of one actor influences the payoff of other actors). Changes in the value of b also determine whether the game is a prisoner's dilemma game. The game can be confirmed as being a prisoner's dilemma game only when b is larger than 1. The scope of interaction r can be regarded as the scope of influence of "decision interdependence." This increases when the decision interdependence increases. In land development, suppose that each cell represents a block and there are only two permissible types of land use for each block, residential or commercial. The payoff matrix for the land development is written as follows.

	C	D
C	1	0
D	b	0

C: cooperate, D: defect

	R	E
R	1	0
E	b	0

R: residential, E: commercial, b: variable in the (D,C) game or (R,E) game

Figure 6.6 Residential-commercial payoff matrix

The above analysis assumes that the payoff of a block is 1 when both blocks are in residential use and b when a block in commercial use interacts with another in residential use. In other situations, the payoff is 0. Nevertheless, this supposed payoff matrix cannot explain all land development patterns, such as agglomeration economy, but rather shows how the results of the simulation can explain real world situations. The increase in the scope of interactions indicates the expansion of the scope of influence of decision relationships. In a new neighborhood, the scope of decision relationships is relatively small and simple in the beginning. However, with population inflow and commercial development, the decision relationships become increasingly complex. The scope of interaction expands and the number of interacting blocks increases. According to the above analysis, when the scope of interaction r increases, the scope of b shrinks. This system is particularly sensitive to changes in b.

Our analysis also shows that the scope of interaction r and the scope of information collection n react differently to the payoff b, which is an exogenous variable and could be controlled. In land development, the government could adjust the value of b through taxation, charges, and the refund of land development fees, and use other tools to induce land use in a certain area to be purely residential (evolution pattern with homogeneous C) or purely commercial (evolution pattern with homogeneous D) or mixed use (with C and D). Further studies need to be performed to discuss in detail the application of CA simulation in policymaking.

6 Conclusions

Based on the one-dimensional CA and the prisoner's dilemma game, this research developed a computer simulation to examine the influence of plans on system evolution. The results suggest that an increase in planning effects increases the scope of b, causing the system to become increasingly diverse. Enlarging the scope of interaction reduces the scope of b. The cells become sensitive to the value of b with regard to the rules. A slight variation in b may result in a large change in the rules. Moreover, the results of simulation also indicate that C has an advantage over D or could not be invaded by D when both of them agglomerate. That advantage is mainly the result of the asymmetry of the structure of the payoff matrix and the emergence of cooperative activities in the iterative prisoner's dilemma game. Previous literature has proven the capability of one-dimensional CA to explain complex systems in the real world. Therefore, the one-dimensional CA model should also be valid for describing and explaining the evolution of urban systems. This was also the basis for the simulation in this research. More precise, in-depth computer simulations and new explanatory concepts must be developed in the future to apply the findings of this research to planning practices.

Appendix: Setting for the Evolution Rules of One-dimensional CA

When $r = 1$ and $n = 3$, there are a total of eight arrays for the values of a cell and its two neighbors: 111, 110, 101, 100, 011, 010, 001 and 000. When each of the two neighbors interacts with its outward neighbor, there are four possibilities for each array, as shown below. The numbers in the brackets denote the payoffs of three cells in the simplified prisoner's dilemma game, as shown in Figure 6.1. The last row shows the sum of the payoffs of the four possibilities of each of the three cells arrays.

01110	01100	01010	01000	00110	00100	00010	00000
(b 0 b)	(b b 2)	(2b 1 2b)	(2b 2 3)	(2 b b)	(2 2b 2)	(3 2 2b)	(3 3 3)
01111	01101	01011	01001	00111	00101	00011	00001
(b 0 0)	(b b 1)	(2b 1 b)	(2b 2 2)	(2 b 0)	(2 2b 1)	(3 2 b)	(3 3 2)
11110	11100	11010	11000	10110	10100	10010	10000
(0 0 b)	(0 b 2)	(b 1 2b)	(b 2 3)	(1 b b)	(1 2b 2)	(2 2 2b)	(2 3 3)
11111	11101	11011	11001	10111	10101	10011	10001
(0 0 0)	(0 b 1)	(b 1 b)	(b 2 2)	(1 b 0)	(1 2b 1)	(2 2 b)	(2 3 2)
(2b 0 2b)	(2b 4b 6)	(6b 4 6b)	(6b 8 10)	(6 4b 2b)	(6 8b 6)	(10 8 6b)	(10 12 10)

Table 6.7 Rules when $r=1$ and $n=3$

Rule b	Binary code	Wolfram's classes
$b \leq 2/3$	10000000	Class 1
$2/3 < b < 3/4$	10100000	Class 1
$3/4 \leq b < 3/2$	10100100	Class 2
$3/2 \leq b \leq 5/3$	11101100	Class 2
$b > 5/3$	11111110	Class 1

Table 6.8 Rules when $r = 2$ and $n = 3$

Rule b	Binary code	Wolfram's classes
$b < 1$	10000000	Class 1
$b = 1$	11001100	Class 2
$b > 1$	11111110	Class 1

Different classes of structure emerge with variations in the value of b, as shown in Figure 6.7. The binary codes denote the values of the middle cell in the eight arrays in the next time frame. For instance, 10000000 indicates 111→1, 110→0, 101→0, 100→0, 011→0, 010→0, 001→0 and 000→0. The variation zones of the value of b in other combinations of r and n are shown in Table 6.8, Table 6.9, and Table 6.10. For example, when $n=5$, 1010110011100100001011100000 00 indicates 11111→1, 11110→0, 11101→1, 11100 →0, 11011→1, 11010→1, 11001→0, 11000→0, 10111→1, 10110→1, 10101→1, 10100→0, 10011→0, 10010→1, 10001→0, 10000→0, 01111→0, 01110→0, 01101 →1, 01100→0, 01011→1, 01010→1, 01001→1, 01000→0, 00111→0, 00110→0, 00101→0, 00100→0, 00011→0, 00010→0, 00001→0, and 00000→0.

Table 6.9 Rules when $r = 1$ and $n = 5$

Rule b	Binary code	Wolfram's classes
$b < 1/2$	10000000000000000000000000000000	Class 1
$1/2 \leq b < 2/3$	10000000001000000000000000000000	Class 1
$2/3 \leq b \leq 3/4$	10100000101000000000000000000000	Class 1
$3/4 < b < 1$	10100100101000000000110000000000	Class 1
$b = 1$	10100100111000000010110000000000	Class 1
$1 < b < 5/4$	10101100111001000010111000000000	Class 1
$5/4 \leq b \leq 4/3$	10101100111101000010111000110000	Class 2
$4/3 < b < 3/2$	10101110111111000010111000110000	Class 2
$b = 3/2$	11101110111111001110111100110100	Class 2
$3/2 < b < 2$	11101110111111001110111100110100	Class 2
$b = 2$	11101110111111001111111100110100	Class 2
$2 < b < 5/2$	11101110111111111111111100110100	Class 1
$5/2 \leq b \leq 3$	11111110111111111111111111110100	Class 1
$b > 3$	11111111111111111111111111111110	Class 1

Table 6.10 Rules when $r = 2$ and $n = 5$

Rule b	Binary code	Wolfram's classes
$b \leq 1/2$	10000000000000000000000000000000	Class 1
$1/2 < b < 3/4$	10001000000000000000000000000000	Class 1
$3/4 \leq b < 4/5$	10101000100000000000000000000000	Class 1
$4/5 \leq b \leq 5/6$	10101000110000000010000000000000	Class 1
$5/6 < b \leq 6/7$	10101010110010000010000000000000	Class 1
$6/7 < b < 7/8$	10101010110011000010001000000000	Class 1
$7/8 \leq b < 1$	10101010110011000010001000010000	Class 2
$1 \leq b \leq 8/7$	10101010110011000111001001010000	Class 2
$8/7 < b < 7/6$	10101010110011000111001101010100	Class 2
$b = 7/6$	10101010110110001110011011110100	Class 2
$7/6 < b \leq 6/5$	10101010110111001110011011110100	Class 2
$6/5 < b < 5/4$	10101010110111001111111101110100	Class 2
$5/4 \leq b \leq 9/7$	10101010111111001111111101110100	Class 2
$9/7 < b < 4/3$	10101010111111001111111101110110	Class 3 or 4
$4/3 \leq b < 3/2$	11101010111111101111111101110110	Class 1
$b = 3/2$	11111010111111101111111111110110	Class 1
$3/2 < b \leq 8/5$	11111110111111111111111111110110	Class 1
$b > 8/5$	11111111111111111111111111111110	Class 1

References

Anas, A., R. Arnott, and K.A. Small. (September) 1998. "Urban Spatial Structure." *Journal of Economic Literature XXXVI* pp. 1426–64.

Axelrod, R. 1984. *The Evolution of Cooperation*. New York: Basic Books & Co.

Batty, M., and Y. Xie. 1994. "From cells to cities." *Environment and Planning B: Planning and Design* 121: pp. 31–48.

Casti, J.L. 1997. *Would-be Worlds: How Simulation Is Changing the Frontiers of Science*. New York: John Wiley & Sons, Inc.

Chen, S-H., and Y-S. Cheng. 1995. "Self-fulfillment expectation, Bayes learning, and economic lie: a simulation and analysis of cellular interactive model." Proceedings of Taiwan Economic Association Annual Meeting, pp. 123–50.

Conway, J.H., R.K. Guy, and E.R. Berlekamp. 1985. *Winning Ways: For Your Mathematical Plays* Volume 2, New York: Academic Press.

Friend, J., and A. Hickling. 1997. *Planning under Pressure*. Oxford: Butterworth/Heinemann.

Hopkins, L.D. 1981. "The decision to plan: Planning activity as public goods." In *Urban Infrastructure, Location, and Housing*, W.R. Lierop, and P. Nijkamp (eds), Sijthoff and Noordhoff, Alphen aan den Rijn pp. 273–96.

Hopkins, L.D. 2001. *Urban Development: The Logic of Making Plans*. London: Island Press.

Kaiser, E.J., D.R. Godschalk, and F.S. Chapin. 1995. *Urban Land Use Planning*. Chicago: University of Illinois Press.

Knaap, G.J., L.D. Hopkins, and K.P. Donaghy. 1998. "Do plans matter? A framework for examining the logic and effects of land use planning." *Journal of Planning Education and Research* 18(1): 25–34.

Lai, S.K., and H.P. Tseng. 1995. "The logic of planning: an interpretation based on Savage's utility theory." *Journal of Planning* 22: 85–97.

Lai, S.K. 1998. "From organized anarchy to controlled structure: effects of planning on the garbage-can decision processes." *Environment and Planning B: Planning and Design* 25: 85–102.

Lai, S.K. 2002. "Information structures exploration as planning for a unitary Organization." *Planning and Market*, http://www-pam.usc.edu, 5(1): 31–42.

Lai, S.K. 2003. "On transition rules of complex structure in one-dimensional cellular automata: Some implications for urban change." *Annals of Regional Science* 37(2): 337–52.

von Neumann, J., and O. Morgenstern. 1996. *Theory of Self-Reproducing Automata*. A.W. Burks (ed.) Urbana: University of Illinois Press.

Nowak, M.A., and R.M. May. 1992. "Evolutionary games and spatial chaos." *Nature* 359: 826.

Nowak. M.A., and R.M. May. 1993. "The spatial dilemmas of evolution." *International Journal of Bifurcation and Chaos* 3(1): 35–78.

Rudel, T.K. 1989. *Situations and Strategies in American Land-Use Planning*. New York: Cambridge University Press.

Schaeffer, P., and L.D. Hopkins. 1987. "Behavior of land developers: planning and the economics of information." *Environment and Planning A* 19: 1221–32.

Wolfram, S. 1984. "Cellular automata as models of complexity." *Nature* 311: 419–24.

Wolfram, S. 1994. "Universality and complexity in cellular automata." In *Cellular Automata and Complexity*. S. Wolfram (ed.) Massachusetts: Addison-Wesley & Co.

Wolfram, S. 2002. *A New Kind of Science*. Champaign, IL: Wolfram Media, Inc.

Wuensche, A., and M. Lesser. 1992. *The Global Dynamics of Cellular Automata: An Atlas of Basin of Attraction Fields of One-dimensional Cellular Automata*. Massachusetts: Addison-Wesley & Co.

Chapter 7
Planning for City Safety and Creativity: Two Metaphors

1 Introduction

Planning is a set of activities to acquire information and to make contingent decisions into the future. It is also considered as procedures for taking actions. Such a definition of planning is consistent with that of intelligence (e.g., Ghallab et al., 2004; LaValle, 2006). Intelligence in the context of planning connotes different meanings (e.g., Mandelbaum, 2008), but we define intelligence as computation so they are used interchangeably here. Can these procedures of planning as intelligence be reduced to steps similar to computer algorithms? Systems in which planning takes place are complex in that there are numerous elements interacting with each other forming a coherent whole. Can such systems be described as complex systems capable of universal computation? If the answers to both questions are yes, then it is possible to model planning effects using simple models, such as cellular automata, and examine the conditions under which making planning is useful.

There may be various answers to the question of what constitutes a creative city? Some might argue that a creative city is an affluent society; some would argue that a creative city is both an efficient and just society, and still others might conceive a creative city as sustainable. The notion of city creativity is full of ambiguity at best. Viewing the city as a complex and large adaptive system, we argue that a creative city is one that is capable of universal computation, and a necessary condition for a creative city is safety. Put simply, a safe city is a place where the number of problems, in particular disastrous ones, is kept at a minimum. Problems can take many forms: landslide, flooding, traffic congestion, crimes, slums, poverty, homelessness, overbuilding, terrorism, and so on. In particular, problems in one form, such as landslide, if not properly solved, could trigger off problems in another form, such as flooding. The city is a container in which decision-makers or agents, solutions, problems, and decision situations interact in an unpredictable way at certain locations. This metaphor of cities is called the spatial garbage-can model and is presented elsewhere (Lai, 2006). More specifically, agents, solutions, problems, and locations meet in various decision situations and, under certain structural constraints, something happens. Problems may or may not be solved in these decision situations depending on whether the solutions and agents match the problems under consideration at certain locations in these decision situations. It is not practical to aim at a problem-free city, but we can strive for anticipating and eliminating problems that may or may not have occurred. A safe city is defined here, therefore, as a place where the number of problems is kept at a minimum. A creative city is, on the other hand, a complex system capable of universal computation where novelty is sustained over time.

The capability of the city in solving problems is distributive. It is not practical to expect the government to solve all the problems. Cities self-organize themselves, and through self-organization, the agents take adaptive actions to solve various problems. Low-income residents adaptively seek locations with lower land rents they can afford. However, what the local government can do is to set up the rules of the game, or institutions, under which the play of the game unfolds. These rules or institutions are nothing but the relationship between the five elements of the city (Lai, 2006). That is, a decision structure specifies which agent has access to which decision situation. An access structure determines which problem is related to which decision situation. A solution structure depicts which solution can appear in which decision situation. A spatial structure describes which decision situation can occur in which location. These structural constraints do not invalidate the random meeting of agents, solutions, problems, decision situations, and locations; rather, they simply provide conditions under which decisions may or may not be made.

The traditional wisdom of city planning can solve certain problems, mainly through the arrangement of the spatial structure of the relationship between decision situations and locations. What is less known is that the other intangible structural constraints, namely, decision structures, access structures, and solution structures, are of more significance in affecting the working of the city (Lai, 2006). In addition, planning investment focused on relating decisions may only increase the efficiency of decision-making, rather than problem-solving (Lai, 1998; 2003b). In order to eliminate the problems that may or may not have occurred in the city, that is, achieving a safe society, we need more than planning.

In short, in order to create a safe place to live as a basis for a creative city by reducing the number of problems that may or may not have occurred, we need to do at least two things: institutional design and problem-focused planning, in addition to the traditional physical planning. In the institutional design, we need to design structural constraints, namely decision structures, access structures, and solution structures, that would render the problems under consideration as attended to by and aired in as many agents and decision situations as possible so they would have higher probabilities of being solved. In the problem-focused planning, we should aim at plans that relate not only to decisions but also to problems. For example, in making plans, we should focus not only on how decisions are related to each other, but also on how the problems associated with these decisions can be solved. On the other hand, planning brings about order (Lai, 1998; 2003b) and too much planning resulting in highly orderly systems might hamper creativity by reducing degree of novelty.

The book is grounded on two assumptions that a city is a discrete dynamical system and that it is capable of universal computation. These two assumptions are based on the fact that there are an increasing number of attempts to model urban spatial evolution through simulations (e.g., White and Engelen, 1993) and the hypothesis that systems showing some level of complexity are computationally equivalent (Wolfram, 2002). It is well known that systems capable of universal computation are inextricable computationally so that the prediction of the behaviors of the systems is impossible. The only way to study such systems is through direct evolution. The two assumptions proposed imply that planning based on forecasts is impossible, or at least difficult, because there is no way we can predict what would happen and do something with it in advance. On the other hand, Hopkins (2001) argues that under the conditions of four I's of decisions in a complex system, that is, interdependence, indivisibility, irreversibility, and imperfect foresight, making plans should lead to different, beneficial outcomes. We would argue in this book that the two seemingly contradictory arguments can be reconciled through investigating computer simulations of elementary cellular automata. An elementary cellular automaton is a one-dimensional cellular automaton with two possible values for each site, $k = 2$, and the transition rule is based on the nearest neighbors, $r = 1$.

In what follows, we will elaborate on institutional design and problem-focused planning for city management focused on city safety and creativity. Section 2 depicts why a city can be viewed as a discrete dynamical system capable of universal computation. Section 3 reviews Wolfram's (2002) recent work on the simulations of the elementary cellular automata. In particular, we focus on how his principle of computational equivalence can help enhance the validity of our simulation design. In Section 4, we depict planning in relation to universal computation. Section 5 shows what planning can achieve in such a relationship. In particular, we demonstrate that planning gives rise to order, which is consistent with previous work (Lai, 1998; 2003b). We will then argue, in Section 6, that institutional design is more effective than physical planning in affecting how cities work and how it can be related to city safety in terms of reducing the number of problems. In Section 7, we will then argue for problem-focused planning that aims at problem-solving, rather than decision-making, through plan making. Discussion and concluding remarks are provided in Sections 8 and 9 respectively.

2 The City as a System Capable of Computation

There is no satisfactory answer to the question of what a city is, but that fact that much has been done recently in simulating urban spatial change suggests that the spatial system of a city can at least be viewed as many agents, fixed in locations or floating in space, interacting with each other forming a complex system. Most of such work is given different names, including cellular automata (e.g., White and Engelen, 1993), agent-based modeling (e.g., Axelrod, 1997), and artificial life (e.g., Langton, 1989). The theme of such work is that a city can be viewed from the bottom up so that the whole spatial phenomena can be simulated by interacting agents based on simple rules forming complex outcomes. This is equivalent to saying that the city can compute in that given initial configurations or data, the results can be traced definitely through the rules. Therefore, these models of the city are also deterministic dynamical systems.

We are mainly interested in cellular automata, in particular the elementary cellular automata, because of their simplicity in construction and complexity in results. However, most urban spatial simulations based on cellular automata seem to deviate from the original construction of cellular automata. In the original cellular automata (e.g. Wolfram, 1994), there is a single set of transition rules in the course of simulation, while in most urban spatial simulations, there may be more than one set of transition rules and the rules become complicated (e.g. Webster and Wu, 1999a; 1999b). Regardless, these models seem to assume that urban spatial systems are capable of computation. Lai (2003a) investigated deductively the characteristics of urban spatial evolution using the elementary cellular automata, and found that among the 256 transition rules only eight rules can result in complex structures with semi-lattice structures in the transition graph. He further argued that these deterministic transition rules could give rise to seemingly stochastic phenomena of urban spatial evolution as we observed in our daily lives. But no satisfactory explanation was provided as to how the elementary cellular automata model fits the real urban spatial system, with an exception of Caruso et al. (2009).

3 Principle of Computational Equivalence

In his recent provocative book, Wolfram (2002) conducted numerous simulations of simple programs, including the elementary cellular automata, to explain persuasively many natural phenomena, including natural evolution and thermodynamics. His interpretation of these simple programs was also extended to explain some social phenomena, such as fluctuations of stock prices. The validity of his theory is yet to be proved, but he proposed an interesting hypothesis: the principle of computational equivalence in that, in the natural world, many phenomena of complexity are capable of universal computation and thus equivalent. We take his hypothesis as the basis on which we propose our simulation design and claim its validity. In particular, we argue that since some elementary cellular automata rules are capable of universal computation, such as rule 30, and urban spatial systems are capable of computation, according to Wolfram's principle of computational equivalence, the two systems are computationally equivalent. Put differently, ignoring the substances of different systems, the elementary cellular automata can be seen as microcosms of a simplified world capable of emulating other complex systems of computation, including urban spatial systems. By simulating the elementary cellular automata, we should be able to gain insight into the characteristics of the transition rules underlying the evolution of real urban spatial systems.

Consider each cell as a decision situation in which there are only two choices represented by two colors or binary values. A one-dimension cellular automaton with two colors and nearest neighbors can be constructed to represent the evolution of the choices in space-time. At time step t, the color of a particular cell in the next time step $t + 1$ is determined by its color at the current time step and the colors of the two nearest neighbors. Assume that the two colors of cells are represented by 0 and 1, forming two possible choices of the decision situation. This simple formulation implies that the choice of a particular cell in the next time step depends on a set of three decision situations. The transition rules specify how the choices of the three decision situations determine the choice of that cell for the next time step. This simple construct can create very complex structures in the evolution of space-time. According to the principle of computational equivalence, a city viewed as a discrete dynamic system can also evolve into spatial patterns that can be emulated by the elementary cellular automata.

4 Planning as Computation in a Universal System

Making plans requires mental, analytic investments. Considering contingent, related actions, guessing moves of others, measuring uncertainty, and making forecasts all require investments in gathering information. We assume for the present purposes that the underlying mechanisms of these mental investments are indistinguishable from the notion of computation, and that the planner does not know the rules based on which the system of interest evolves. Put differently, the planner makes plans according to a logic different from the rules underlying the system evolution. This assumption is plausible because in reality planners do not have the complete knowledge of how the spatial change of the city takes place. They make forecasts and plans and act accordingly depending on the information gathered, not the complete knowledge of how the system works. Therefore, there are two types of logic: the logic of how plans are made and the logic of how the system evolves.

The value of a plan depends on the cost of making the plan and the benefit it might yield compared to that without the plan (Hopkins, 2001). The benefit of a plan can be calculated as the difference through a decision tree between the expected value of an optimal path with the plan and that without the plan. This notion is equivalent to the calculation of the value of sample information in any management science textbook (e.g., Anderson et al, 2003). Schaeffer and Hopkins (1987) applied the Bayesian approach to describing how a land developer manipulated right during the investment process to yield profit. This approach can be used for the present purposes to describe the logic of making plans in the elementary cellular automata. Consider a space–time plot of ten cells and ten time steps based on rule 30 of nearest neighbors as shown below. The initial state is given randomly where 0 and 1 represent two possible states for a cell.

124   Urban Complexity and Planning

Time	State
1	1001101000
2	1111001101
3	0000111000
4	0001100100
5	0011011110
6	0110010001
7	0101111011
8	0101000010
9	1101100111
10	0001011100

In order to apply the Bayesian approach to the simple system, the state of the system at each time step is given a benefit index, which could be the mapping between the states and a set of integers. The greater the index, the more self-organized the state is, and the more preferred the state is. This index of self-organization can be measured by entropy (Wolfram, 1994). The probability of the state of a cell to be zero or one at a particular time step can be evaluated through the Bayesian theorem based on the values of the state at previous time steps. Given the planning logic, we can set the number of time steps backward before the current time step for calculating the Bayesian probabilities as the information gathering scope. We can also set the number of time steps forward after the current time step for predicting the Bayesian probabilities as the planning horizon. Making a plan according to this definition is equivalent to changing the values of the cell states based on the results calculated from the Bayesian theorem. In this way, the logic of planning is blended into the system evolution.

Similar to the self-organization index for a particular state of the system, the effects of planning can be measured by comparing the global index as defined by entropy for the space-time plot with planning with that without planning. Information gathering scope and planning horizon are parameters in the simulation design that we can manipulate in order to evaluate the sensitivity of the system behavior to the level of investment of planning. The greater the information gathering scope or planning horizon, the greater the level of planning investment: all this can be done on the Mathematica platform (Wolfram, 1999).

It is possible to test hypotheses regarding planning effects for urban development in the simulation design proposed because in the elementary cellular automata, decisions (or states of the cells in the cellular automaton) are interrelated; the states of the cells at one time step are partially irreversible in time; actions are indivisible and thus discrete in space–time; and unpredictability and thus uncertainty defies perfect foresight, which together characterize urban development decisions (Hopkins, 2001). We can also expect that making plans defined here does not affect the system's fundamental characteristics, including universality. We are particularly interested in how planning defined here would affect the pattern of space-time evolution.

5 Planning Brings about Order

It is difficult to make forecasts in the elementary cellular automata systems; that is, to predict the value of the state of a particular cell at a particular time step. This is because the effects of the rules propagate throughout the system after some time steps, making forecasting difficult. In particular, the 'cone' where the values of the states are determined by the initial states shrinks at the speed of two cells a time step, and vanishes eventually. If we view the spatial evolution of a city as a cellular automata model, this observation is consistent with the fact that urban spatial change is extremely difficult to predict. Without knowing the initial condition *and* the transition rules, it is impossible to acquire the complete knowledge of how the system works. Unfortunately, in reality we usually do not know both, and, as a result, effective forecasting is impossible, or at least prohibitively costly. The type of research proposed in the present book could, however, shed some light on resolving such difficulty.

Entropy has long been an interesting topic for planning theorists (e.g. Wilson, 1970). In modeling land-use/transportation activities, maximizing entropy is treated as the objective function, implying that without intervention, agents should find themselves in locations so that the aggregate patterns approach random, chaotic distribution. Planning, in contrast, seeks order so as to minimize entropy. Therefore, maximizing entropy is equivalent to assuming that the system lacks planning, which is not true in most real urban developments. The proposed simulation design blends planning logic into the underlying rules of the elementary cellular automata evolution so it is close to reality. Entropy can be used, however, as an index of the degree of self-organization. For example, low entropy means agents are less randomly distributed, and are thus highly self-organized. In the simulation design, we assume self-organization is a desired characteristic of the distribution pattern of the system because it might enhance computation capacity of the system and make the system more capable of universal computation. For example, agglomerative economy is a type of self-organization, and is a result of interactive agents maximizing self-interests.

According to Wolfram (1994), there are four classes of the elementary cellular automata rules. Class 1 rules quickly result in homogeneous states. Class 2 rules fix to a periodic patterns. Class 3 rules create chaotic patterns. Only class 4 rules are capable of universal computation evolving into complex structures. We argue that urban spatial change can be thought of as cellular automata models of class 4 rules because none of the other three classes of rules can characterize the spatial evolution of a city. Universal computation is also a fundamental characteristic of urban spatial change, which cannot be modified regardless of planning.

Given the above conception and the simulation design, we conducted a set of simulations using rule 110 as defined by Wolfram in one-dimensional cellular automata. rule 110 is one of the simplest 256 elementary rules that is capable of universal computation and belongs to the class 4 rules. More specifically, it specifies that 000 → 0, 001 → 1, 010 → 1, 011 → 1, 100 → 0, 101 → 0, 110 →1, 111 → 0, where the three values on the left-hand side of the arrow sign are the initial states of the triplet of cells and the value on the right hand-side is the state of the central cell in the triplet at the next step after transformation. We considered the 100×100 space–time plot, meaning that there are 100 cells evolving over 100 time steps. The initial values were assigned randomly to the 100 cells at time step zero. Planning as computation was defined by the following Bayesian rule:

$$P(S_i/X) = \frac{P(X/S_i) \cdot P(S_i)}{\sum_{i=1}^{n} P(X/S_i) \times P(S_i)} = \frac{P(X/S_i) \cdot P(S_i)}{P(X)} \tag{1}$$

where S_i are the possible states of each cell for i = 1, 2, ..., n,
X is the sample information gathered through planning,
$P(S_i)$ is the prior probability,
P(X) is the probability of the sample outcome,
$P(X/S_i)$ is the probability of the sample outcome under the condition that S_i obtains, and
$P(S_i/X)$ is the posterior probability.

In the simulations, we considered two states: zero and one, and when $P(S_i/X) \geq 0.5$, the value of the cell becomes one. If $P(S_i/X) \leq 0.5$, the value of the cell becomes zero. In addition, we considered three regimes of planning: time-driven, event-driven, and random planning. The *time-driven* system requires that planning take place at a particular time step within a fixed time interval. The *event-driven* system demands that planning be undertaken when a pre-specified event comes about, which is the condition that at any time step if the number of states with values of zero is not equal to that of one. The *random* system simply requires that planning take place at any time step in a random fashion.

In order to assess the evolutions of the universal system under the three regimes of planning, following Wolfram (1994), we computed the spatial set entropy for each simulation given as below:

$$S^{(x)}(X) = -\frac{1}{X} \sum_{j=1}^{|A|^x} p_j^{(x)} \log_{|A|} P_j^{(x)}, \tag{2}$$

where $P_j^{(x)}$ represents the probability that over the length of X, all the neighboring cells have the outcomes $|A|^x$.

In other words, in a sequence of cells spanning the length of X with all neighboring cells classified into $|A|^x$, the frequency distribution can be calculated by $P(X) = \{P_j\}$. The distribution remains the same in the case of a circular system. Wolfram (1994) applied a set dimension to estimate the density of the overall structural evolution to indicate the degree of information content. In the case of an infinite number of cells, the degree of information content is approximately equivalent to the spatial set entropy as shown below:

$$d^{(x)} = \lim_{x \to \infty} S^x(X). \tag{3}$$

Note in (3) that when the probability that all states occur remains the same, $d^{(X)}$ is equal to one; if the states of all the cells are the same (homogeneous structures), then $d^{(X)}$ is equal to zero. In our experiments, the degree of information content was used as a measurement of effectiveness of planning to examine whether planning resulted in reduction of spatial set entropy and set dimension.

In addition to three regimes of planning, two other control variables considered in the simulations were planning intervals and planning scopes. Planning intervals indicate the fixed number of time steps between those at which planning takes place in the time-driven system, whereas planning scopes specify the number of neighboring cells considered in planning behavior. Since the planning intervals were increased incrementally up to time step 50 and the planning scopes up to 25 neighboring cells on each side of a central cell, there were totally 25×50 = 1,250 simulation runs for each regime of planning, which in turn resulted in 3,750 simulation runs.

A multiple regression analysis was conducted considering information content as the independent variable and all other control variables as the dependent variables, including planning scope, planning interval, and planning regime. The results showed that an increase in a unit of planning scope reduced information content in 0.12 units and an increase in a unit of planning interval increased information content in 0.212 units. The more information content, the less effective planning performs. As to the three regimes of planning, the time-driven system was less effective than the event-driven system by 0.236 units; the random system was less effective than the event-driven system by 0.798 units; and the event-driven system was more effective than the time-driven and random systems by 0.236 and 0.798 units, respectively. In short, the event-driven planning was most effective in reducing information content and entropy. A sample of illustrations of the simulation runs is provided in Figure 7.1. Apparently, either graphically or analytically, planning gives rise to order in that the system tends toward more fixed patterns or smaller information content through planning than without it. For example, in the space-time plot of time-driven planning in panel (b), the evolution of the system changes dramatically from a complex structure into a nearly uniformed one at the time when planning takes place.

128   Urban Complexity and Planning

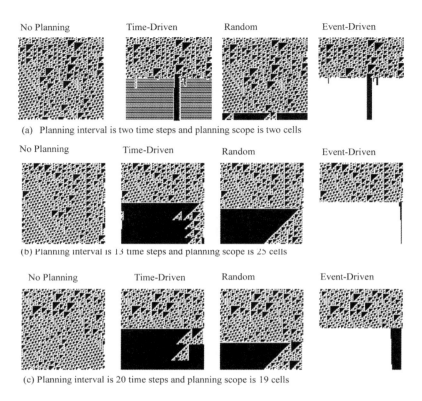

Figure 7.1   A sample of illustrations of the simulation runs

6   Institutional Design

Returning now to our spatial garbage-can metaphor of cities, in the simplest form, an institution is a set of rules that confine the agents' rights in taking certain actions in the complex system under consideration. For example, an institution can be set up to codify which agent is eligible for participating in which decision situation. This simple institution can be represented by a matrix as shown in Figure 7.2. Consider Matrix 1 where rows are agents and columns are decision situations. A "1" means that the associated agent in the row is eligible for participating in the associated decision situation in the column; whereas a "0" means that the agent is not eligible for participating in that decision situation. Assume that there exist ten decision situations and ten agents and that there is a monitoring cost of preventing a particular agent from participating in a particular decision situation and call this cost the cost of delineating the right in participating. Following Cohen et al. (1972), there are three prototypical structures of the matrix: unsegmented, hierarchical, and specialized, where the unsegmented and specialized structures are the two extreme institutional designs and the hierarchical structure is the intermediate design. In the unsegemented structure, all agents have access to each decision situation, whereas in the specialized structure, each agent is allowed to participate in one and only one decision situation. It can be easily shown that the specialized structure gives rise to the highest delineation cost of right because the agents are prevented from participating in most of the decision situations, whereas the unsegmented structure imposes the lowest delineation cost of right because there is no restriction as to which decision situation the agents can participate in. The delineation cost of right for the hierarchical structure falls in between the two extremes. The implication is that the more restrictive the institution is, the more delineated the rights are, and the more the delineation cost is.

```
1111111111        1111111111        1000000000
1111111111        0111111111        0100000000
1111111111        0011111111        0010000000
1111111111        0001111111        0001000000
1111111111        0000111111        0000100000
1111111111        0000011111        0000010000
1111111111        0000001111        0000001000
1111111111        0000000111        0000000100
1111111111        0000000011        0000000010
1111111111        0000000001        0000000001

 Unsegmented      Hierarchical       Specialized
```

Figure 7.2   Three prototypes of institutional structure

In addition, fewer problems would be solved by more restrictive institutions because the probability is smaller under which an agent is eligible for participating in a particular decision situation. Thus, we can expect in terms of problem-solving that the unsegmented structure would allow the largest number of problems to be solved, whereas the specialized structure would render the smallest number of problems to be solved. The hierarchical structure would result in an intermediate number of problems to be solved. Table 7.1 summarizes the results of the analysis.

Table 7.1   A Summary of effects of different institutional designs

	Delineation cost	**Right delineated**	**Number of problems solved**
Unsegmented	Low	Low	High
Hierarchical	Intermediate	Intermediate	Intermediate
Specialized	High	High	Low

On the face of it, one would argue that the unsegemented structure is more desirable because it results in the lowest delineation cost with a highest number of problems solved. However, that structure also renders the right delineated as the least. As argued by Barzel (1997), when right is not appropriately delineated, much of it will be left in the public domain and the agents would spend resources to acquire such right during transactions, resulting in higher transaction cost. Therefore, the question of which prototypical structure is most effective really depends on the trade-offs between the various costs and the number of problems solved. Solely focusing on the increase in the number of problems solved would increase transaction cost, which would in turn decrease the performance of the city. Furthermore, it is arguably plausible that institutional design is more significant than spatial structure in affecting how the city works because the former set the constraints as to whether decisions can be made and our previous simulations demonstrated that it is indeed so (Lai, 2006).

For concreteness, compare the zoning system and permit system as two contrasting institutions. The zoning system is reminiscent of the specialized, or at least the hierarchical, form of the decision structure, while the permit system the unsegmented form. They could also correspond, to some extent, to different forms of spatial structure, but for our purposes we regard them as institutions of rules as defined here. Referring to Table 7.1, we could infer that the zoning system would have a higher right delineation cost in land use with right in land use more clearly specified, but solve fewer problems emerging from daily activities than the permit system. However, the permit system with right in land use less clearly delineated would cause a higher transaction cost in the land market. Whether the zoning system is superior to the permit system depends on which dimension we are looking at.

7 Problem-focused Planning

The traditional decision analysis develops, on the one hand, decision-making techniques under the presumption that problems are fixed and given, and the decision-maker is to seek appropriate actions that can solve the problems. On the other hand, the traditional planning analysis focuses on interdependence of decisions in that the selection of the action in a particular decision situation depends on the outcome of the selection of the action in another decision situation, also presuming that the problems associated with the decision situations are fixed and given. In the real situations, problems are fluid that flow between decision situations so that the optimization approach to planning might result in enhancing the efficiency of decision-making, rather than problem-solving. For example, decisions might be made without regard to associated problems.

One way of countering the bias toward decision-making while ignoring the significance of problem-solving in planning analysis is to apply weights to disutility resulting from problems in decision situations. More specifically, in a decision situation utilities are associated with the agents, solutions, and locations, while disutilities are associated with problems. If the total amount of utilities is greater than the total amount of disutilities, then a decision is made. Otherwise, no decision is made. In problem-focused planning, weights are assigned to these disutilities so that the arrangement of decision situations in time, thus plans, would result in the largest number of decisions solved, albeit through decision choices. Lai (2003b) ran a computer simulation specifically for examining the effects of problem-focused planning. The results show that the more weights placed on problem disutilities, the greater the number of problems solved, and the more active the problems are in the system evolution. Indeed, we could improve planning by highlighting the significance of problems through assigning weights to problem disutilities, so that the behavior of problem activities are appropriately attended to and a higher proportion of problems are solved.

For example, in determining the urban growth boundaries for urban development, one might prefer the event-driven approach to the time-driven approach to the land inventory problem (Lai and Han, 2010), because the former in essence makes the urban boundaries plan by considering the interdependence of the expansion decisions in time, while the latter makes these decisions independently. However, if we apply weights to the problem disutilities associated with these decisions or decision situations, such as holding cost, expansion cost, overbuilding, and inflation, the resulting plan would be different if these problems were considered as commeasurable to the revenues gained.

8 Discussion

The one-dimensional cellular automata model presented here is an abstract one capable of universal computation and planning as intelligence intervenes in the evolution of the system. The model represents, to some extent, the real urban dynamics in that the four I's of urban development decisions as observed by Hopkins (2001) are well captured by the model: interdependence, indivisibility, irreversibility, and imperfect foresight. Interdependence can be thought of as the propagating principle of the cells in time and space so that a change in the state of a cell would cause the changes of the states in other cells over time. Indivisibility can be characterized by discrete units of time and space. Irreversibility can be modeled by the second law of thermodynamics of the one-dimensional cellular automata system, which is known to be irreversible. Imperfect foresight can be represented by the unpredictability of the evolution of the system.

To attain realism, the one-dimensional cellular automata model proposed here can be explained in the context of urban change. For example, the zero- or one-state of the cells could be explained as "developed" or "undeveloped" spatial units as proposed by Lai (2003a). In addition, the model could be extended to be coupled with economic theory to explain economic behavior of spatial change. For example, Caruso et al. (2009) extend Lai's (2003a) formulation by using rules derived from economic theory in the one-dimensional cellular automata model to bring time and distance dependences of urban structures to explain how discontinuous spatial patterns would emerge.

The notion of creative cities is relatively new and there is no consensus on its meanings. For example, the Creative Cities Network was first launched by the United Nations Educational, Scientific, and Cultural Organization in 2004 to "promote the social, economic, and cultural development of cities in both the developed and the developing world" (UNESCO, 2010). The crux of a creative city is diversity, either economic or cultural, a desired characteristic of cities which can be traced in the writings by as early as Jacobs (1993). We argue that creativity as manifested by diversity correlates with novelty which is in turn characterized by the class 4 rules according to Wolfram's (2002) classification of the elementary one-dimensional cellular automata. As demonstrated in our simulations, too much planning that gives rise to orderly evolution of the space–time plot would destroy the fabric of the complex structure capable of universal computation. By the same token, too much planning would also result in a complex system that would, albeit with orderly development, solve fewer problems than one without planning.

9 Conclusions

Urban spatial change can be modeled as cellular automata simulations. Effects of planning can be examined through such simulations. The simple programs of the elementary cellular automata can serve as a metaphor based on which urban spatial change can be studied. The principle of computational equivalence implies that this approach is plausible because these simple programs capable of universal computation can emulate cellular automata models of urban spatial change. In order to incorporate planning behavior into the simple programs, we need, however, to distinguish between the logic of planning and the underlying rules based on which the elementary cellular automata systems evolve. The simulation design proposed here intends to achieve this aim by testing the hypotheses regarding planning effects. Insight can be gained through such simulations as to when making plans is useful, how it affects system behavior, and whether it works. The simulation results imply that increase in planning investment in terms of shortened planning intervals and widened planning scopes enhances planning effectiveness, whereas the event-driven system is more effective than the time-driven system. Regardless, planning brings about order as manifested by fixed patterns and little information content in the space-time plot. Under the presumption that creativity connotes novelty derived from universal computation, too much planning might hamper rather than enhancing this goal.

On the other hand, city safety is an issue that cannot be coped with by planning per se. It should, among others, be dealt with through institutions and problem-focused planning. Viewing the city as a large, complex system and city safety as reducing the number of problems arising in the evolution of the system, we argue that institutional design for urban development is the key toward a safe place to live. In addition, we propose a problem-focused approach to planning for city safety that enhances problem-solving, rather than decision-making, in making plans through applying weights to the disutilities associated with problems. How these approaches to city safety and creativity can be operationalized begs future work. However, both metaphors of cities presented in this book seem to imply that too much planning might not be desired and there would exist an optimal level of planning in relation to safety and creativity.

Acknowledgements

The authors are grateful to Chi-Hsu Yeh for his help in conducting the simulations and analyzing the results.

References

Anderson, D.R., D.J. Sweeney, and T.A. Williams. 2003. *An Introduction to Management Science*. Mason, OH: South-Western.
Axelrod, R. 1997. *The Complexity of Cooperation*. Princeton, NJ: Princeton University Press.
Barzel, Y. 1997. *Economic Analysis of Property Rights*. Cambridge University Press, Cambridge, UK.
Caruso, G., D. Peeters, J. Cavailhès, and M. Rounsevell. 2009. "Space-time patterns of urban sprawl, a 1D cellular automata and microeconomic approach." *Environment and Planning B: Planning and Design* 36(6): 968–88.
Cohen, M.D., J.G. March, and J.P. Olsen. 1972. "A garbage can model of organizational choice." *Administrative Science Quarterly* 17: 1–25.
Ghallab, M., D. Nau, and P. Traverso. 2004. *Automated Planning: Theory and Practice*. San Francisco, CA: Morgan Kaufmann Publishers.
Hopkins, L.D. 2001. *Urban Development: The Logic of Making Plans*. London: Island Press.
Jacobs, J. 1993. *The Death and Life of Great American Cities*. New York: The Modern Library.
Lai, S-K., and H. Han. 2010. "Reformulation and assessment of the inventory approach to urban growth boundaries: a decision network framework." Paper submitted to Environment and Planning B: Planning and Design for possible publication.
Lai, S-K. 1998. "From organized anarchy to controlled structure: effects of planning on the garbage-can processes." *Environment and Planning B: Planning and Design* 25: 85–102.

Lai, S-K. 2003a. "On transition rules of complex structure in one-dimensional cellular automata: Some implications for urban change." *Annals of Regional Science* 37: 337–52.

Lai, S-K. 2003b. "Effects of planning on the garbage-can decision processes: a reformulation and extension." *Environment and Planning B: Planning and Design* 30: 379–89.

Lai, S-K. 2006. "A spatial garbage-can model." *Environment and Planning B: Planning and Design* 33: 141–56.

Langton, C. 1989. *Artificial Life*. Reading, MA: Addison-Wesley.

LaValle, S.M. 2006. *Planning Algorithms*. Cambridge, England: Cambridge University Press.

Mandelbaum, S.J. 2008. "Planning intelligence." *Planning Theory* 7(3): 318–22.

Schaeffer, P.V., and L.D. Hopkins. 1987. "Planning behavior: the economics of information and land development." *Environment and Planning A* 19: 1221–32.

UNESCO. 2010. "What is the creative cities network?" at http://portal.unesco.org/culture/en/ev.php-URL_ID=36746&URL_DO=DO_TOPIC&URL_SECTION=201.html.

Webster, C.J., and F. Wu. 1999a. "Regulation, land-use mix, and urban performance. Part 1: theory." *Environment and Planning A* 31: 1433–42.

Webster, C.J., and F. Wu. 1999b. "Regulation, land-use mix, and urban performance. Part 2: simulation." *Environment and Planning A* 31: 1529–45.

Wilson, A.G. 1970. *Entropy in Urban and Regional Modeling*. London: Pion Ltd.

White, R., and G. Englen. 1993. "Cellular automata and fractal urban form: a cellular modelling approach to the evolution of urban land-use pattern." *Environment and Planning B: Planning and Design* 25: 1175–99.

Wolfram, S. 1994. *Cellular automata and Complexity*. New York: Addison-Wesley Publishing Company.

Wolfram, S. 1999. *The Mathematica Book*. 4th ed. Champaign, IL: Wolfram Media, Inc.

Wolfram, S. 2002. *A New Kind of Science*. Champaign, IL: Wolfram Media, Inc.

Chapter 8
Emergent Macro-structures of Path-dependent Location Adoptions Processes of Firms[1]

1 Introduction

On a website of the department that I am currently affiliated with, a bulletin board is constructed so that any student can post a message on it to express his or her opinions. There are two pieces of information in each of the message: the subject of the message and the number of people who have read the message. Presumably a student visiting the website would select a message to read based on the two pieces of information: whether the message subject attracts him or her and how many other students have read that message. An interesting question is: would the distribution of the numbers of students who have read the messages follow a particular pattern? I conducted a regression analysis on the logarithmic scale of the numbers and the ranks of these numbers.[2] What I found was that the rank-size relation as depicted by Zipf (1949) applied to this case with an R^2 value equal to 0.89 and a slope -1.1715. The surprising finding leads me to speculate that what Professor Krugman (1996a) named the mystery of urban hierarchy and explained it as order from random growth (1996b) resembles the formulation of the above phenomenon of what I call the bulletin board mystery. Consider each message on the board as a potential location from which a student as a firm is to select to read. The firm's preferences for locations depend on two components: geographical benefit and agglomeration benefit reminiscent of the curious student in selecting a particular message to view: the inherent attractiveness of the subject and the popularity of the message in terms of the number of people who have read it. Indeed, Arthur (1990) has constructed mathematical models to analyze what spatial patterns would emerge from firms entering into alternative locations under

---

 1 This chapter has been published in *Annals of Regional Science* 2006, Vol. 40, No. 3, pages 545–58.
 2 The numbers of students viewing the 53 messages were, in a descending order, 680, 185, 159, 153, 148, 147, 134, 124, 122, 110, 102, 92, 87, 87, 85, 83, 83, 81, 80, 75, 72, 69, 66, 61, 60, 59, 57, 54, 49, 46, 45, 44, 41, 41, 40, 40, 38, 36, 36, 35, 34, 33, 32, 29, 27, 27, 26, 23, 19, 18, 16, and 14.

the assumption of increasing returns. The results are insightful in that a monopoly outcome is to emerge, but which location would win is unpredictable.

Cities are spatial agglomerations of individual agents acting in particular facilities and buildings. It is still in debate as to how these spatial agglomerations come about and how they evolve. There are at least two camps of such explanations: deterministic and path-dependent (Batten, 2001). On the one hand, traditional models of urban economics assume homogeneous agents that share some common behavioral assumptions, such as rationality in terms of profit or utility maximization (O'Sullivan, 1993). These models can at best depict in a static way that regional spatial agglomerations are equilibriums or solutions of economic models built on such assumptions, ignoring the dynamic trajectories of the economic systems in spatial evolution. One condition under which such spatial equilibriums exist is decreasing returns or diminishing marginal rate of substitution functions. Decreasing returns are without doubt present in many economic activities, such as agricultural land cultivation, but in some economic activities, such as technological competition, increasing returns or positive feedback is the driving force of market domination (Arthur, 1994).

On the other hand, the market sharing processes of competing technologies are subject to increasing returns resulting in multiple equilibriums, and which of these equilibriums emerges depends on small events (Arthur, 1994). The pathdependence models of describing the market competition of technologies can readily be transposed into models depicting spatial competition of locations. This has been done by Arthur (1990) through a mathematical model to describe the stochastic processes of firms in choosing locations under the assumption of increasing returns to agglomeration economies. In his model, Arthur concludes that where there is no upper bound to locational increasing returns due to agglomeration, there will indeed be a dominant outcome, and that where there is an upper bound to increasing returns due to agglomeration, either dominance by one region or regional sharing of the industry exactly as if the agglomeration effects were absent could occur.

In the present book, I follow the second camp of explanations of agglomeration, reminiscent of choices among technologies. The immediate question following the increasing returns and path-dependent model is: what macro-structures of locations of agglomeration would emerge from micro-behaviors of agents that give rise to small events? The result derived from Arthur's model simply argues that there is a dominant location depending on the entry order of firms to form the industry, but no claim is made as to what properties the emergent locational patterns have. If there exists an envelope of certain properties within which all the emergent locational patterns fall, and we could trace the mechanisms based on which small events in the increasing returns regime are accumulated to lead the system to the envelope of all locational patterns, then that insight should enhance our understanding of how and why cities form and scatter spatially in the way they do.

The present book is not going to provide such an answer, but through two sets of simulations designed under some plausible assumptions, it attempts to throw some light on the question. In short, the simulation results strongly suggest that increasing returns to agglomeration lead not only to a dominant outcome of locational patterns (which is consistent with the result of Arthur's theoretical model), but to a locational pattern that is close to a power law of frequency-size distribution of cities. Section 2 reviews current work on the power law distribution of cities and depicts the relationship between increasing returns and spatial evolution. Section 3 introduces the research design of the computer simulations. Section 4 shows the results. Section 5 discusses some relevant issues. Section 6 concludes.

2 Power Law, Increasing Returns, and Spatial Evolution

The fact that the size distribution of metropolitan areas is regular in relation to the ranking of the sizes is not a new story. Zipf (1949) found out the regularity about half a century ago. The regularity indicates that the population of a city is inversely proportional to its rank. The rank-size rule seems very stable over time regardless of technological and economical transformations. Krugman (1996a and b), confronted by the mystery of urban hierarchy, attempted to search for a plausible explanation of the mechanisms underlying the regularity. Specifically, he traced back to Simon's (1955) earlier work on probability mechanisms underlying five such empirical distributions: distributions of words in prose samples by their frequency of occurrences, distributions of scientists by number of papers published, distributions of cities by population, distributions of incomes by size, and distributions of biological genera by number of species. All these five examples show a commonality of underlying probability mechanisms based on which Krugman (1996b) attempted to explain the emerging power law of city sizes distribution of what he called order from random growth.[3]

In his seminal work on competing technologies, Arthur (1994) argues that when returns to choosing among two technologies, say A and B, are increasing, which technology would dominate the market is unpredictable depending on small events that occur in the process of competition. When these returns are decreasing, it is possible that the two technologies coexist with respective market shares over time. Increasing returns to additional adoptions of a particular technology are proportional with respect to the number of previous adoptions of that technology. More specifically, assume that there are two types of agents, R and S, and two technologies to adopt, A and B. The payoff table for the market is as follows:

---

3   Krugman notes one example of order from random growth as Bak's (1996) earthquake model of self-organized criticality. A more widely known metaphor is a sand pile growing in height because of external dropping of grains of sand on top of it, which results in different scales of avalanches whose frequency is inversely proportional to its scale logarithmically, an apparent case of a power law phenomenon.

Table 8.1 Returns to choosing *A* or *B* given previous adoptions

	Technology A	Technology B
R-Agent	$a_R + rn_A$	$b_R + rn_B$
S-Agent	$a_S + sn_A$	$b_S + sn_B$

In the payoff table, a_R, b_R, a_S, and b_S are the initial payoffs for *R*-agent and *S*-agent adopting A and B respectively; n_A and n_B are the numbers of agents already having adopted A and B respectively; and r and s are rates of returns which can be increasing, diminishing, or constant, depending on whether r and s are positive, negative, or zero simultaneously.

Assuming increasing returns to agglomeration in the spatial context, this formulation can be readily transformed into spatial choices of two types of firms among two competing locations. We can relabel the Technology row as Location in Table 8.1.

Though one might argue that the adoption of agent among competing technologies is distinct behaviorally from the choice of firms among competing locations, the similarity of the formulations of the two decision problems is so obvious that at a higher level, the two problems could indeed bear some resemblance. The literature on urban economies or scale economies implies that urban agglomeration results in part from externalities of firms' moving nearby each other (O'Sullivan, 1993). These phenomena are called order from random growth (e.g., Krugman, 1996b). Regardless, the research design described in the next section considers the payoff table in Table 8.1 as the behavioral basis for the firms to locate themselves. By conducting computer simulations through varying the values of the parameters in the locational model, we can observe how regional agglomerations emerge, and, more importantly, how lawful macro-structures would emerge from such simple rules as depicted in Table 8.1.

3 Research Design

In the research design, I conducted two types of computer simulations, one across regions while the other within regions. Consider four regions on an island (Taiwan). There are two types of firms, *R* (basic industry) and *S* (non-basic industry), each of which has different initial locational preferences among the four regions. Firms enter into these regions in a random order.

3.1 Moving across Regions

The first type of simulations of firms' choosing locations across regions was based on the following payoff table.

Table 8.2 Returns of firms to choosing locations (regions) A, B, C, or D, given previous decisions

	Region A	Region B	Region C	Region D
R-Firm	$\pi_{RA}+r_a n_{RA}$	$\pi_{RB}+r_b n_{RB}$	$\pi_{RC}+r_c n_{RC}$	$\pi_{RD}+r_d n_{RD}$
S-Firm	$\pi_{SA}+s_a n_{SA}$	$\pi_{SB}+s_b n_{SB}$	$\pi_{SC}+s_c n_{SC}$	$\pi_{SD}+s_d n_{SD}$

The variables and parameters in the payoff table are modified slightly in order to reflect differences in locations and firms. For example, the initial payoffs for R and S firms to choose locations A, B, C, and D, are different with respect to firms and locations, that is, π_{RA}, π_{RB}, π_{RC}, π_{RD}, π_{SA}, π_{SB}, π_{SC}, and π_{SD} are distinct. So are rates of returns, that is, r_a, r_b, r_c, r_d, s_a, s_b, s_c, and s_d are distinct. Drawing on random and empirical data of firms of two types in basic and non-basic industries over a period of 21 time steps (years in real data), and given different values of these parameters, I conducted a set of simulations of firms' movement among the four regions. The random data were generated by a random number generator so the probability distribution of these numbers was uniform.

A decision rule of movement or immigration among the four regions is given. Consider a firm originally located in Region A. In speculating whether to move to the other regions, the firm must take into account two costs: a distance cost that prohibits it from moving if the distance between the two regions is too great, and an opportunity cost that is incurred because the firm, on deciding to move, must give up the payoff of residing in the original region. After considering these two costs for each target region, the net payoff is computed by subtracting these costs from the payoff of moving to the target region. The firm should then move to the region resulting in the maximum positive net payoff. Mathematically, let $\pi_{net(A \rightarrow B)}$ denote the net payoff for the firm located in region A that intends to move to region B, so that:

$$\pi_{net(A \rightarrow B)} = \pi_B - \pi_A - C_{AB} \qquad (1)$$

where π_A and π_B are the initial payoffs of the firm located in regions A and B respectively according to the payoff functions in Table 8.2, and C_{AB} is the cost of moving from regions A to B indicating distance cost. The decision rule for moving becomes:

$$\text{Max}[\pi_{net(A \rightarrow B)}, \pi_{net(A \rightarrow C)}, \pi_{net(A \rightarrow D)}], \text{ for all } \pi\text{'s greater than zero.} \qquad (2)$$

Note that the cost of moving is referred to as the one-time cost of moving in the period in which the move occurs during a time step of the simulation. In the context of the real data, a time step can be thought of as per annum so whenever the net payoff of moving for a firm is greater than zero during that year, the firm will move.

3.2 Moving Within Regions

Once certain firms have decided to move into a region, it is interesting to observe how these firms are distributed spatially. To put it simply, but without loss of generalizability, in this experiment I incorporated the notion of increasing returns into a cellular automata simulation, but not in the geographic context of Taiwan. More specific, in a grid system of 100×100 = 10000 cells, initially the sequence of the firms moving to the region are randomly located. The initial assignment was random so the probability distribution among the cells of being occupied was uniform. But once a firm is located in a cell, the payoffs or values of the eight neighbors surrounding that cell would increase according to the payoff functions shown in Table 8.2. For example, in Figure 8.1 two types of firms, shown as a dark and a gray cells, are located nearby with their neighbors overlapping, each with a distinct rate of returns, that is, r_i or s_i. The payoff of their neighbors is the sum of the rates of returns associated with these firms, that is, r_i+s_i. Therefore, the more firms located nearby forming clusters, the more attractive these clusters to newcomers. This formulation is conceptually equivalent to the payoff functions depicted in Table 8.2, but it can be shown spatially. The movement of the firms among clusters is again based on the decision rule shown in (1) and (2), with regions replaced by clusters.

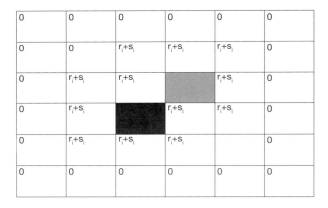

Figure 8.1   Payoffs resulting from emerging clusters

4   Results

4.1   Moving across Regions

In the first set of experiments, I manipulated the values of the parameters of distances, initial payoffs, rates of returns across regions, regional and technological differences in terms of rates of returns in order to simulate real regional and technological change as exogenous conditions. Note, however, that these values do not connote any realistic meanings because they are assigned without referring to any specific units. They are determined only to show how sensitive the simulation outcome is to variation of the values of the parameters. For example, the distance cost is varied from 700 to 0 decrementally with other parameters being set at unity. It does not mean that the distance cost is unrealistically high relative to rates of return, but that it indicates how decremental changes in distance cost would affect the simulation outcome. All simulations were conducted using two sets of data, random and real numbers of firms in basic and non-basic industries in Taiwan from 1977 to 1997 (see Tables 8.3 and 8.4). Each year stood for a time step in the simulations, and the numbers of the firms measured in hundreds in the data represented the sequence based on which the firms entered into the market. The lock-in effects were calculated according to the locational decision rule based on the sequence.

Table 8.3   The random data of firms entering the market (from 1 to 40 in hundreds)

	North Basic	North Non-basic	Central Basic	Central Non-basic	South Basic	South Non-basic	East Basic	East Non-basic
1977	9	12	13	11	12	34	11	28
1978	36	26	3	30	24	17	8	22
1979	28	29	32	10	2	27	5	6
1980	32	18	13	31	19	20	6	9
1981	2	40	18	4	9	33	14	31
1982	24	1	35	7	15	18	34	16
1983	27	14	1	33	13	5	13	29
1984	14	15	28	32	36	12	32	28
1985	40	32	10	36	35	35	23	4
1986	3	5	21	19	27	28	16	28
1987	18	5	25	9	14	29	20	21
1988	7	29	24	32	6	20	30	20
1989	26	16	20	23	29	25	5	24
1990	2	37	22	8	28	22	30	23
1991	4	17	19	12	17	32	1	9
1992	18	34	10	38	16	37	21	12
1993	35	20	16	8	9	23	13	13
1994	14	6	4	6	15	7	3	31
1995	29	25	15	7	8	28	25	4
1996	11	30	29	33	34	24	4	25
1997	19	24	4	25	28	0	3	9

142   Urban Complexity and Planning

Table 8.4 The real data of firms entering the market (in hundreds)

	North		Central		South		East	
	Basic	Non-basic	Basic	Non-basic	Basic	Non-basic	Basic	Non-basic
1977	4	62	3	31	0	156	0	6
1978	0	73	0	29	0	30	0	4
1979	5	89	7	44	1	57	0	8
1980	5	101	6	55	3	77	0	11
1981	2	108	10	47	2	75	0	10
1982	3	109	5	49	0	45	0	9
1983	4	134	3	0	51	78	0	10
1984	9	108	1	100	0	62	0	7
1985	2	114	3	445	1	60	0	5
1986	7	88	8	39	7	65	0	5
1987	6	100	7	37	4	59	0	6
1988	2	88	2	37	2	42	0	1
1989	2	46	0	8	0	23	0	3
1990	0	38	1	16	0	12	1	6
1991	0	20	2	36	2	23	1	7
1992	4	88	1	43	8	70	1	7
1993	0	61	1	32	12	65	1	8
1994	4	19	2	28	10	54	1	9
1995	2	30	0	0	0	4	0	0
1996	0	39	0	14	0	3	0	1
1997	0	38	0	30	0	31	0	6

The geographic map of how the four regions, that is North, Central, South, and East, are delineated in Taiwan is shown in Figure 8.2.

Figure 8.2 A map of delineation of regions in Taiwan

When distance cost changed from 700 toward 0, firms tended to agglomerate in Region North for both random and real data, given that the rates of returns and the initial payoff were set to unity. In particular, for the random data, the four regions coexisted until the distance cost dropped from 700 to 30 (see Table 8.5).

Table 8.5 Lock-in regions for the random and real data with different distance costs (A "-" means no regions dominate; N stands for north; and S for south)

Distance cost	0	1	5	10	30	40	50	100	300	500	700
Random data	N	N	N	N	-	-	-	-	-	-	-
Real data	N	N	N	N	N	N	S	S	S	S	S

With the initial payoffs for Regions Central, South, and East increasing from one through 50, the firms would agglomerate in the respective regions where the associated initial payoffs increased, given that rates of returns and distance cost were set to unity. This was true for both the random and real data sets, with only one exception where the increase in the initial payoff for Region East using the empirical data set resulted in agglomeration in Region South instead of Region East (see Table 8.6).

Table 8.6 Lock-in regions for random and real data with different initial payoffs by regions (N stands for north; C for central; S for south; and E for east)

Initial Payoffs		1	2	3	4	5	6	7	8	9	10	15	20	25	30	35	40	50
Region central	Random	N	N	N	N	N	N	N	N	N	N	N	N	N	C	C	C	C
	Real	N	S	S	S	S	S	S	S	S	S	S	C	C	C	C	C	C
Region south	Random	N	N	N	N	N	N	N	N	N	N	S	S	S	S	S	S	S
	Real	N	S	S	S	S	S	S	S	S	S	S	S	S	S	S	S	S
Region east	Random	N	N	N	N	N	N	N	N	N	N	N	N	E	E	E	E	E
	Real	N	N	N	N	N	S	S	S	S	S	S	S	S	S	S	S	S

When the rates of returns across region increased from one through 50, reflecting economic growth, the random data set resulted in agglomeration in Region North, while the empirical data resulted in Region South, given that the initial payoff and distance cost were set to unity (see Table 8.7).

Table 8.7 Lock-in regions for random and real data with different rates of returns

Rates of returns	1	2	3	4	5	6	7	8	9	10	15	20	25	30	35	40	50
Random	N	N	N	N	N	N	N	N	N	N	N	N	N	N	N	N	N
Real	N	S	S	S	S	S	S	S	S	S	S	S	S	S	S	S	S

When the rates of returns in Regions Central, South, and East increased respectively, holding the rates in the other regions constant, reflecting regional differences, agglomeration occurred in the respective regions both for the random and real data sets, given that the initial payoff and distance cost were set to unity (see Table 8.8).

Table 8.8 Lock-in regions for random and real data with different rates of returns by regions

Rates of returns		1	2	3	4	5	6	7	8	9	10	15	20	25	30	35	40	50
Region central	Random	N	C	C	C	C	C	C	C	C	C	C	C	C	C	C	C	C
	Real	N	C	C	C	C	C	C	C	C	C	C	C	C	C	C	C	C
Region south	Random	N	S	S	S	S	S	S	S	S	S	S	S	S	S	S	S	S
	Real	N	S	S	S	S	S	S	S	S	S	S	S	S	S	S	S	S
Region east	Random	N	E	E	E	E	E	E	E	E	E	E	E	E	E	E	E	E
	Real	N	S	S	S	S	S	S	E	E	E	E	E	E	E	E	E	E

When the rates of returns associated with the firms of an industry, say basic industry, increased, holding the rate of the other industry constant to reflect a technological change, agglomeration occurred in Region North, except that with the increase in the rates of returns for non-basic firms, using the empirical data set resulted in agglomeration in Region South (see Table 8.9).

Table 8.9 Lock-in regions for random and real data with different rates of returns by industries

Rates of returns		1	2	3	4	5	6	7	8	9	10	15	20	25	30	35	40	50
Random data	Basic	N	N	N	N	N	N	N	N	N	N	N	N	N	N	N	N	N
	Non-basic	N	N	N	N	N	N	N	N	N	N	N	N	N	N	N	N	N
Real data	Basic	N	N	N	N	N	N	N	N	N	N	N	N	N	N	N	N	N
	Non-basic	N	N	N	N	N	N	S	S	S	S	S	S	S	S	S	S	S

In short, the behaviors of agglomeration were apparently different between the two data sets, and exogenous factors indeed changed such behaviors. This implies that small events matter that created the history of how the firms entered into the market as manifested in the real data, in contrast to the random data where no historical meanings of the numbers exist. As to realism, the results coincide somewhat with the regional development situations in Taiwan. For example, the Taipei metropolitan area, the largest on the island, is located in Region North. The second largest metropolitan area, Kaoshung, is located in Region South. The simulation results clearly show the comparative advantage of the two regions. The explanations of the subtle differences in the simulation results in terms of shifts in lock-in regions as a result of the change in parameter values is beyond the scope of the book. My main purpose here is, however, to show how regions are locked in based on the decision rule of equations (1) and (2), and how sensitive they are to the change in the values of the parameters in these equations. Note that there were no multiple equilibriums in all conditions where more than one region existed.

4.2 Moving within Regions

Once located in a particular region, it is interesting to observe how firms mutually adjusted to each other spatially and whether orderly patterns would emerge. Again, in this set of simulations I used two behavioral models of spatial choices, random and increasing returns. In the former model, the firms chose randomly the cells in the grid system to locate themselves in sequence, while in the latter model, firms chose the cells to locate themselves according to the decision rule of equations (1) and (2). Setting the rates of returns to unity for both types of firms in the two industries and increasing the distance cost from zero through 50, I found that in the random model, no spatial patterns emerged. More specifically, the locations where the firms chose scattered evenly in the grid system. However, in the increasing returns model, clusters of the firms emerged and the greater the distance cost, the more scattered the clusters were. One of the intriguing findings was that the spatial patterns showed a tendency of self-organization in that the size of clusters linearly correlated with the numbers of clusters in the logarithmic scale. Figure 8.3 shows the R^2 values of the power law functions generated by the random and increasing returns models, plotted against distance cost. The increasing returns model apparently resulted in higher R^2 values than the random model, meaning that the linear form is more significant in the former. Since I was interested in the resulting power law in general, not any specific one with a coefficient at -1 that Zipf found, I did not investigate to what extent the coefficients derived from the simulation deviate from that of Zipf's law, that is, -1. Such attempts have been done and reported elsewhere (e.g., Yu and Lai, 2005).

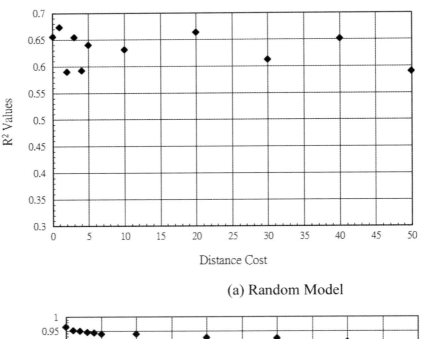

(a) Random Model

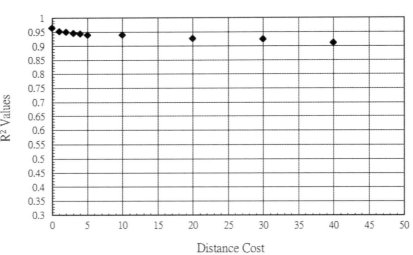

(b) Increasing Returns Model

Figure 8.3   Two plots of the R^2 values in relation to distance costs for the random and increasing returns models

5 Discussion

It might be arguably true that the behavioral model of firms in choosing locations depicted here is too simple. In particular, the direct translation of the decision rule for technology choices into that for location choices might seem irrelevant at first because, in the latter, transportation costs and the spatial distribution of buyers matter. However, in both types of the simulations the locational factors of transportation costs and the spatial distribution of buyers are considered to some extent by including a distance cost in equation (1) and considering the effects of spatial distribution of clustering as shown in Figures 8.1 and 8.2. The crux of the research design is, however, to show that complex phenomena may result from simple rules, a theme of an emerging science of complexity (Simon, 1998). Although the spatial configurations used in the simulations were assumed homogeneous without features of a real landscape, such as rivers, hills, and transportation networks, it may be argued that most, if not all, such factors could be reflected in the distance cost, so the model may be robust regardless of the variations in the landscape. Similar modeling approaches were adopted elsewhere (Krugman, 1996b).

In the simulations of firms' movement across regions, agglomeration in one region is essentially a lock-in phenomenon in Arthur's original model of agents' choosing among competing technologies. Under the assumption of increasing returns, when the number of agents adopting one of the technologies is greater than those of other technologies, that technology might eventually dominate the market. In our transformed model of regional development, regions are considered as technologies and firms as agents. The lock-in processes imply that eventually all firms would reside in a particular region forming a sweeping agglomeration where all firms move into that region. Similar implication can be derived from considering firms' spatial behavior within regions. The lock-in processes imply that there would be a super metropolitan area that attracts all firms to that area. But in reality, no such a metropolitan area exists. That super metropolitan area can only be found in the simulations when the distance cost is set to zero. With the increase in the distance cost, the resulting clusters scatter in a more fragmented pattern. Except for the case of subsidy policies where movement is encouraged, in most cases in the real world the distance cost is nothing but positive, and the sweeping metropolitan area cannot exist. We could infer from the simulation results that spatial agglomeration is path-dependent and unpredictable in that we cannot predict where agglomeration would occur except for explaining the process *after the fact*. Small events of firms choosing locations would be magnified over time resulting in agglomeration in particular locations. More important, the results of the simulations using the empirical data of firms resemble to some extent the real regional development in Taiwan, so we could argue that the path-dependence characteristic of the model is already embedded in the data. Note, however, that small events are referred to here as those events that cannot be modeled explicitly in the clustering process, that is, they are invisible in the model. For example, decisions in a firm concerning hiring and budgeting at various times might not be directly related to location choices, but the effects of a sequence of such small events might propagate and eventually affect the firm's locational choices.

When examining more closely the patterns of particular agglomerations or clusters of firms, I found a power law relation between the numbers of clusters and their sizes. Similar patterns were found in simulations elsewhere (Lai and Gao, 2001), but the underlying interactions among agents are different. In the simulations conducted here, the interaction among the firms is mainly based on increasing returns as a function of cluster sizes. In other simulations designed by Lai and Gao, the agents interacted through a payoff table according to a questionnaire survey and learned over time the best land development strategy contingent on the development pattern in the neighbors of the site. Based on the empirical data of land uses in Taipei, Lai and Lin (1999) also found the power law relation between the numbers of clusters and the cluster sizes in fractal scales. These findings strongly support the hypothesis that simple, reasonable interacting rules among the agents result in the spatial patterns that bear significant similarity, regardless of how the rules are constructed. There is no accepted theory yet to explain the fact that the complex spatial systems of interacting agents tend to self-organize themselves, such as a power law relation, but the increasing returns and cellular automata models might indeed share a common underlying mechanism yet to be found.

6 Conclusions

I have conducted two sets of simulations focusing on how the firms would choose locations to form agglomeration as a way of observing spatial evolution both across regions and within regions. Instead of investigating in depth the behavioral rules of the firms' movement, I concentrated on how simple behavioral models of the firms interacting with each other give rise to complex, but orderly, spatial patterns. Based on the principle of increasing returns to choosing among competing locations, agglomeration of the firms is explained as a function of the initial payoffs of the regions as well as the opportunity and distance costs of moving. By manipulating the values of parameters of the model to reflect the change in exogenous factors, the simulations of the firms moving across the regions based on the real data resulted in lock-in processes of agglomeration distinct from that using random data. In the second set of simulations considering the firms' moving within regions, I found that distance cost played an important role in agglomeration of the firms. The evidence of self-organization in terms of a power law relation prompts me to speculate that there may be a common, underlying mechanism yet to be found, whether in an urban or regional context. Similar attempts have been made (e.g., Simon, 1955). To yield results useful for understanding spatial evolution, we should aim at uncovering such a mechanism in a formal, rigorous way.

Acknowledgement

The author is grateful to Tzeng-Long Chen's help for coding and analyzing the simulations.

References

Arthur, W.B. 1990. "'Silicon valley' locational clusters: When do increasing returns imply monopoly?" *Mathematical Social Sciences* 19: 235–51.
Arthur, W.B. 1994. *Increasing Returns and Path Dependence in the Economy.* Ann Arbor, Michigan: The University of Michigan Press.
Bak, P. 1996. *How Nature Works.* New York: Springer-Verlag New York, Inc.
Batten, D.F. 2001. "Complex landscapes of spatial interaction." *The Annals of Regional Science* 35: 81–111.
Garreau, J. 1992. *Edge City.* New York: Anchor Books.
Krugman, P. 1996a. "Confronting the mystery of urban hierarchy." *Journal of the Japanese and International Economies* 10: 399–418.
Krugman, P. 1996b. *The Self-organizing Economy.* Cambridge, Massachusetts: Blackwell Publishers.
Lai, S-K, and H-H Gao. 2001. "Self-organized criticality in urban complex spatial systems." *Journal of Building and Planning* 10: 31–43. (in Chinese).
Lai, S-K, and J-J Lin. 1999. "A study of complex spatial structures of urban land uses." *Man and Land* April: 16–25. (in Chinese).
O'Sullivan, A. 1993. *Urban Economics*, Second Edition. Homewood, IL: IRWIN.
Simon, H.A. 1955. "On a class of skew distribution functions." *Biometrika* 52: 425–40.
Simon, H.A. 1998. *The Sciences of the Artificial.* Third Edition. Cambridge, Massachusetts: The MIT Press.
Yu, J-L, and S-K Lai. 2005. "Power law distribution of human settlements: an explanation based on increasing returns." CUPUM05. CASA, University College London.
Zipf, G.K. 1949. *Human Behavior and the Principle of Least Effort.* New York: Addison-Wesley Press

Chapter 9
The Formation of Urban Settlement Systems: Computer Experiments and Mathematical Proofs of the Increasing-returns Approach to Power Law

1 Introduction

Throughout history, urban systems have developed in which a small number of well-developed large cities have coexisted with a large number of smaller settlements. A degree of order appears to govern these settlements, as though they had been distributed deliberately (Batty, 2006). Previous studies have described the formation of urban settlements using theories such as rank-size rule (Zipf, 1949; Gibaix, 1999; Chen, 2000) and power law (Bak, 1989; 1991); however, the underlying mechanisms still require further exploration. Simon (1955) proposed a famous interpretive model, in which it was assumed that cities grow through the addition of one urban lump at a time, which would either join an existing city or form as a new settlement. The probability that a lump will become a new settlement is represented as the constant π and the derived variable $\alpha = 1 / (1-\pi)$. The value of α drawn from the statistical data of settlements in the real world is close to 1; therefore, the value of π should be close to 0. However, in such circumstances new settlements tend not to be produced, which precludes the formation of urban settlements and renders the model unable to effectively explain the causes of the power law.

This research is an attempt to fill this gap in explaining the self-organization of urban settlements. This research attempts to discover how such urban systems were formed through the use of computer and mathematical simulations. In recent years, increasing return has been successfully applied to explain a number of self-organized phenomena in complex systems, and in this study, increasing return is used to explain the power law. Thus, we designed a simplified urban settlement on a homogeneous plain and applied computer simulation programs and mathematical calculations to analyze the rules associated with its evolution. Our aim was to examine whether increasing return is the basic reason for the power law in urban settlements.

2 Basic Theory of Increasing Return and Power Law

2.1 Rank-size Rule and Power Law

Zipf proposed the rank-size rule in 1949 to describe the correlation between the scale and size of a city. That was denoted in the following equation:

$P_r = P_1 / r$

in which P_r represents the population of a city at level r in the region;

P_1 represents the population of the largest city (primary city) in the region; and

r represents the level of development of cities with population P_r.

It has been proven by many scholars that this equation, obtained through observation, is capable of describing the hierarchical relationship within urban systems to a large extent.

Power law indicates the relationship between the scale and frequency of an event. If the scale of an event is denoted as S, the frequency can be represented as S^{-a}. This suggests that the larger the scale of an event is, the less frequent it will be, and vice versa. The most famous examples of the power law are earthquakes and sand pile experiments. The frequency of earthquakes and the energy they release follows the power law. In the sand experiment, the scale and frequency of the collapses of sand pile also obey the power law.

Power law also exists in urban systems and the rank-size rule is a manifestation of it. Krugman (1996) developed a statistical analysis of American cities. After sorting those cities by size and double-logging the orders and sizes, he found that they were significantly linearly correlated. That proved that the order and size of cities obey the power law.

2.2 The Theory of Increasing Return

Arthur (1990) was the first to introduce the concept of increasing return to modern economics. Increasing return is highly related to agglomeration in urban economics. For manufacturers or producers, external economy of scale is the main reason for agglomeration. For example, the increase of production in a certain industry will result in the decrease in price of the raw materials so that every manufacturer in this industry can access the cheaper raw material. The forces acting on firms in a single industry together are called localization economies, which are external for manufacturers while internal for the whole industry. Urbanization economies mean every industry in a city can benefit from the enlargement of the city scale; for example, some high-level urban facilities (such as concert halls, stadiums) that only exist in large cities can benefit all their citizens.

The two basic causes of economies of agglomeration, the scale effect and increasing return, are closely related to each other. In terms of increasing return, the so-called "camps" may have no correlation in space, such as users of a product. In other words, the increasing return does not only function in agglomeration. However, the indivisibility of urban construction is only valid in agglomeration, so there is still difference between those two causes.

In terms of space aggregation behavior, Arthur regarded it as an increasing return phenomenon. Manufacturers prefer regions with better conditions for production. Those entering later would locate around existing manufacturers in order to reduce the development cost and acquire more profit. It is called the agglomeration economy effect and can be expressed as follows:

$\pi_i + g(N_i)$

in which, π_i represents the geographic advantage of region i; and

$g(N_i)$ represents the aggregation profit when N_i manufacturers agglomerate in region i. The profit of aggregation becomes larger as the number of manufacturers increases. Arthur concluded that if the aggregation profit is unbounded, all industries would gather in one region. However, he did not explain the spatial structure of the location.

3 Research Design of Computer Experiment

In this research, based on Krugman and Arthur's theoretical framework, we designed a computer experiment in a two-dimensional space. The logic for the experiment is to view the formation of an urban settlement system as a randomly growing process. In our computer experiment, we adopted Arthur's analytical framework, which divided the attraction of location into the characteristics of location and the aggregation of profit. To simplify the model and focus on the relationship between increasing return and the power law, the simulation space is designed on a homogeneous plane, without considering the characteristics of location. In that simplified model, location attraction is purely the result of the aggregation of profit. In addition, the number and division of regions in Arthur's model are predetermined; while in this simplified model, the number of urban settlements was produced by the system and the profit of aggregation of each settlement was proportional to its size. Each settlement in this simplified model can be regarded as a small region in Arthur's (1990) model.

The space in the model was designed as a checkerboard composed of uniform grids. Each grid represents a cell (in the cellular automata) or the smallest unit associated with land development. An increase in the number of cells would result in increased computation. However, from the perspective of statistical analysis, a larger statistical sample would be more convincing. Within the limit of computation, this research greatly increased the number of cells, establishing a matrix of 200×200, for a total of 40,000 cells.

In the simulation, a cell has either of the two states: undeveloped or developed. All of the cells were undeveloped in the initial state with some being developed according to the rules of simulation. In each round of the experiment, a cell develops in the system and selects a location of residence. That location consequently switches from an undeveloped to a developed state. Thus, the number of developed cells increases by one after each round and this increase in the number of cells continues until the 2,000th round. The simulation was set to 2,000 rounds due to the following considerations:

1. A total of 2,000 rounds are capable of providing sufficient statistical data to observe the evolutionary patterns of the system within a tolerable duration.
2. The region would not be too crowded. By keeping the number of iterations below 2,000 rounds, less than 5% of the region would developed, which would help to avoid the merging of settlements due to limited developmental space. When two settlements merge into one, the scale of the settlements increases. That would violate the rules of the experiment in which only one developed cell is added to the system in each round, with detrimental effects on the experimental results.

A number of basic presumptions were adopted for this experiment:

1. The development of a cell was irreversible. This means that after an undeveloped cell has been developed, it would never switch back to an undeveloped state during the simulation. This indicates that land development is irreversible and once land has been developed, it is not easily converted to its initial state.
2. In their initial state, all cells in a region are undeveloped and one developed cell is added to the region in each round, regardless of whether it is generated within the system or incorporated from outside the system. In this research, it was crucial to determine where a cell chooses to locate. The rules for the selection of location are elaborated in Section 2 of Chapter 3.

The computer simulation in this research was developed from Monte Carlo simulation methods and programmed by the authors using Microsoft Visual Basic 6.0. We employed a fixed-sequence series of random numbers to compare the simulation results drawn from various models using various parameters. With such a series of numbers, all numbers were randomly generated, but the sequence remained unchanged through each iteration. Consequently, the same parameters would result in the same experimental results. This helped to reduce the degree to which the random numbers cause variations in the results. For a location with high developmental potential, one grid was assigned several random numbers to increase its chances of being developed.

We designed three computer models, according to three patterns of cell attraction, as explained below.

3.1 Neighborhood Attraction

In the neighborhood attraction model, we assumed that one cell only interacts with its 8 neighbors. This means that a cell only considers the relationship with its 8 neighbors in its selection of location. The following rules were adopted for the neighborhood attraction model:

1. Suppose that a homogeneous space exists in the region, and in the initial state each cell has an equal chance of being developed. With no developed

cells in the region in the beginning, the potential for development is 1 and the probability of growth is 1/40000 for each cell.
2. Following the development of a cell, the development potential of its 8 neighbors increases to N, which is called "aggregation strength" in this simulation (as shown in Figure 9.1, the grid in gray indicates a state of development). Moreover, if a cell is developed, its development potential becomes 0, which demonstrates that this location can never be converted back to its initial state.
3. The first cell has an identical chance of development in the selection of its location within the entire region. However, when one developed cell exists in the region, the development potential is no longer homogeneous. The grid around the already developed cell will have higher developmental potential. Moreover, development potential can accumulate. When a grid is adjacent to 2 developed cells, its development potential increases to 2N. Similarly, if a grid is surrounded by 8 developed cells, its development potential will be 8N, which represents the highest probability for development (Figure 9.2).

1	1	1	1	1	1	1
1	1	1	1	1	1	1
1	1	N	N	N	1	1
1	1	N	░	N	1	1
1	1	N	N	N	1	1
1	1	1	1	1	1	1
1	1	1	1	1	1	1

1	1	1	1	1	1	1
1	N	2N	3N	2N	N	1
1	2N	░	░	░	2N	1
1	3N	░	8N	░	3N	1
1	2N	░	░	░	2N	1
1	N	2N	3N	2N	N	1
1	1	1	1	1	1	1

1	1	1	1	1	1	1
1	3N	3N	3N	3N	1	1
1	3N	░	░	3N	1	1
1	3N	░	3N	3N	1	1
1	3N	3N	3N	1	1	1
1	1	1	1	1	1	1
1	1	1	1	1	1	1

Figure 9.1 An example of attractiveness scores with a single developed cell

Figure 9.2 An example of attractiveness scores with a regular cluster of developed cells

Figure 9.3 An example of attractiveness scores with an irregular cluster of developed cells

3.2 Scale Attraction

The basic concept behind increasing return is that the payoff rate increases when more members join the camp. Therefore, the larger a camp is, the more attractive it would be to new members. Scale attraction means that the attraction of a city to new urban settlement is proportional to the scale of the city. Scale attraction considers the selection of cell location in a scale larger than that used in neighborhood attraction, by considering not only the number of neighboring cells but also the scale of agglomeration.

For example, if a grid is next to a developed agglomeration with a scale of 3 (comprising 3 adjacent developed cells), its development potential will increase to 3N, as shown in Figure 9.3. If the scale of agglomeration is M, the development potential of its neighbors increases to M×N.

According to the above logic, cells new to the region are more likely to select a location with high development potential adjacent to large-scale settlements.

3.3 Mixed Attraction

In the real world, both neighborhood attraction and scale attraction are considered in the selection of location. People choose to live in large cities with aggregation profits, in which the factor of scale is considered, at least at a basic level. Meanwhile, when selecting regional location, people tend to choose a place with neighbors, in which neighborhood attraction is the primary consideration. Based on these mixed considerations, we designed a mixed attraction model for this study.

We used the following formula to calculate the development potential of a location (a grid).

$$Q = J \times \sqrt{S \times T}$$

in which
Q denotes its development potential;
J denotes aggregation strength;
S denotes the number of developed cells of its 8 neighbors;
T denotes the scale of the largest agglomeration adjacent to it; and
$\sqrt{S \times T}$ denotes the geometric mean of S and T.

In the three above patterns, the probability of location selection is decided by the value of development potential. The higher the value, the higher the probability that a location will be selected by a new cell. Location advantage can accumulate, representing the basic principle of increasing return.

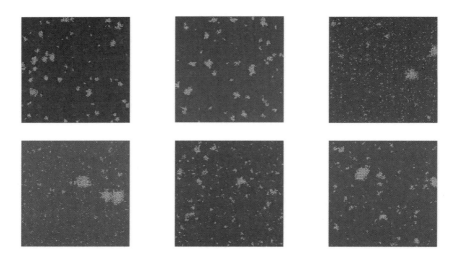

Figure 9.4 Examples of simulation results with different attractiveness scores

4 Results of Simulation

As shown in Figure 9.4 (gray indicates undeveloped cells and white indicates developed cells), we selected typical sections to illustrate the simulation results.

To explore whether the scale and rank of settlements (agglomerations of cells) follow the power law, both scale and rank were math logged into a simple linear regression with rank as the dependent variable (Y) and scale as the independent variable (X). We used statistics provided by the experiment to determine whether the distribution of urban settlements follows a power law distribution. It should be noted that the aggregation strengths of the three models varied between 1 and 5,000 to denote different features of the models. Otherwise, it would not have been possible to acquire typical results from those models.

The simulation results for the neighborhood attraction model, scale attraction model and mixed model are shown in Tables 9.1–9.3.

Table 9.1 Indices for the neighboring attraction model

Aggregation strength	Scale of primary city	R^2	Coefficient	Average scale of urban settlements	Standard deviation of urban settlement scales	Variation coefficient of urban settlement scales
50	34	0.8893	-1.4378	6.35	6.45	1.0473
100	84	0.9257	-1.2087	9.08	11.21	1.2337
200	105	0.8645	-0.9360	15.72	18.21	1.1582
500	138	0.8718	-0.7632	25.82	29.85	1.1560
1000	164	0.8589	-0.6432	38.42	39.03	1.0158
2000	262	0.8251	-0.4650	74.04	78.67	1.0626
5000	348	0.8254	-0.4702	90.91	89.06	0.9797

Table 9.2 Indices for the scale-attraction model

Aggregation strength	Scale of primary city	R^2	Coefficient	Average scale of urban settlements	Standard deviation of urban settlement scales	Variation coefficient of urban settlement scales
1	12	0.9937	-2.1485	1.25	0.78	0.6254
2	164	0.9569	-1.2622	1.69	4.99	2.9554
3	174	0.9953	-1.0732	2.12	7.12	3.3550
5	286	0.9841	-0.9645	2.80	13.39	4.7873
7	720	0.9677	-0.8921	3.53	30.52	8.6546
10	651	0.9488	-0.7890	4.69	36.33	7.7492
20	1235	0.9607	-0.7202	7.34	74.82	10.1908

Table 9.3 Indices for the mixed-relation model of neighboring attraction and scale-attraction

Aggregation strength	Scale of primary city	R^2	Coefficient	Average scale of urban settlements	Standard deviation of urban settlement scales	Variation coefficient of urban settlement scales
10	31	0.9546	-1.6155	3.17	3.86	1.2789
20	88	0.9598	-1.1812	4.65	8.84	1.9001
40	172	0.9710	-0.9920	7.32	16.96	2.3170
50	238	0.9724	-0.8781	9.85	25.13	2.5516
70	448	0.9863	-0.8400	11.82	39.61	3.3520
100	812	0.9280	-0.7814	15.91	72.86	4.5789
500	994	0.9801	-0.4781	55.53	190.39	3.4287

4.1 Comparison of Three Models

From the simulations results for the three models, we find the following characteristics:

1. In the three models, both the scale of the primary city the average scale of urban settlements tend to enlarge with an increase in aggregation strength. This demonstrates that when the location of an adjacent settlement has high development potential, new developments tend to gather there, resulting in very few large settlements. However, it does not always occur that the primary city becomes larger as the aggregation strength increases in the simulation. This is a model of probability with interference from random variables, in which the emergence of unexpected cases influences the subsequent results. Moreover, a sudden increase in the scale of a settlement due to the merging of two settlements also has the potential to influence the result.
2. With an increase in aggregation strength, the absolute value of the coefficient of regression is reduced in the three models. That eventually results in the "polarization" of the urban system, indicating that urban development is concentrated in a few large cities with enormous gaps between large and small cities. The implication is, more and larger settlements will occur if areas adjacent to existing settlements are given higher development potential. Moreover, the intensity of aggregation is proportional to the increase in development potential.
3. R^2 was used to test whether simulated urban settlements meet the power law. With R^2 values between 0.83 and 0.99, all three models produced distribution patterns in accordance with the power law; however, significant differences were noted among the three models. Neighborhood attraction has a much lower R^2 than scale attraction or mixed attraction. Statistical

tests confirm that there is a significant difference between neighborhood attraction and the other two models and no significant difference between scale attraction and mixed attraction (at the significance level of 5%). Moreover, because both the R^2 of scale attraction and that of mixed attraction are over 0.9, we conclude that scale effect is a determining factor in the formation of a settlement system. This expresses the basic spirit of increasing return.

4. The variation coefficient (the average divided by the standard deviation) was applied to the three models to examine whether the distribution of simulated urban settlements is homogeneous or polarized. Among the three models, scale attraction has the largest variation coefficient and neighborhood attraction has the least. In the scale attraction model, the attraction of a settlement for new residents is proportional to its scale; therefore, the gap between large and small settlements quickly expands. However, in the neighborhood attraction model, the strength of attraction is never more than eight times larger; therefore, the gap between large and small settlements is relatively small.

4.2 Comparison Over Time

Table 9.4 Changes in parameters for different rounds of simulation

Type of attraction	Round	Scale of primary city	R^2	Coefficient
Neighborhood attraction (aggregation strength: 500)	300	29	0.9010	-0.9515
	500	45	0.9113	-0.9331
	700	57	0.9139	-0.8838
	1000	73	0.8919	-0.8287
	1200	83	0.8847	-0.8125
	1500	105	0.8751	0.7949
	2000	138	0.8718	-0.7632
Scale attraction (aggregation strength: 5)	300	4	0.9916	-2.4704
	500	5	0.9518	-2.4039
	700	9	0.9789	-2.0510
	1000	29	0.9962	-1.5166
	1200	46	0.9932	-1.3912
	1500	105	0.9940	-1.4216
	2000	286	0.9841	-0.9645
Mixed attraction (aggregation strength: 40)	300	10	0.9744	-1.5426
	500	20	0.9640	-1.5069
	700	43	0.9673	-1.3670
	1000	37	0.9766	-1.2079
	1200	87	0.9759	-1.1270
	1500	111	0.9732	-1.0777
	2000	172	0.9710	-0.9920

Table 9.4 shows the simulation results of three models from Round 500 to Round 2,000. By observing variations in the coefficients and R^2 in the three models, we obtain the following results:

1. R^2 did not vary linearly over time in any of the models.
2. This suggests the universality and stability of the power law. The distribution of urban settlements follows the power law distribution from the beginning to the end of the simulation, rather than by "gradually approaching."
3. In scale attraction, the absolute value of the coefficient decreased over time, but remained nearly the same for neighborhood attraction and mixed attraction.

In neighborhood attraction, whether new developments will be attracted around existing settlements is determined by the relationships among existing cells. Therefore, settlements which have different scales but the same relationship with their neighbors will have the same attraction for new developments. The attractiveness of a settlement is not determined directly by its scale. In addition, the difference in attractiveness among neighboring cells never exceeds eight times, which enables settlements of different scale to grow together. The difference among them remains stable and does not increase over time.

In scale attraction, the attractiveness of a settlement to new residents is proportional to its scale. Thus, the larger a settlement is, the faster it grows. Moreover, the difference between large and small settlements increases over time, as shown in the regression model in which the slope (coefficient) decreases over time.

For the mixed attraction model, the attraction of scale is influenced by neighborhood attraction; therefore, differences among settlements do not change significantly over time.

4.3 Comparison of the Primary City's Growth

Table 9.5 Growth of the primary city in three models

Type of attraction	Neighborhood attraction		Scale attraction		Mixed attraction	
Aggregation strength	500	1000	5	10	40	70
Round 100	13	24	2	2	3	14
Round 500	45	63	5	11	20	66
Round 1000	73	115	29	80	73	186
Round 1500	105	137	105	319	111	295
Round 2000	138	164	286	651	172	448
Growth ratio at the second half phase	1.89	1.43	9.86	8.14	2.36	2.41

Table 9.5 shows the growth of the primary city in the three models. In terms of the growth rate during the second half of the simulation period, the scale of the region doubled from 1,000 to 2,000, but the growth rate of the primary city varied significantly between 200% and 1000% in the three models. The primary city grew the quickest in scale attraction and slowest in neighborhood attraction. The growth rate of the latter was even below average (double for all settlements). We also noted that setting a high aggregation strength resulted in the emergence of a number of small settlements, which grew at a rate similar to neighborhood attraction; while in scale attraction, settlements grew very slowly in the beginning and Increased dramatically when their scales increased to a certain level. The growth rate of mixed attraction was between that of neighborhood attraction and scale attraction.

This also proves what has been discussed above. In neighborhood attraction, settlements of different scales grew simultaneously; while in scale attraction, the growth rate of large settlements far exceeded that of small settlements, resulting in an increased difference in scale.

In the real world, the speed at which the primary city grows definitely exceeds the average. This is contradicted by the simulation results of neighborhood attraction in which the primary city grew slower than average. Thus, we can conclude that scale attraction and mixed attraction are more appropriate than neighborhood attraction in revealing the growth of urban settlements in the real world.

5 Mathematical Simulation Calculation

According to the growth logic of neighborhood attraction in the last section, we designed a two-dimensional model to simulate the growth of urban settlement. We explored the relationship between the scale and frequency of urban settlement in a random growth process, in which different scales of settlements are formed by allowing new residents or manufacturers to randomly select their location. The frequency of the scales can be calculated by the expectation of an occurrence. When a new cell, resident, or manufacturer enters an area, the expectation of its occurrence can provide information related to optional locations. This information enables it to select a location near or far from the developed cells. Different growth paths occur during the evolution from time t to time $t+n$ (Figure 9.5).

As shown in Figure 9.5, there are 9 optional grids in the initial state t_0 (all grids were undeveloped). Therefore, the number of possibilities for growth is 9. When one cell is occupied, there are 8 possibilities for growth in following state t_1. The total number of paths to grow becomes 9×8. By parity of reasoning, this calculation can continue until all 9 grids are developed. There are a total of 362,880 paths (9×8×7×...×2×1, or P(9,9)). In addition, this model simulated the growth process of urban settlements within a limited space. The development of a particular grid will influence the one developed in the next state. Thus, the development is path-dependent.

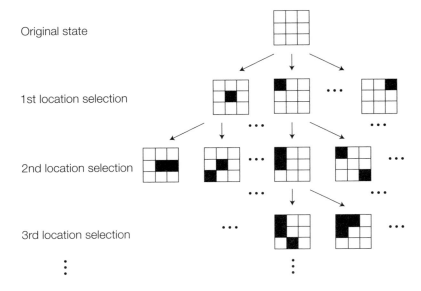

Figure 9.5 Stochastic paths of growth in the 9-grid lattice model

5.1   Power Law Coefficients and Significance Analysis

As discussed above, the power law in urban settlements refers to the linear correlation between the logarithm of urban scale and its rank. Because the sample size of the 9-grid lattice is too small in this mathematical simulation, we adopted the logarithm of scale and its frequency of occurrence instead, regarding scale as the independent variable (X) and frequency as the dependent variable (Y). We developed a statistical analysis using linear regression, considering the changes in the distribution pattern over time and examining variations in the coefficient and R^2. The results are shown in Table 9.6.

The probability of blocks occurring at a particular scale was calculated by dividing the aggregation strength of each grid by the sum aggregation strengths of all grids. We then calculated the expectation of the occurrence of each scale distribution pattern by summing up all of the above probabilities. As the model evolved from its initial state t_0 to t_3, the largest possible scale of urban settlement was 3 (three blocks adjacent to each other) and the smallest was 1 (one independent block). By summing up the probabilities of all developmental states, we acquired the initial data for our statistical analysis (Table 9.6).

In Table 9.6, the dimension of time denoted the range of times or states being considered. Adjusted R^2 was the variable used to determine whether the distribution of urban settlements followed the power law. The higher the adjusted R^2 is, the more closely the distribution of urban settlement follows the power law.

Table 9.6 Coefficients and R squares in the regression model

Time dimension	n=3	n=4	n=5	n=6	n=7	n=8	n=9
Coefficient	-1.6501	-1.2276	-1.0116	-0.8653	-0.7247	-0.6198	-0.5421
Adjusted R^2	0.99998	0.97477	0.95282	0.90113	0.77732	0.68058	0.61004

The absolute value of the coefficient decreased with time. Empirically, this would lead to polarization, in which urban development agglomerates mainly in a small number of large cities with enormous potential gaps in the scale of urban settlements. The R^2 of the model (indicating the significance of the regression) could exceed 0.9 in the initial state but decreased sharply to below 0.7 in the second half period. This might be the result of limitations in development space. As an increasing number of blocks were occupied and fewer blocks remained, the entire region would result in one large settlement without urban settlements of other sizes.

5.2 Comparison with the Calculation of Non-increasing Return

We also examined whether the distribution of probability changes with aggregation effect (N). We calculated the distribution of settlements in a purely random growth pattern (without increasing return) as a comparison group and observed the variation in the variables (coefficient and R^2) in models with and without increasing return (Table 9.7). In the model without increasing return, it was assumed that the value of aggregation effect (N) is 0, denoting that a block can be randomly developed. In this model, every newcomer may freely choose its location; the formation depended entirely on the location.

Table 9.7 Models with and without the consideration of increasing return

Time frame	With increasing return		Without increasing return	
	Coefficient	R^2	Coefficient	R^2
n=3	-1.65011	0.999976	-2.30206	0.995191
n=4	-1.22763	0.974766	-1.94798	0.988797
n=5	-1.0116	0.952817	-1.95853	0.994604
n=6	-0.8653	0.901126	-1.26534	0.950884
n=7	-0.72466	0.777319	-1.02343	0.790182
n=8	-0.61981	0.680579	-0.85451	0.657108
n=9	-0.5421	0.61004	-0.73247	0.564107

Table 9.7 shows that in the non-increasing-return model, the results of the regression obeyed the power law (regression is mostly significant), but the values of the coefficients were smaller than those in the increasing-return model. In another words, the formation of urban settlements is more dispersed in urban development without increasing return than with increasing return. According to the statistical analysis, the power law is less significant in the late period of evolution due to limitations in space. By comparing only the results with significance exceeding 0.9 in the two models, we find that even if urban settlements lack motivation to aggregate, their distribution still follows the power law. However, that distribution pattern differs considerably from the distribution pattern of urban settlements in the real world. Highly agglomerated large cities cannot be produced in the non-increasing-return model, as they do in the real world.

In addition, in the model with increasing return, the coefficient of regression was close to 1, showing a trend of polarization. That is very similar to the urban settlements in the real world. Therefore, we may conclude that increasing return is one of the reasons for the power law.

6 Discussion

Empirical statistics in the US indicate that urban systems follow a power law distribution perfectly and it has not changed over the past century. The coefficient in the linear regression model of the size and rank of US cities remained at -1. However, in our computer simulation, different aggregation strengths resulted in coefficients of different values. In the scale attraction and mixed attraction models, the coefficients were very close to -1 and the R^2s were over 0.95, suggesting that the simulation results were very similar to the real world. For example, when the aggregation strength was 5 in scale attraction, the coefficient became -0.9645 (Figure 9.6). After it was increased to 40 in mixed attraction, the coefficient was -0.9920 (Table 9.8). In our simulation, the distribution patterns of many urban settlements followed a power law distribution, but we obtained coefficients close to those of the real world only under specific circumstances. This may suggest that the profit and influence of aggregation are fixed in the real world, neither too small nor too big. If the profit and influence of aggregation were too small, there would be only groups of small urban settlements. If they were too big, there would be just one enormous primary city.

An appropriate coefficient is capable of producing results close to those found in the real world. Empirical data also show that the coefficient remained nearly unchanged over the past century. Therefore, we can say that, to some extent, the coefficient closest to that found in the real world is the best result.

To explore the gap between the model and the real world, we developed the comparison listed below (Table 9.8). Data from the seven largest cities in Taiwan and the ten largest cities in Zhejiang province, China, were listed and compared with the simulation results. In the ideal model of rank-size rule, it was assumed that the scale of the primary city is 100. The seven largest cities in Taiwan in 2003 were Taipei, Kaohsiung, Taichung, Tainan, Keelung, Hsinchu, and Chiayi according to the *Collections of Statistical Data for Urban and Regional Development* (Wang, 2003); while the ten largest cities in Zhejiang Province in 2006 were Hangzhou, Wenzhou, Ningbo, Yiwu, Ruian, Taizhou, Shaoxing, Huzhou, Jinhua, and Jiaxing according to the *Study on the Urban and Rural Construction Land Scale and Utilization of Spatial Distribution in Zhejiang Province* (Shao and Pan, 2006). The coefficient of the linear regression model of the former was -0.811, representing a slight deviation from -1, which may be the result of a small number of samples. The coefficient of the linear regression model of the latter was -1.0960, which is highly consistent with the rank-size rule.

The unit for the scale of urban settlement in Taiwan and Zhejiang Province: 1000 people. Data for Taiwan from the *Collections of Statistical Data for Urban and Regional Development*, 2003. Data for Zhejiang Province from the *Urban and Rural Construction Land Area and the Improvement of Its Spatial Distribution in Zhejiang Province*, 2006.

We need to determine which model is superior: scale attraction or mixed attraction. In terms of interpretation, the two models did not differ significantly. In terms of statistics, scale attraction is preferable, due to its simplicity.

However, it was found that the coefficient in scale attraction changed largely over time, which contradicts the empirical data from US cities. Although the paucity of data available from only one century makes it difficult to conclude that the coefficient in the empirical model of US cities does not change, the coefficient should remain stable over a given period. The coefficient in the mixed attraction model appears to be more stable. Table 9.4 suggests that the coefficient in the mixed

Table 9.8 Comparison of the models and the real urban settlement systems

Item	Scale of 10 largest urban settlements									R^2	Coefficient
Rank-size rule	100	50	33	25	20	17	14	13	11	10	1.0000	-1.0000
7 large cities in Taiwan	2641	1475	940	728	385	361	265	-	-	-	0.9836	-0.8111
10 largest cities in Zhejiang Province, China	2647	1951	1556	694	615	612	607	523	520	402	0.9280	-1.0960
Scale attraction (5)	286	195	48	45	37	35	32	23	17	16	0.9841	-0.9645
Mixed attraction (40)	172	111	99	87	68	62	61	53	51	45	0.9710	-0.9920

attraction model remained nearly unchanged between rounds 1,500 and 2,000, which more closely relates to the real world. Thus, both regional relationships and scale should probably be considered in the process of selecting locations in the real world.

Although the computer experiments and mathematical simulations were based on the presumption that the simulation space is a homogeneous plane, the same results should be obtained when topography or changes in public infrastructure, such as transportation networks, are considered. We predict that changes in topography will not alter the power law distribution of urban settlements; however, it will change their spatial distribution.

7 Conclusions

The power law is a common phenomenon in the natural and social sciences as well as in urban systems found in the real world. To explore the correlation between power law and increasing return, we simulated the formation of urban settlement systems using random growth models based on computer experimentation and mathematical simulation. Based on the concept of increasing return, these simulations included three different approaches to model the means by which development is attracted to specific locations, including neighborhood attraction (a cell is only influenced by its eight neighbors in the selection of location), scale attraction (the larger scale a settlement has, the more attractive it is to new developments), and mixed attraction (considering both neighborhood attraction and scale attraction). According to the results from the R^2, all three models produce urban settlement systems that obey the power law, as also proven by mathematical simulation.

By considering R^2 and the speed of growth of the primary city, it was found that the neighborhood attraction model was not in strong accordance with the real world. Both the scale and mixed attraction models were well adapted and demonstrated explanatory power. With regard to the explanatory power of the models, scale was determined to be more important than neighborhood, representing the key explanatory variable. This indicates the influence of increasing return. It can be concluded from the simulation results that increasing return did produce settlement systems that follow the power law distribution. This might be a basic reason for the power law distribution in the real world. According to the results of mathematical simulation, we conclude that the existence of the power law may be a statistical phenomenon, and will not be influenced by factors such as urban economics. Economic or other factors could alter the distribution of power law, but not its existence.

In their research on increasing return, Arthur et al. (1987) discussed the distribution of space by establishing a mathematical model showing the impact of increasing return on aggregation interests. From a different approach, this research proved the existence of a close relationship between increasing return and the power law through computer experimentation and mathematical simulation. We will continue our research by combining the results of this research with Arthur's mathematical model. Moreover, we made several assumptions to simplify the simulation. In future studies, we will attempt to release a number of assumed restrictions; for instance, by considering migration behaviors and heterogeneous space as a means of making our simulation closer to the real world.

References

Arthur, W.B. 1990. *Increasing Returns and Path Dependence in the Economy*. Ann Arbor, Michigan: The University of Michigan Press.
Arthur, W.B. 1990. "'Silicon Valley' locational clusters: when do increasing returns imply monopoly?" *Mathematical Social Sciences* 19:.235–51.
Bak, P., and K. Chen. 1989. "Self-organization criticality phenomenon." *Journal of Geophysical Studies* 94: 15635–7.
Bak, P. 1991. "Self-organizing criticality." *Scientific American* 1: pp. 26–33.
Batty, M. 2006. "Rank clock." *Nature* 444: 592–6.
Chen, H.P. 2000. Zipf's Law and the Spatial Interaction Models, Proceedings of Annual Meeting for Regional Science Association, A1-III-1–30, Taipei.
Gibaix, X. 1999. "Zipf's law for cities: an explanation." *Quarterly Journal of Economics* 14(3): 739–67.
Krugman, P. 1996. *The Self-organizing Economy*. Cambridge, Massachusetts: Blackwell Publishers Inc.
Shao, Bo., and Q. Pan 2006. *Urban and Rural Construction Land Area and the Improvement of Its Spatial Distribution in Zhejiang Province*. Hangzhou: Zhejiang University Press, 2006.
Simon H.A., "On a class of skew distribution function," *Biometrika*, No.52 (1955), pp. 425–440.
Wang, Z.Y. 2003. Collections of Statistical Data for Urban and Regional Development, Taipei: City and Housing Development Division. Economic Construction Commission, The Executive Council.
Zipf, G.K. 1949. *Human Behavior and the Principle of Least Effort*. New York: Addison-Wesley Press.

Chapter 10
Power Law Distribution of Human Settlements: An Explanation Based on Increasing Returns

1 Introduction

Understanding how urban systems evolve is important to make good plans for urban developments. The spatial evolution of urban systems appears to be regular because the urban hierarchic system seems to exist everywhere in that cities of various sizes are in proportional order, as if they were placed after a delicate artificial design. As early as 1933, German geologist Walter Christaller pointed this out in his classic central place theory. In 1949, Zipf posed his rank-size rule. These two theories can be considered as the pioneers of the theory of urban formation. There is a resurgence of attempts in the literature of the explanations of how the Zipf law, or the power law in general, emerges in natural systems (e.g., Bak, 1996; Gabaix, 1999; Barabási and Bonabeau, 2003; and Chen, 2004). In particular, recent efforts have been made in modeling deductively or empirically how the Zipf law emerges from random growth processes of urban systems; there seems no explicit explanatory mechanism existing that explains the emergence of the Zipf law from a disaggregate, spatial perspective. The main objective of the present chapter is to provide such an explanation based on the notion of increasing returns, first by simulation and then by mathematical deduction, that takes into account the dynamic processes of individual agents in choosing locations spatially resulting in an amazingly robust order. A similar approach to explaining the lock-in effects of agglomeration of firms based on increasing returns was reported elsewhere that confirms with the real situations in regional development in Taiwan (Lai, 2006).

In recent years, the impact of the sciences of complexity pervades in many fields (see, e.g. Kauffman 1995; Simon 1998; Batten 2001). The sciences of complexity emphasize that the whole system is composed of many individual agents, and its complexity emerges from the interaction of the individual agents. An urban system is a complex spatial system where many agents interact. The sciences of complexity also postulate that many systems in natural and social sciences have the feature of self-organization, and that in suitable situations systems will evolve from chaos spontaneously into ordered patterns. Such patterns are not originated from physical or economic principles, but are inherent in the details of the system's individual agents. The power law is one of such self-organizing phenomena. It means that the frequencies of occurrence are often related to the scales S of objects of interests in a way that they are proportional to $S^{-\alpha}$, where α is a constant. Therefore, large-scale occurrences happen infrequently, while small-scale cases are more common, in a special way that is characterized by the power law. In nature, occurrences and scales of earthquakes and meteorites appear to obey a power law and so do stock markets in the social science. Zipf's rank-size rule is an example of power law, relating the sizes of cities to their ranks. Specifically, let P(r) be the size of the r-th largest city. The rule depicts:

$$P(r) = K * r^{-q} \qquad (1)$$

for constants K and q, where K is the size (population) of the largest city, and q is referred to as the Zipf force, and is often assumed to be 1. According to this rule, if we take the logarithms of the sizes and the ranks of a set of cities, the resulting relation is linear (Savage, 1997; Black, 2001).

This special form of power law does prevail in most urban systems, and is consistent with the conception of the rank-size rule postulated by the pioneering scholars: namely, larger cities are rarer. However, such a rule is only a result of empirical observations, and has not been verified deductively in the framework of self-organization.

In a competitive market, we can observe the effects of "positive feedback" or "increasing returns" and the resulting lock-in processes of products or protocols. The competition of the two standards of video tape systems, VHS versus Beta in a market, is a classic example. Due to the positive-feedback effect, everybody tends to follow the market leader, and eventually the leader takes over the whole market. In a commercial market, the competing camps may be products of different protocols (e.g. VHS and Beta). In urban systems, cities with their locations are the competing camps, and we would observe the same effects. For example, the reason why the English colonists chose the cold, stormy, and rocky Bay of Massachusetts is simply because it was the anchoring location of the Mayflower, the very first ship arriving there (purely by chance after getting lost). But after the site was locked-in, increasing returns would make sure that it remained as a dominating city. Similarly, we can also observe an urban development process shaped by the early investment of retailers.

When Arthur (1990a) introduced "increasing returns" into modern economics, it had a significant impact on the field. The traditional economics emphasizes on "decreasing returns"; namely, the more one puts into effort, the smaller in production the profit becomes. For example, applying twice the amount of fertilizer in cultivations of land would not yield twice the amount of crop. Negative feedback and decreasing returns are the necessary components of neoclassical economics for harmony, stability, and balance.

Arthur (1990b) also considered the behavior of spatial concentration as a case of increasing returns: the location choices of manufacturers, based on manufacturing conditions, may give priorities to the surroundings of the existing manufacturers, to reduce the cost of development and have a greater profit margin. This is the effect of agglomeration economy, and can be formulated as follows—the attractiveness of region i is:

$$\pi_i + g(N_i) \tag{2}$$

where π_i represents the geological resourcefulness of region i, and $g(N_i)$ represents the advantage of having N_i manufacturers established in region i. When $g(N_i)$ increases with N_i, the total attractiveness increases in that region. Arthur (1990b) showed by theoretical deductions that if the advantage of concentration was unbounded, eventually one region might monopolize the whole business. However, he did not elaborate on the structure of the final spatial distribution, which we intend to explain in the book.

The power law is a general phenomenon seen in many natural and social settings, including urban systems, as was discussed by Krugman (1996). The most celebrated examples of power laws are the cases of earthquakes and sand piles (Bak et al., 1991). The frequency of earthquakes and the energy released by them are related by a power law. In sand pile experiments, the frequency of collapsing sand piles and their scales are also governed by a power law. Krugman has studied the scales of American cities according to statistical data, and observed a similar power law. He did this by ranking cities according to their scales, and then looking at the logarithms of ranks and logarithms of scales. He then noticed a linear relation between these two quantities with a slope close to -1 (see Figure 10.1, where the horizontal axis represents the logarithms of city scales, and the vertical axis the logarithms of ranks).

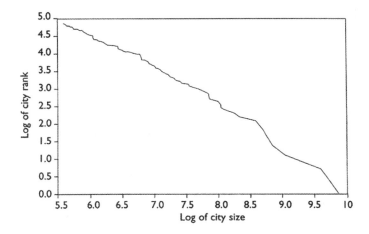

Figure 10.1 The logarithmic linear relation of rank-size (adopted from Krugman (1996), p. 40)

Zipf's law is a special case of power laws. The question is not completely answered as to what mechanisms give rise to the phenomenon. By reviewing the literature, one finds two approaches to explaining Zipf's law (Gabaix1999). One approach is purely from the viewpoint of statistical distributions, for example Gibrat's Law. Gibrat's Law was first presented by Robert Gibrat (1931) to model the relation between the dynamics of firm size and industry structure. Gibrat's Law indicates that cities with a homogeneous growth process would converge to Zipf's law distribution. The other is based on random growth models, as represented by Simon's (1955) model. These models show how random growth produces a power law.

Krugman (1996) considers Simon's model as one of the best explanations of how the power law emerges. In particular, Simon (1955) assumed that cities grew in lumps, and each lump might choose to become part of an existing city, or to form a new city. By assuming that the probability of forming a new city was a fixed value π, Simon deduced that α, the power law coefficient, is equal to $1/(1 - \pi)$. However, in the real world α is estimated to be very close to 1, which is only possible when π is very small. From the observations of the real world examples, we see that small cities are formed frequently, indicating that π is not too small. The assumption that α is close to 1 and π close to 0 is therefore inconsistent with the real world observations. We suspect that Simon's model does not explain completely the driving forces of the urban systems as depicted in the power law distribution. Using a different approach, we will provide a mathematical model to explain partially why the power law distribution emerges, following computer simulation experiments based on increasing returns.

2 Computer Simulation

In this book we designed computer simulation experiments, based on the notion of increasing returns, to investigate how the power law distribution of human settlements would emerge. The presumption of the experiments is to view the forming of urban systems as a random growth process (Krugman 1996). To simplify without loss of generality, we assume that the model is a two-dimensional uniform plane. That is, the differential spatial characteristics of a site are not considered, and the attractiveness of the site is purely derived from the advantage of concentration, that is, the term $g(N_i)$ in (2). We divide the uniform plane into cells of the same size. Each cell represents a minimal spatial unit. Each cell may have two states: "undeveloped" or "developed". Initially, all cells are undeveloped. Some will become developed later according to our simulation rules. This process is irreversible, that is, once a cell becomes developed, it cannot resume its original state. We consider a square region of 200×200 cells (a total of 40,000 cells) with a sufficiently large number of samples. In each round or time step, only one household enters the region and the cell occupied based on a selection rule becomes developed. Thus in each round, the number of developed cells increases by one. After 2,000 rounds of the simulation, we then examine the spatial structure of the urban system formed by those developed cells.

Power Law Distribution of Human Settlements 173

According to the notion of increasing returns, an urban area becomes more attractive as its size grows. We quantify the attractiveness of a cluster of developed cells as proportional to its size. Therefore, our simulations are based on the following location decision rule:

Step 1: Initially, based on the uniform assumption, each cell has an equal potential of being developed, which is represented by a score of 1. Therefore, the probability that each cell becomes developed is 1/40,000.

Step 2: If one cell becomes developed while its surrounding cells are undeveloped, we consider this cell to form an urban area of size one, and the eight surrounding cell's scores of potential will be increased to a fixed value N, which we call "the concentration intensity coefficient." That coefficient is a controlled variable in the simulations. By "the eight surrounding cells," we mean the eight cells adjacent to the central cell in a 3×3 matrix of cells. The developed cell is given the potential score of zero, so that it will not be selected as occupied in later time steps.

Step 3: After the first household occupies a cell, the region is no longer uniform in terms of potential scores. The cells surrounding the "developed urban area" have higher potential scores. A "developed urban area" is a cluster of developed cells connected spatially to each other, whose attractiveness is proportional to its size. For example, as shown in Figure 10.2, suppose that one cell is to be attached to a developed urban area of three cells. The potential score of the undeveloped cells surrounding the urban area will be increased from 1 to 3N. Similarly, an urban area of size M gives its surrounding cells the potential score of M×N.

Given the location decision rule, the cells entering the region after the first cell is occupied are more likely to select the sites of higher potential scores.

The computer simulation experiments were written in the Microsoft Visual Basic 6.0 (VB for short) programming language. We have repeated the experiments with different models and different parameters many times. Because of limit of space, we will only report here some representative results. Figures 10.3 and 10.4 show two examples of urban spatial structures that emerged with and without the location decision rule of increasing returns. The dark cells are undeveloped sites, while the light cells are developed sites.

To see whether the simulation result is consistent with the power law distribution, we took the logarithms of ranks and sizes of the developed urban areas emerging from the experiments. Consider the logarithms of ranks as the dependent variable Y, and those of sizes as the independent variable X. We performed a linear regression analysis. The resulting statistical number would verify whether the developed urban systems self-organize themselves into a power law distribution. The result is show in Table 10.1.

1	1	1	1	1	1	1
1	3N	3N	3N	3N	1	1
1	3N			3N	1	1
1	3N		3N	3N	1	1
1	3N	3N	3N	1	1	1
1	1	1	1	1	1	1
1	1	1	1	1	1	1

Figure 10.2 An example of attractiveness scores

Table 10.1   The results of the computer simulation

The concentration intensity coefficient	City size of largest city	Averaged city size	Correlation coefficient	Slope
1	12	1.25	0.9937	-2.1485
2	164	1.69	0.9569	-1.2622
3	174	2.12	0.9953	-1.0732
5	286	2.80	0.9841	-0.9645
7	720	3.53	0.9677	-0.8921
10	651	4.69	0.9488	-0.7890
20	1235	7.34	0.9607	-0.7202

From the simulation results and statistical analysis, we summarize some observations as follows:

1. Given the two-dimensional uniform spatial configuration, the computer simulations do generate spatial distributions of clusters of developed urban areas following power law distributions. In particular, the correlation coefficients are at least as high as 0.95.

Figure 10.3   An example of the random growth model with an increasing returns mechanism

2. As the concentration intensity coefficient (N) increases, the largest city and the averaged city sizes both become larger. This means that if we give the surrounding cells of developed urban areas higher priorities of development, the tendency of concentration increases. Therefore, we tend to see larger urban areas and a smaller

number of cities for higher N than lower N. For example, Table 10.1 shows that when the concentration intensity coefficient is 1, the largest city is of size 12. But this increases to 1235 when the concentration intensity coefficient is raised to 20.

3. When the concentration intensity coefficient N is increased, the slope in the linear regression equation decreases in absolute value. We can interpret this slope as the averaged difference between the ranks of cities with respect to various sizes (in logarithms). Therefore, a smaller slope in absolute value represents a tendency of polarization. Urban developments are concentrated on few large cities, and the difference in size between large cities and small ones is widened. For example, Table 10.1 shows that the slope is -2.1485 when the concentration intensity coefficient is 1, while it is -0.7202 when the concentration intensity coefficient is 20. The latter signifies greater diversity in size among the cities.

4. The correlation coefficient does not change with time (see Table 10.2). We can interpret this as the generality and stability of the power law. That is, at any time point, the spatial distribution of urban systems obeys an approximate power law. The system does not converge to the power law gradually. It happens at any value of concentration intensity coefficient.

The computer simulations show that under the mechanism of increasing returns, we do get a spatial system that is highly consistent with a power law. But what about the random growth model without the increasing returns mechanism? That is, what about our model with the concentration intensity coefficient N equal to 0? We conducted this experiment as well and the result is as shown in the Figure 10.4. One can see that the developed cells are scattered and concentrated areas are hardly visible. However, based on a regression analysis, we found the result to be a good fit to a power law as well, and the correlation coefficient is as high as 0.97. However, the slope is -4.0, which deviates from -1 given by Zipf's law. It is possible that when no increasing returns mechanism is present, the system would not result in a spatial distribution with enough concentrated urban areas similar to those of the real world systems that give rise to a flatter slope. The implication is that increasing returns might be a necessary condition underlying the power law distribution of urban systems.

Table 10.2   One sample with $N = 5$

Rounds (steps)	City size of largest city	Correlation coefficient	Slope
300	4	0.9916	-2.4704
500	5	0.9518	-2.4039
700	9	0.9789	-2.0510
1000	29	0.9962	-1.5166
1200	46	0.9932	-1.3912
1500	105	0.9940	-1.4216
2000	286	0.9841	-0.9645

176   Urban Complexity and Planning

Figure 10.4 An example of the random growth model without an increasing returns mechanism

3   Mathematical Approximation

The aim of this part is to seek a mathematical explanation of the power law distribution about the sizes of cities. This has been verified partially by our earlier computer experiments in the previous section. Deductive verification can confirm our earlier findings. Let s(X) denote the size of city X, and l(X) its perimeter. The basic assumption is that the probability that a new resident joins city X should be proportional to $s(X)^\alpha \times l(X)^\beta$ for some constants α and β which are independent of the city. This theorizes and generalizes our computer simulation model: a sizable city makes its boundary locations more attractive. It is reasonable to assume that the number of boundary locations is proportional to $l(X)^\beta$, and that the attractiveness is proportional to $s(X)^\alpha$. In our computer experiments, we took $\alpha = \beta = 1$. But here we can easily proceed with greater generality.

It is reasonable to assume that l(X) is proportional to s(X)d. Indeed, if the shape of X is fairly smooth, d is equal to 1/2. However, X often looks like a fractal in nature, in which case d is greater than 1/2. In any case, it is reasonable to postulate that the cities in the region being studied share similar fractal geometry and fractal dimension, and this is precisely our assumption that l(X) is proportional to $s(X)^d$. By combining our two assumptions, we arrive at a new assumption: the probability that a new resident joins city X is proportional to $s(X)^\gamma$, where $\gamma = \alpha + d\beta$. From now on, this is our working assumption. For simplicity, we will not consider the situation where two cities may merge into one.

It is also possible that the new resident would start a new city. This probability depends on the availability of the unused lands, and the attractiveness of the existing cities. That is, it is a function of U and A, where U is equal to C - Σs(X); A is equal to Σs(X) $^{\gamma}$; and C is the total capacity of land. In our computer experiment, the probability is proportional to U/(U + c×A) for some constant c. By putting the above formulas together, we get a mathematical model, which we will analyze further below. The mathematical model is simpler than the computer model, but it approximates the latter fairly well.

It should be noticed that in our model the power law is an intermediate phenomenon, not a final one. We begin to see a power law emerging after quite some time (e.g. after 10% of the total capacity is occupied; i.e., after urban formation really starts). But after a very long time, the power law no longer holds. This is so both for the computer simulation and the mathematical model, and the reason is obvious: The occupied land grows linearly with time and it will exhaust the whole region in a finite amount of time; and at that point certainly it is meaningless to expect a power law. Therefore, we think that the non-linear Polya process which Arthur et al. (1987) used is not an adequate tool here, as it only addresses the behavior after an indefinitely long period of time.

We should also observe the path-dependent nature of both the simulation and the computer model. That is, if the experiment is repeated ten times, we get ten different results. Each result fits closely to a power law. However, the realized size of the largest city and the slope of the power law vary significantly from one experiment to another. These are determined by small events in the early stage of urban development. However, after the early stage, the probabilistic, discrete computer model can be reasonably approximated by a deterministic, continuous model which can be represented by differential equations. Put differently, our mathematical model depicts the evolution of the urban system after the power has emerged in the early development.

Consider an arbitrary city, say city X. Its size is s(X, t) at time t. The probability that the next batch of new population chooses this city is:

$$\frac{cs(X,t)^{\gamma}}{U+cA} \tag{3}$$

We can regard equation (3) as the rate of change of city population. Therefore:

$$\frac{ds(X,t)}{dt}=\frac{cs(X,t)^{\gamma}}{U+cA} \tag{4}$$

This is a system of ordinary differential equations, with variable functions s(X, t) as the size of city X. Let X_1 be the largest city and X_2 the second largest city, and so on. Let $s_i(t)$ be $s(X_i, t)$. For any i and j, we have:

$$\frac{ds_i}{dt} = \frac{cs_i(t)^\gamma}{U+cA}$$
$$\frac{ds_j}{dt} = \frac{cs_j(t)^\gamma}{U+cA}$$
(5)

Taking the quotient of the above two equations in (5), and applying the chain rule for differentiation, that is:

$$\frac{\frac{ds_i}{dt}}{\frac{ds_j}{dt}} = \frac{ds_i}{ds_j}$$
(6)

we get the differential equation:

$$\frac{ds_i}{ds_j} = \frac{s_i^\gamma}{s_j^\gamma}$$
(7)

This is the differential equation describing the trajectory of $(s_i(t), s_j(t))$ on the $s_i s_j$ plane.

Theorem 1: the solutions to differential equations of $s_i(t)$ and $s_j(t)$ in equation (7) lie on the following trajectory:

$$s_i^{1-\gamma} - s_j^{1-\gamma}$$
(8)

Proof: we apply the method of "separation of variables" to solve the differential equation. That is, we first rewrite equation (7) as:

$$\frac{ds_i}{s_i^\gamma} = \frac{ds_j}{s_j^\gamma}$$
(9)

Then we integrate both sides using the simple formula:

$$\int \frac{dx}{x^\gamma} = \int x^{-\gamma} dx = \frac{x^{1-\gamma}}{1-\gamma} + \text{a constant}$$
(10)

Thus, we obtain:

$$\frac{s_i^{1-\gamma}}{1-\gamma} + C_1 = \frac{s_j^{1-\gamma}}{1-\gamma} + C_2$$
(11)

In other words:

$$s_i^{1-\gamma} - s_j^{1-\gamma} = (1-\gamma)(C_2 - C_1) = \text{a constant} \tag{12}$$

This model allows us to compute $\{s_1(t_1), s_2(t_1), s_3(t_1), \ldots\}$ from $\{s_1(t_0), s_2(t_0), s_3(t_0), \ldots\}$ and $s_i(t_1)$ for any single i, assuming that t_0 and t_1 represent the times when the cities are reasonably developed, and t_1 is not too far away after t_0. We illustrate this in the following example.

Example: in a computer simulation with $\gamma = 1.5$, after 2,400 rounds, we get the following result as show in Table 10.3.

Table 10.3 The difference between excepted values and actual values

	s_1	s_2	s_3	s_4	s_5	s_6	s_7	s_8
Computer simulation result with $\gamma = 1.5$, after 2400 rounds	1000	208	102	56	38	35	30	26
When s_1 is 2374, the expected values of s_i (According to trajectory equation)	2374	295	129	67	44	40	34	29
When s_1 is 2374, the actual values of s_i (Computer simulation result)	2374	301	125	69	47	40	32	23

We would like to know what happens when the largest city grows to the size, say 2374. According to our trajectory equation (8), we have:
(new s_i)$^{-0.5}$ - 1000$^{-0.5}$ = 2374$^{-0.5}$ - $s_i^{-0.5}$.

From this, we can compute the expected values of s_i (see Table 10.3). We then continue the simulation till $s_1 = 2374$, and we have the actual values (see Table 10.3).

We see that our trajectory equations predict the future developments of the cities very well. In particular, we can compute the power law emerging at t_1 derived from t_0. This is the aim of the next theorem.

Theorem 2: suppose that $\{s_1(t_0), s_2(t_0), s_3(t_0), \ldots\}$ satisfies a power law:

$$s_i(t_0) \simeq h_0 i^{-e_0} \tag{13}$$

Then $\{s_1(t_1), s_2(t_1), s_3(t_1), \ldots\}$ also satisfies a power law:

$$s_i(t_1) \simeq h_1 i^{-e_1} \tag{14}$$

with $e_1 \geq e_0$.
Proof: we have $s_1(t_0) = h_0$, and:

$$s_i(t_0)^{1-\gamma} - s_1(t_0)^{1-\gamma} = h_0^{1-\gamma}(i^{e_0(\gamma-1)} - 1) \tag{15}$$

According to Theorem 1:

$$s_i(t_1)^{1-\gamma} - s_1(t_1)^{1-\gamma} \qquad (16)$$
$$= s_i(t_1)^{1-\gamma} - h_1^{1-\gamma}$$
$$= h_0^{1-\gamma}(i^{e_0(\gamma-1)} - 1)$$

where $h_1 = s_1(t_1)$. This gives:

$$s_i(t_1)^{1-\gamma} = h_0^{1-\gamma}(i^{e_0(\gamma-1)} - 1) + h_1^{1-\gamma} \qquad (17)$$

We can rewrite this as:

$$s_i(t_1) = h_1\left(\left(\frac{h_0}{h_1}\right)^{1-\gamma}(i^{e_0(\gamma-1)} - 1) + 1\right)^{\frac{1}{1-\gamma}} \qquad (18)$$

We can regard the above expression as a function of log i, by setting x to log i, that is:

$$F(x) - h_1\left(\left(\frac{h_0}{h_1}\right)^{1-\gamma}(e^{xe_0(\gamma-1)} - 1 + 1\right)^{\frac{1}{1-\gamma}} \qquad (19)$$

so that F(log i) is equal to the above expression for $s_i(t_1)$. Let f(x) = log F(x). The theorem says that f(x) is almost a linear function of x, with slope -e_1, and $e_1 \geq e_0$.

It remains to compute f'(x).
Let:

$$k = 1/(1-\gamma), g(x) = (h_0/h_1)^{1-\gamma}(e^{xe_0(\gamma-1)} - 1) + 1 \qquad (20)$$

We observe that f(x) is of the form of log $(h_1 g(x)^k)$, and hence:

$$f'(x) = \frac{(h_1 g(x)^k)'}{h_1 g(x)^k} \qquad (21)$$
$$= \frac{h_1 k g(x)^{k-1} g'(x)}{h_1 g(x)^k}$$
$$= k\frac{g'(x)}{g(x)}$$

thus:

$$f'(x) = \frac{1}{1-\gamma}\frac{(h_0/h_1)^{1-\gamma}(\gamma-1)e_0^{xe_0(\gamma-1)}}{(h_0/h_1)^{1-\gamma}(e_0^{xe_0(\gamma-1)} - 1) + 1} \qquad (22)$$

After cancellation, we get:

$$f'(x) = -e_0 \frac{e^{e_0(\gamma-1)x}(h_1/h_0)^{\gamma-1}}{1+(e^{e_0(\gamma-1)x}-1)(h_1/h_0)^{\gamma-1}} \quad (23)$$

For reasonably large x (e.g. log 2, log 3, and so on), the term 1 in the denominator can be ignored and we have:

$$-f'(x) \simeq e_0 \frac{e^{e_0(\gamma-1)x}(h_1/h_0)^{\gamma-1}}{(e^{e_0(\gamma-1)x}-1)(h_1/h_0)^{\gamma-1}} \quad (24)$$

$$= e_0 \frac{1}{1-e^{-e_0(\gamma-1)x}}$$

$$= e_0(1+e^{-e_0(\gamma-1)x}+e^{-2e_0(\gamma-1)x}+e^{-3e_0(\gamma-1)x}+...)$$

Clearly, $-f'(x) \geq e_0$ and is almost a constant. This proves the theorem.
The argument can be reversed to give the following result.
Theorem 3: with the above assumptions, suppose that $\{s_1(t_1), s_2(t_1), s_3(t_1), ...\}$ satisfies a power law of:

$$s_i(t_1) \simeq h_1 i^{-e_1} \quad (25)$$

Then $\{s_1(t_0), s_2(t_0), s_3(t_0), ...\}$ also satisfies a power law:

$$s_i(t_0) \simeq h_0 i^{-e_0} \quad (26)$$

with $e_0 \leq e_1$.
Proof: the calculation is the same as the preceding theorem, because we can simply reverse the role of t_0 and t_1. We have:

$$-f'(x) = e_1 \frac{e^{e_1(\gamma-1)x}(h_0/h_1)^{\gamma-1}}{1+(e^{e_1(\gamma-1)x}-1)(h_0/h_1)^{\gamma-1}} \quad (27)$$

$$= e_1 \frac{e^{e_1(\gamma-1)x}}{e^{e_1(\gamma-1)x}+((h_0/h_1)^{\gamma-1}-1)}$$

Since $(h_1/h_0)^{(\gamma-1)} - 1$ is greater than or equal to 0, it is clear that $f'(x) \geq e_1$. For x to be reasonably large, the term $(h_1/h_0)^{(\gamma-1)}$ can be ignored, and we see that f'(x) is almost a constant.

The above results show that the power law, once formed, will persist through time. If the power law is observed after a long period, it can also be backtracked through time. The theory of Simon (1955), as presented by Krugman (1996), argued that the power law is valid in the long run. Therefore, it is observable, once emerging, almost all the time according to our theorems.

4 Discussion

Krugman (1996) considered Simon's (1955) model to be the best explanation so far of the power law phenomenon of urban systems. Our mathematical model is also based on the concepts of Simon's model. However, we suspect that the basic assumption of Simon's model is not reasonable as depicted earlier, and hence the conclusion thus derived does not fit the real world well. As mentioned in Section 1, it can never generate a power law with coefficient α equal to 1 (as in standard Zipf's law). Our mathematical model can produce the results that fit Zipf's law with α equal to 1, hence can be considered as an improvement on Simon's model.

The deduction of Simon's model is based on the assumption that in the long run s(X)/P, where P is the total population, remains a constant. This assumption is not supported by other theory or empirical data, and appears to be inconsistent with the real world observations. The assumption means that the cities continue to grow in the same rate. But in the studies of the real world examples, one usually observes that larger cities grow faster than smaller ones, in particular the largest city. The percentage of population in large cities in relation to the total population usually increases with time. This phenomenon is consistent with our computer simulations and mathematical model. For example, in Table 10.2 we see that as we go from the 1,000th round to the 2,000th round, the total scale is doubled, but the largest city grows from 29 to 286 in size, showing a growth of nearly 10 times. Therefore, in this aspect our model also appears to be closer to the real world than Simon's model.

Also, under the assumption of Simon's model, all the cities grow at the same rate. Therefore, if the system obeys a power law, it will continue to do so with the same power law coefficient. But in our simulation and mathematical analysis, the exponent of the power law should increase with time in absolute value, that is, $e_1 \geq e_0$. Note that in the literature, the regression is often done by imposing logarithmic scales on the ranks in the vertical axis, and the same for the sizes in the horizontal axis. Then the slope of the regression equation is the reciprocal of the above-mentioned exponent. Therefore, it should decrease with time in absolute value. This result shows that the urban system evolves toward centralization, and the gap between big cities and small ones in terms of population widens with time.

We do not find any discussion in the literature of whether this coefficient should change with time in a particular pattern. In fact, most scholars seem to believe that the coefficient is a time-independent constant. In particular, Zipf's law says that it should be 1. But our model supports decreasing slopes in absolute values and polarization of urban systems. It is worth exploring into empirical data to understand the behavior of the coefficient.

According to Hsueh and Lai (2002), the spatial distribution of cities in Taiwan, based on populations of towns and counties from 1971 to 2000, is consistent with the power law, where the correlation coefficients are 0.8795 in 1971, 0.9015 in 2000, and the slope changed from -0.9821 in 1971 to -0.7967 in 2000. Thus, it fits the power law well, and the slope decreases in absolute value with time, representing the tendency of concentration of the Taiwan population. But this tendency is not significant statistically. Given a longer time horizon, we argue that the slope would change significantly, and thus would be consistent with the prediction of our models.

On the other hand, the empirical data in the United States (Bureau of the Census, 1989) show that the slope moves in the other direction. From the historical data of US populations in 1890 to 1970, we took urban places with a population of 50,000 or higher to study whether the system would obey a power law. The result is shown in Figure 10.5. In the nine sampling years, the correlation coefficients are all higher than 0.99, satisfying the power law requirement. The slope changes from -1.03736 in 1890 toward -1.33228 in 1970, a significant difference of over 30%. It is also significant statistically. Therefore, we can assert that in the past hundred years, the urban systems in the United States have a tendency of decentralization. In Figure 10.5, we see a limited growth of large cities, and an impressive increase in the number of smaller cities. Of course, when the small cities are booming, the developments of the large ones are prohibited relatively.

Given that most of the literature assumes a constant slope in the power law, our finding from the US data is quite intriguing. Regardless, the power law distribution of urban systems is confirmed both in our computer experiments and mathematical model. It is also examined and validated using empirical data in Taiwan and the US.

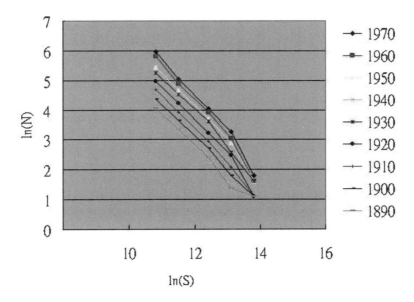

Figure 10.5 **The logarithmic linear relation of the rank-size rule for the US (1890–1970)**

5 Conclusions

The power law distribution of objects is a phenomenon seen widely across many areas of natural and social systems. In particular it has been observed in the spatial distribution of urban systems as shown in Zipf's law. In the literature, the underlying mechanism of power law remains a mystery. In this book, we use computer simulations and a mathematical model to show that there is a close relation between increasing returns and the power law phenomenon.

Specifically, both the computer simulations and the mathematical model based on the locational assumption of increasing returns support the emergence of the power law distribution of urban systems. The empirical data from two case studies also show the robustness of the power law phenomenon. A recent study on scale-free networks by Barabási and Bonabeau (2003) provides further evidence that the mechanism similar to increasing returns is the cause of the power law distribution. We conclude from our models and research elsewhere that the power law distribution in urban systems is a universal phenomenon and increasing returns is the main underlying mechanism. Whether the power law coefficient, or slope, tends to shift upward or downward remains to be shown in the future.

References

Arthur, W.B. 1990a. *Increasing Returns and Path Dependence in the Economy*. The University of Michigan Press, Ann Arbor, Michigan.
Arthur, W.B. 1990b. "'Silicon Valley' locational clusters: When do increasing returns imply monopoly ?" *Mathematical Social Sciences* 19: 235–51.
Arthur, W.B., Y.M. Ermoliev, and Y.M. Kaniovski. 1987. "Path-dependent processes and the emergence of macro-structure." *European Journal of Operational Research* 30: 294–303.
Bak, P. 1996. *How Nature Works: The Science of Self-organized Criticality*. Copernicus, New York.
Bak, P., K. Chen, M. Creutz. 1991. "Self-organized criticality." *Scientific American* Jan 26–33.
Barabási, A-L., E. Bonabeau. 2003. "Scale-free networks." *Scientific American* May 50–59.
Batten, D.F. 2001. "Complex landscapes of spatial interaction." *The Annals of Regional Science* 35: 81–111.
Black, P.E. 2001. "Zipf's Law." http://hissa.nist.gov/dads/HTML/zipfslaw.html.
Bureau of the Census. 1989. *Historical Statistics of the United States, Colonial Times to 1970*. Kraus International Publications, White Plains, New York.
Chen, H.P. 2004. "Path-dependent processes and the emergence of the rank-size rule." *The Annals of Regional Science* 38(3): 433–50.
Gabaix, X. 1999. "Zipf's law for cities: an explanation." *Quarterly Journal of Economics* 114(3): 739–67.

Hsueh, M-S., S-K. Lai. 2002. "Invariability and universality of the power law of population distribution in time and space: a case study of the Taiwan island." *Journal of Taiwan Land Research* 5: 67–86 (in Chinese).

Kauffman, S. 1995. *At Home in the Universe: The Search for the Laws of Self-Organization and Complexity*. Oxford University Press, New York.

Krugman, P. 1996. *The Self-Organizing Economy*. Blackwell Publishers Inc., Cambridge, Massachusetts.

Lai, S-K. 2006. "Emergent macro-structures of path-dependent location adoptions processes of firms." *The Annals of Regional Science* 40(3): pp. 545–558.

Savage, S.H. 1997. "Assessing departures from log-normality in the rank-size rule." *Journal of Archaeological Science* 24: 233–44.

Simon, H.A. 1955. "On a class of skew distribution function." *Biometrika* 52: 425–40.

Simon, H.A. 1998. *The Sciences of the Artificial*. The MIT Press, Cambridge, Massachusetts.

Zipf, G.K. 1949. *Human Behavior and the Principle of Least Effort*. Addison-Wesley Press, New York.

Chapter 11

A Preliminary Exploration on Self-organized Criticality of Urban Complex Spatial Systems

1 Introduction

Urban development is the result of the interactions among numerous individuals in many sectors engaging in complex decision-making behaviors. Previously, much of the planning and many of the spatial models used for urban development were based on traditional economic rationalism, which includes the assumption of *homo economicus* who seeks maximum profits and has perfect information. Urban spatial models derived from this assumption are capable of partially depicting urban development; however, the simulation is far from perfect. In recent years, urban economics based on econometrics has sought a balance between individual maximum utility (profit) and constraints using a Lagrange polynomial. This methodology is also based on the assumption that individuals are rational and always pursue maximum utility or profits. However, this assumption has been called into question, particularly within the field of descriptive decision making (Robin and Melvin, 1987).

The present research observes the development of cities by considering its spatial evolution from a bottom-up perspective. By emphasizing the variation in the component elements, we discuss the self-organization of city spaces from the perspective of bounded rationality, and explore the rules in urban space evolution using the dynamic simulation of the development of land parcels with cellular automata (CA).

The application of the concept of CA to cities can be traced back to the initial simulations of urban systems. In Chapin's simulation of land development, similar to the neighborhood effect in CA, change in the use of land parcels was influenced by the use of surrounding land (Chapin and Kaiser, 1979). A more holistic application of CA in the simulation of spatial evolution was in theoretical geographimetrics. Tobler (1979) established a cell-space model for Detroit and explained his method of applying CA to the geographic spatial system in his book *Cellular Geography*. In the late 1980s, with the development of computer image processing along with theories on fractals, chaos and complexity, CA was further adopted within the simulation of urban space evolution.

For example, White and Engelen (1993) observed a power law distribution in the simulation of changes in urban land use, in which the rule was based on a series of mathematical formulas and a weighted matrix. The simulation was developed on a 50×50 grid. Four types of land use were allowed: residential, industrial, commercial, and vacant. The land use of a parcel was only allowed to change from a lower to a higher level (for instance, a vacant lot could be converted to residential use, but not vice versa). The equation was established according to probability theory using the rules of two-dimensional CA and parameters determined from real data.

The results of the simulation show that the scale and frequency of commercial land parcels obeys a power law. This was further confirmed by the statistical data of four US cities (Atlanta, Cincinnati, Houston, and Milwaukee) in 1971. White and Engelen proved that if such a correlation were linear (before or after the logarithmic transformation), the spatial structure was fractal (Bak et al., 1989).

Our research started from an analysis of the characteristics, definition, and recent development of complexity science to discover how complexity is related to space. Moving beyond the assumption of perfect rationality in traditional spatial models, we attempted to integrate the application of bounded rationality and adaptive systems within the computer simulation of spatial evolution. By referring to the development of CA in the analysis of self-organization in the evolution of urban space in recent years, we also explored the rules of spatial evolution in the system of self-organization using computer simulation.

2 Complexity Science and Self-organization

This research explores whether self-organized spatial structures can emerge from the perspective of spatial evolution as described in complexity science. Self-organization exists in complex systems. In the theory of complexity science, order can emerge from chaotic systems under specific situations. The order does not originate from specific theorems or propositions in physics or economics, but from the interactions of molecules in the system. However, the emergence of a system with order cannot be explained by an understanding of the behavior of individual molecules without understanding the laws of their interaction. To judge whether a system is self-organized, we must observe whether the order that manifests itself in the system evolves according to bottom-up rules. The self-organization of a system usually has the following basic characteristics:

(1) Local Interaction

A system comprises many agents. The behavior of individual agents is influenced by other agents, and vice versa. The final form of the system results from continuous interaction among the individual agents. Causes for the interactions of different types of agents vary. For example, the interactions of atoms and molecules result from applied forces. Economic interaction results from the desire to make a profit through the exchange of commodities. In land development, interactions involve the mutual spatial and functional influence of neighboring land parcels. In this research, these mutually influencing processes are generally defined as "interactions." Interactions also lead to emergent properties: therefore, the whole is greater than the sum of the parts in a complex system.

(2) Non-linear Dynamics

Elements in a complex system interact with one another. A small disturbance can be greatly and unpredictably magnified. Self-organization exists in a system with local interactions and positive feedback (Arthur, 1990). A system with positive feedback can only be described by the equations of non-linear dynamics. These equations used to be extremely difficult to solve; however, they can now be solved more easily using computers.

(3) Many Agents

Self-organization is based on connections, interactions, and feedback among elements within a system. This means that many agents are required for a complex system to achieve self-organization. An agent could be a molecule, a nerve cell, a consumer, or an enterprise. Regardless of what they are, the agents can form enormous structures through self-organization. Molecules can form cells. Nerve cells can form a brain. Species can form an ecological system, and consumers and enterprises can form an economy. Different levels of newly established structures have different behavioral models.

(4) Emergence

A system is more than the sum of all its elements. The holistic structure and order of the system emerges from the interaction of its component elements and is not identical to that of the individual elements (Green, 1993). Inspired by the positive effect of emergence, organisms cooperate or compete with each other, thereby driving evolution, and allowing ecological systems to form. In addition, people trade with each other to satisfy their own needs, thereby creating markets as an emergent structure.

(5) Global-local Interactions

The concept of emergence also suggests the influence of global-local interactions in a self-organized system. The local interaction of individuals results in the holistic structure and form of the system. In turn, they influence the individual behaviors and rules for their interaction.

Using the theory of complexity science, Bak and Chen (1991) developed a concept to explain behavior in composite systems, in which millions of elements interact with each other within a limited time and space. They called the concept "self-organized criticality." Many composite systems evolve naturally to a critical state, in which tiny variations can result in a chain reaction followed by enormous changes that influence all elements in the system. According to this theory, the mechanism that causes small events and large variations is the same and equilibrium does not exist in a composite system. However, the system can continuously evolve into a metastable state.

Bak and Chen (1991) explained self-organization through observations and experiments related to sand piles. Fixed instruments were used to release a sand particle from the same height each time, which then fell to the ground. Eventually, the sand pile reached a roughly stable state. Although the dropped sand particles continued to influence other sand particles, resulting in collapses on various scales, the surface of the sand pile maintained the same slope. The scale and frequency of the collapse obeyed a power law distribution. A sand particle would remain static until it was bumped by other sand particles or the sand pile collapsed. It is uncertain when and where a sand particle will be bumped by other sand particles; however, the entire system represents a nearly stable state, which is called "self-organized criticality." The results of the experiment also show that an event is not always driven by direct causes, but may be caused by a chain of events involving the interaction of other events.

3 Bounded Rationality

Many definitions have been provided for bounded rationality. Simon termed bounded rational as behaviors in which an individual maximizes his utility function subject to the constraints faced (e.g., budget constraints, or limited choices) in pursuit of self-interest (Kreps, 1990). This is reflected in the theory of SEU (subjective expected utility). Bounded rationality is used to designate rational choice, taking into account the both cognitive and computational limitations. Literature on the adjustment of SEU is expansive. After analyzing individual decision-making processes involved in complex events using economic theories, Arthur (1994) argued that two factors prevent an individual from achieving absolute rationality in decision-making:

1. An individual's ability to use logical thinking decreases when the decision becomes more complex. For instance, it is easy for a player in tick-tack-toe to know what his opponent will do at the next step, but very difficult to know that in a complex game, such as chess, Chinese chess, or I-go.
2. One has to guess the actions of the other people since he/she does not know what decisions they will make. Therefore, his/her behaviors are actually

limited, and can be regarded as the selection of an optimal decision in a game.

Arthur (1994) argued that inductive logic is adaptive. People are completely rational only under very specific circumstances. People simplify complex problems and establish a presumed logic or model (they are still completely rational during this process). After they obtain results, they consolidate or adjust the existing logic or model (they exhibit bounded rationality during this process). That is, when the situation is too complex for people to make a decision through deductive logic, they use inductive logic. For example, a chess player will usually look at the position on the chessboard and remember his/her opponent's previous moves to induce his/her action for the next move.

Based on the concept of bounded rationality, Arthur designed a computer experiment to simulate decision-making in a simplified complex system and observed its characteristics as it evolved. The assumptions and rules for the computer experiment are as follows:

1. There are 100 people who like to visit a bar at night on weekends. If the population in the bar is no more than 60, meaning that the bar is not crowded, all the people in the bar will be satisfied.
2. A customer cannot predict the number of people who will be in the bar next weekend. He/she will choose to visit the bar if he/she predicts that it will not be crowded (has no more than 60 people in it). Otherwise, he/she will not go.
3. There is no collusion among those 100 people. Customers do not discuss with each other or set a time to visit the bar.
4. The number of people who visited the bar last weekend is the only information that all 100 people have.

Next, all the customers predict what they think will be the number of customers on the weekend. Customer A may think that the number of customers will be 35, which is the same as the number last week. Customer B may think that the number will be 49, which is the average number over the past four weeks. Customer C might think that the number will be 76, the number of customers five weeks ago (the simulation is repeated every five weeks). Each person chooses to use the most successful prediction rule out of his/her previous predictions for their current prediction. For Customer A, his/her prediction is that the number of people in the bar is 35 or smaller than the crowded threshold (60 people) last weekend. If the actual number of costumers is smaller than that, it means that the prediction is correct. Therefore, Customer A will continue to use this prediction rule, which is to choose the number of customers in the previous week as the predicted number for this week. Otherwise, Customer A will change to another prediction rule if the prediction is incorrect.

The results show that the simulated complex system achieved uniform order. The number of customers fluctuated stably around the threshold number of 60: 40% of people predicted that the number of customers next weekend would be more than 60; and 60% of people predicted that the number would be less than 60. The individual predictions represent a dynamic equilibrium. The 60/40 ratio can be regarded as the attractor or critical state in the complex system or Nash equilibrium from the perspective of game theory (Figure 11.1). Although we can easily predict that the number of customers in the bar will remain around 60 through traditional methods, such a result is difficult to obtain in a complex system operating through the interaction of individual behaviors when there is no collusion among customers and the predictions are based on bounded rationality.

The primary contribution of Arthur's computer simulation is the demonstration of bounded rational behavior in a simplified complex system. Surprisingly, order emerges through simple adjustment and the interactions of individual behaviors. However, Arthur's computer simulation did not consider spatial factors. Further examination would be required to determine whether self-organized rules can emerge from decision-making behaviors related to spatial issues, such as land development. Referring to the design of bounded rationality in Arthur's simulation, Casti (1999) projected a future artificial world where cities can be regarded as complex adaptive systems, which are restored through computer simulation.

In real world land development, bounded rationality can be described by the processes of collecting information and the maneuvering of property rights. Developers collect information about the surrounding environment for future decision-making. Their primary objective is to acquire property rights from the public domain through real estate transactions (Lai, 1998). Although economic

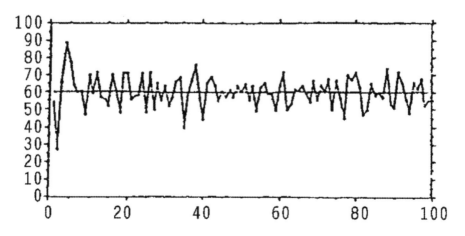

Figure 11.1   Changes in the number of customers in the bar in Arthur's simulation

implications are not considered in our computer simulation, the concept of bounded rationality is integrated into our computer program to more closely simulate the real world. For instance, a land parcel for development only interacts with its neighboring parcels, showing that developers only have limited information available for land development.

4 Research Design

In this research, we designed a two-dimensional grid to simulate land development behavior based on bounded rationality and adaptability. The rules for land development behaviors in the simulation were established from the simplified neighborhood environment profit-and-loss or payoff matrix. They were investigated through questionnaires and reflect the characteristics of bounded rationality and adaptability in land development.

The aim of this research was not to establish models for urban space evolution, but to explore self-organization in complex spatial systems. Therefore, land development patterns were simplified: the spatial configuration was assumed to be a grid. However, this does not undermine the explanation of the evolution of land development because no large difference exists between a regular site and an irregular one (e.g., both can denote the neighborhood adjacency of spatial units through a contiguity matrix). Moreover, we applied Arthur's research on individual behavior in land development to analyze the ability of individual developers to select optimal strategies through induction. To compare different assumptions of development behaviors, we also considered both fixed development rules and random ones.

This research adopted two-dimensional CA for the computer simulation. Each cell in the CA was considered a land parcel. To make the model more easily comprehensible and operable, only two types of land use for each land parcel could be selected: residential or commercial. Unlike those in traditional CA, the rules for land-use change were based on bounded rationality, as implied by Arthur's study (individual developers have the ability to study through deduction). This research adopted such rules in computer programming as the basic tools of empirical analysis.

The inclusion of a large number of land parcels in the simulation resulted in longer simulation times and unnecessary procedures. Therefore, with reference to White and Engelen's (1993) simulation design, this research set the simulation area as 50 parcels long and 50 parcels wide, representing 2,500 land parcels in total. The rules for land development were acquired from questionnaires and saved in the decision database. The land development status of each land parcel in each time frame was decided by the holistic land development status of its surrounding land parcels at the previous time frame. At the next time frame, the satisfaction calculated from the profit-loss matrix in the database was used to decide whether a land parcel should continue to use the rules in the present time frame. From the simulation results, we observed the variation in the proportion of residential and commercial land use in different time frames and explored whether the system manifested fractal structures. We also examined whether self-organization emerged in our simulated system by comparing the characteristics of this system with those in other typical complex systems.

Although this research was based on Arthur's behavioral experiment, it took into account spatial factors. To explore the decision-making model through bounded rationality, this research designed a spatial evolution experiment based on the random speculation decision model and the fixed decision-making model. By comparing the results with those in the bounded rationality model, we sought to discover the reasons for the emergence of the critical state of self-organization. More specifically, we presumed that the land development decisions of a land parcel in our simulation were made according to its surrounding environment. At the beginning of the simulation, a decision was randomly selected from a group of development decisions corresponding to the surrounding environment of the land parcel. Next, after considering the sum payoff of the interactions between development behaviors and the base as feedback, developers decided whether they should retain the previous decision or randomly select another development decision from the database when they faced the same land development situation. The development procedures are illustrated as follows.

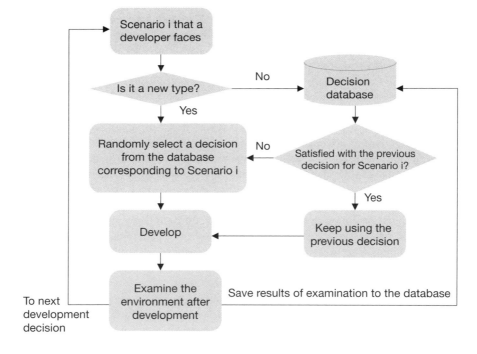

Figure 11.2   **Procedures for land development in the bounded rationality model**

This research defined basic constraints for the computer simulation as follows:

1. The simulation was confined to a two-dimensional plane and does not consider three-dimensional factors.
2. All land parcels were homogeneous with the same form and size and represented as grids of the same size. Roads were represented by lines on the grid. Thus, each land parcel was adjacent to eight neighboring land parcels.
3. There were only two types of land use: residential and commercial.
4. The system of simulation was closed, self-driven, and undisturbed by outer forces.

The above four constraints did not undermine the explanation of the simulation results in the real world, since the rules for land development simulation were acquired from questionnaires.

In addition, the basic assumptions about the interaction of each land parcel with its surrounding parcels are as follows:

1. Whether a development decision for a land parcel continues to be used in the next step depends on its surrounding environment. For example, after a developer applies decision j, if the sum credit of the development profit-loss matrix for the interactions between that land parcel and its surrounding parcels is smaller than the average of all its neighborhood land parcels, a new development decision is chosen from the decision database. Otherwise, the previous decision is retained, indicating that the developer is satisfied with it.
2. Developers could not predict the land development environment at the next time frame and could only randomly select a decision from the decision database or retain the previous decision at the last time frame. For example, when a developer selects decision j from the decision database for a particular development pattern at time frame t, he would continue to use decision j when he encountered the same development pattern in the next time frame, if the evaluation of the land development at this time frame was satisfactory. Otherwise, he would randomly select another decision from the decision database.
3. Developers did not collude by discussing their development plans.
4. The only information that a developer could refer to was the development results at the previous time frame.

The payoff matrix is calculated based on Nowak and May's (1993) study, which integrated the prisoner's dilemma to two-dimensional CA. First of all, the prisoner dilemma matrix was simplified. Each cell interacts with its neighboring cells within distance r. Its neighboring cells continue to interact with other cells within distance r. The result of this interaction is calculated by the prisoner's dilemma matrix. As shown in Figure 11.3, the number of neighboring cells for a1 is 4. The credits for the interactions between those five cells (a1, a2, a3, a4, a5) and their neighboring cells, which are denoted by $a_{s1}, a_{s2}, a_{s3}, a_{s4}$ and a_{s5}, determine the strategy that a_1 will adopt in the following time frame. For example, if a_{s5} is the largest credit and adopts the strategy of "cooperation," a1 selects cooperation in the next time frame (Lai and Chen, 1996).

In accordance with Nowak and May's study, this research sets the interaction scale r as 1. Each cell interacts with its surrounding eight cells. Therefore, there are a total of nine credits for each cell: $a_{s1}, a_{s2}, a_{s3}, a_{s4}, a_{s5}, a_{s6}, a_{s7}, a_{s8}$ and a_{s9} (Figure 11.4). At the end of each time frame, if the credit of a land parcel is higher than the average credit of all its surrounding land parcels, the decision is considered successful. This decision is again adopted when the development environment is the same in the following time frame. Otherwise, a new decision is randomly selected from the decision database.

White and Engelen (1993) found that the scale and frequency of commercial land use obey a power law distribution. This was further confirmed by their subsequent study of land-use data for four US cities in 1960. Bak and Chen (1991) argued that the power law distribution is evidence of the critical

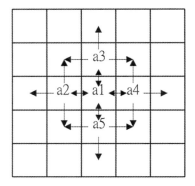

Figure 11.3 Interaction of cells in Nowak and May's study

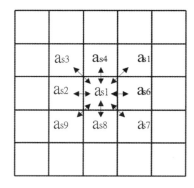

Figure 11.4 Payoff matrix for the computer simulation

state of self-organization. The simulation in White and Engelen's study relied on a transformation variable matrix, based on real land-use data. Although the matrix was adjusted later by the land-use data for Cincinnati in 1971 and resulted in the same power law distribution, the transformation rules were deterministic and fixed. They are unable to depict the characteristics of the study on the selection of behavior. Based on the bounded rationality of individuals, this research designed transformation rules capable of changing according to the study of individuals over time. The transformation rules are explained in detail as follows:

(1) Questionnaires for Transformation Rules

This research listed all possible scenarios for land development in the computer simulation. The preferences of the interviewees were then surveyed and saved in the decision database. The constraints and assumptions of the simulation resulted in a total of nine scenarios as the neighborhood situations of a land development.

Table 11.1 Land development scenarios in the computer simulation

Item	Scenario 0	Scenario 1	Scenario 2	Scenario 3	Scenario 4	Scenario 5	Scenario 6	Scenario 7	Scenario 8
Number of Adjacent Residential Land Parcles	0	1	2	3	4	5	6	7	8
Number of Adjacent Residential Land Parcels	8	7	6	5	4	3	2	1	0

In each scenario, interviewees were asked for their preference of residential or commercial use in the next time frame and the reason for this preference. The answers were then coded and added to the database. For instance, when the development situation was Scenario 3 (with three adjacent commercial land parcels and five adjacent residential land parcels) and the interviewee's preference was "to choose commercial use when the number of adjacent commercial land parcels is 3-5," (3, 5) would be recorded in the database for the selection of decisions in future steps. In total, we interviewed 60 developers and obtained 46 filled-in questionnaires, 40 of which were valid. Half (20) of the interviewees who submitted valid questionnaires had a background in planning (having received planning education or undertaken work related to planning). The other half had no such background.

(2) Profit-loss Matrix

In our computer simulation, a land parcel continues using its current transformation rule in the next time frame according to the total credits calculated upon the profit-loss matrices, which are established based on the average preference for the development of a land parcel derived from all possible scenarios that a developer may face. The credits are determined by taking the average of the payoffs of all various developers. The profit-loss matrix must be checked for each land parcel to select the development decision in each time frame. If as1 > (a_{s2}+ a_{s3}+ a_{s4}+ a_{s5}+ a_{s6}+ a_{s7}+ a_{s8}+ a_{s9}) / 8, the current decision is used in the following time frame. Otherwise, a new decision is selected from the decision database.

In the profit-loss matrix, $a_{s1}, a_{s2}, a_{s3}, a_{s4}, a_{s5}, a_{s6}, a_{s7}, a_{s8}$ and a_{s9} indicate the sum credits for nine adjacent parcels of land.

5 Results of Simulation

The computer simulation in this research was programmed in Microsoft Visual Basic 4.0, which is an object-oriented programming language. The computer program comprises three parts: random setting of the original frame, the database for land development decisions, and the framing of land development decisions. A development gain-loss matrix was established to evaluate the development in the previous frame and the rules of land transition were saved in a Microsoft Excel 7.0 file as the basis for transferring land to the following frames. As with the rules in most CAs, the world in the simulation wraps horizontally and vertically. The results are shown in Figures 11.5–11.9.

The left part is the spatial pattern of the simulation (gray cells indicate commercial use, white cells indicate residential use), while the right part graphically displays the distribution of the clusters of cells (the vertical axis is the logarithm of frequency, the horizontal axis is the scale of the cell clusters, the dots show the distribution of the actual cell clusters, and the line is plotted according to a linear regression of the above two variables).

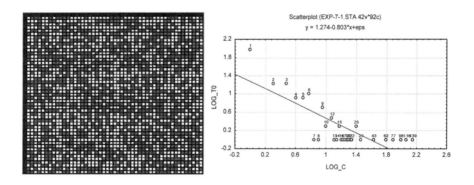

Figure 11.5 Spatial patterns and cluster patterns from the simulation (frame 0)

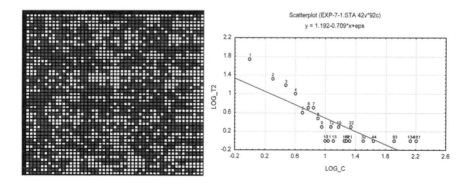

Figure 11.6 Spatial patterns and cluster patterns from the simulation (frame 1)

A Preliminary Exploration 199

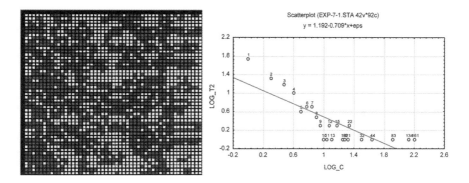

Figure 11.7 Spatial patterns and cluster patterns from the simulation (frame 2)

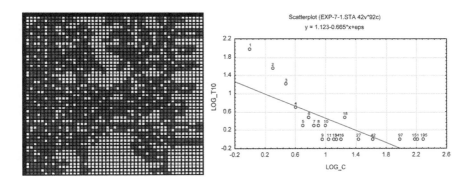

Figure 11.8 Spatial patterns and cluster patterns from the simulation (frame 10)

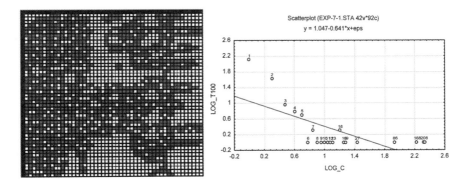

Figure 11.9 Spatial patterns and cluster patterns from the simulation (frame 100)

The above simulation illustrates how the spatial distribution of cells was random at the beginning and congregated in several clusters in the following frames. The power law distribution of the cells was most evident when the average scale of cells (representing scale of land parcels) was small at the beginning of the simulation. As the scale increased, the power law distribution became less obvious. We also found that the long-term transition of the number of cell clusters is similar to Arthur's research on the number of customers in a bar (Figure 11.10). The number of cell clusters fluctuated stably within a specific range, although the spatial pattern of the clusters continued to change.

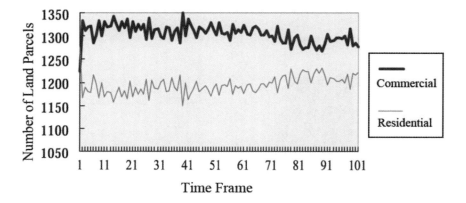

Figure 11.10 Long-term transition of the number of cell clusters

In addition, we analyzed the relationship between the ranks and sizes of land parcels (cells) by classifying all land parcels into several ranks as shown in Table 11.2:

Table 11.2 Rank-size classification of land parcels

Number of cells in a land parcel	Rank
1	1
2~4	2
5~8	3
9~16	4
17~32	5
33~64	6
...	...

A Preliminary Exploration

201

The typical equation for the power law $Y = b_0 \times t^{b_1}$ was used to examine the relationship between the ranks and sizes, where t is time, and b_0 and b_1 are constants. By taking the logarithm of both sides of the equation, we obtain the equation $\log(Y) = \log(b_0) + b_1 \times \log(t)$, which we use to analyze how closely the ranks and sizes of the land parcels obey a power law distribution. The results are shown in the following graphics, in which the X axis is log (size) and the Y axis is log (rank).

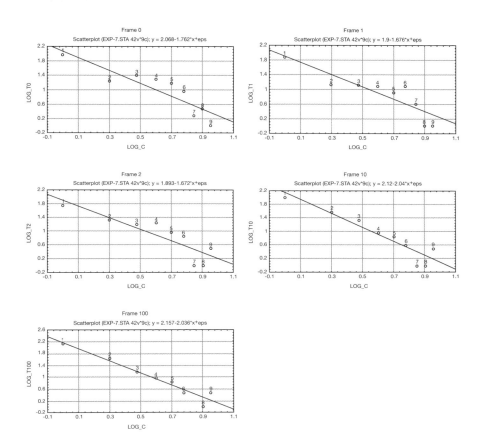

Figure 11.11 Logarithmic relationship of rank-size for residential land parcels in bounded rationality decision mode

The figures demonstrate that the relationship between the logarithms of ranks and sizes of land parcels can be fitted using a linear regression equation. The adjusted R^2 value of the linear regression model approached 1, indicating that the ranks and sizes of land parcels obey a power law (Figure 11.12). This did not occur in the other two experiments (random and fixed decision modes). In the random decision mode, developers selected random decision strategies in each frame. In the fixed decision mode, developers were unable to select decision strategies, and followed the same rule in each frame. In those two extremes, the evolution of the spatial structure did not converge to a self-organized critical state as occurred in the case of bounded rationality (see Gao, 1998 for those two modes).

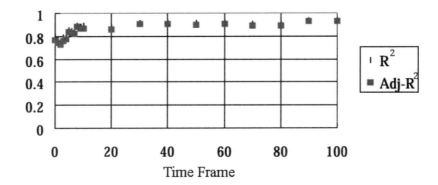

Figure 11.12 Plot of R^2 and adjusted R^2

6 Discussion

Our analysis of how city space evolves in this research is based on a simplified two-dimensional CA and appears to require more precise examination. However, as opposed to previous experiments, this research integrates computer simulation with experiments on development behavior, which makes the simulation better implicate the operation in the real world. The results support those found in White and Engelen's (1993) research.

Moreover, although this research discusses two-dimensional space, the methods and findings could be extended to a three-dimensional space. According to one-dimensional analysis (e.g., Lai, 2003), Wolfram's four types of complex structure are closely related to self-organization. Wolfram's research (1994; 2002) also implies that all cellular automata can be included in those four types. Because a complex system comprises numerous molecules and emergence is most evident in large complex systems, the inclusion of more molecules in the computer simulation could result in more reliable results. However, because we were limited in computational speed and complexity of the data processing we were able to perform, this research set the grid number to be the same as an ordinary two-dimensional CA (50x50=2500). Moreover, to make the simulation more closely resemble real world conditions, the rules for computer simulation were not designed by the authors, but were summarized from questionnaires filled out by both specialists in urban planning and local people without any background in planning. The questionnaires was designed with simple logic so that the rules could be precisely and easily acquired. Other factors considered in the normal development process, such as neighborhood environment adaptability, economic aggregation, and development profits, were also included in our research, but mostly as part of other terms, such as local interactions, clusters, and the profit-loss matrix.

In the past two decades, the way that urban development is viewed by scholars in geography and planning has significantly changed. Observation of the holistic manifestation of systems based on individual decision-makers has attracted increased attention. The spatial structure of cities is regarded as a typical example of self-organization emerging from individuals or agents (Holland, 1995). A basic characteristic of self-organization, the power law, has been studied or referred to in much of the previous literature (e.g., Krugman, 1996). This research refused to accept the assumption of "full collected information" and "absolute rationality" because neither exists in the real world. Instead, we regarded bounded rationality as the basis for the consideration of the behavior of individual decision-makers. The results show that under such an assumption, the interaction of individuals gradually evolves to the critical point of self-organization, which is a perfect example of the dynamic equilibrium of a system, although its implications in terms of space and planning require further exploration. Moreover, the purely rational way of thinking about economics has been criticized in recent years. More attention has been paid to considering individual characteristics, such as bounded rationality, with which to better model the real world. To further explore such research, the definition of the critical point of self-organization must first be carefully explained.

Wolfram (1984) classified the patterns of CA into four basic classes. In the first class, behavior is very simple, and nearly all initial conditions lead to exactly the same uniform final state. In the second class, there are many different possible final states, but all of them comprise only a particular set of simple structures that either remain the same forever or repeat every few steps. In the third class, the behavior is more complex, and appears in many respects to be random, although small-scale structures are always seen at some level. The fourth class involves a mixture of order and randomness: localized structures are produced, which on their own are fairly simple, but these structures move around and interact with each other in highly complex ways.

Kauffman (1995) explained why complex structures of the fourth class exist only in the area between order and chaos through random Boolean networks. In these networks, the form of each node is decided by the Boolean rule of logic transformation and constrained by the other nodes connected with it. When specific rules cause some nodes to be locked in a particular state, part of the network will be frozen. When there are few such rules, the network remains in a state of chaos.

When there are many such rules, the network becomes static or changes in a stable manner within a certain cycle. If the proportion of frozen rules reaches a critical point where some nodes are locked and some begin to percolate and revitalize, the network is dynamically stable and order emerges. Only when a system reaches such a state can dynamic evolution continue successfully. Otherwise, the system will either die or remain in chaos. This means that the equilibrium of order and chaos creates the complex structure that emerges from self-organization (White and Engelen, 1993). The characteristics of self-organization and the power law in this research were found after data transformation or classification. This is probably because after transformation or classification the data simultaneously have less noise and useful information, and thus can reach equilibrium between the two extremes of order and chaos.

Fractals and power law distributions are characteristics of a system that lies between order and chaos (Bak and Chen, 1991; Kauffman, 1996). By reviewing the literature on urban spatial studies, this research found that in addition to the manifestation of cities as fractal distributions, a simulated urban system, such as the single-center city developed by White and Engelen, also shows fractal patterns. Kauffman's (1996) analysis of cities based on random Boolean networks also suggests that the long-term maintenance of urban spatial structures at the critical point of phase transition occurs because cities can only continuously evolve at such a point. Moreover, Krugman (1996) found that the ranks and sizes of US cities obeyed a power law distribution from 1890 to 1990. Other properties of certain events, such as the scale and frequency of earthquakes also obey a power law distribution. Until now, the study of complexity has been primarily limited to the discovery of rules, and has seldom been connected to the exploration of their causes (apart from Simon, 1955). The economic implication of complexity is that complex economic, political, and ecological systems may evolve toward the attractor or critical state of self-organization.

7 Conclusions

This research designed and developed a computer simulation of urban evolution and self-organization. The research design focused on individual behaviors and the basic characteristics of urban space evolution, although the research into land development behavior was somewhat simplified. The results indicate that the critical state of self-organization emerges from local bottom-up interactions and that specific rules, such as bounded rationality, can lead to a power law distribution. For example, in land development, bounded rationality means that developers cannot comprehensively acquire all information and must gradually learn (through induction) from their experience to achieve satisfactory development strategies. The power law distribution in the computer simulation in this research is very similar to the common fractal distribution in real urban systems. Therefore, bounded rationality may be the basic cause for the interaction of local agents.

Further examination of the detailed transformation rule of each land parcel still need to be performed in future studies. At the same time, Lin's (1998) study on mixed land use in Sanchong City and Nantou County in Taiwan, which was based on fractals, demonstrated a power law distribution. This suggests that urban spatial structures are self-organized using empirical data. The results of our research also suggest that land-use distribution evolves toward a critical state of equilibrium over time when the complex spatial systems are self-organized and do not undergo interruptions by outside forces. In other words, the critical state is the attractor in the evolution of space.

References

Arthur, B.W. 1990. "Positive Feedback in the Economy." *Scientific America* (2): pp. 92–9.
Arthur, B.W. 1994. "Complexity in Economic Theory: Inductive Reasoning and Bounded Rationality." *American Economic Association Papers and Proceedings*, pp. 406–11.
Bak, P., and K. Chen. 1989. "Self-Organization Criticality Phenomenon." *Journal of Geophysical Studies* (94): pp. 15635–7.
Bak, P., and K. Chen. 1991. "Self-Organized Criticality." *Scientific American* (1): pp. 26–33.
Bak, P., K. Chen, and M. Creutz. 1989. "Self-Organized Criticality in the Game Of Life." *Nature* (342): pp. 780–781.
Casti, J.L. 1999. "Would-be Words : The Science and Surprise of Artificial Worlds." *Computers, Environment, and Urban Systems* 23(3): pp. 193–203.
Chapin, F.S. Jnr, and E. Kaiser. 1979. *Urban Land Use Planning*. Urbana, Illinois: University of Illinois Press.
Gao, H. 1998. Critical State of Self-Organization for Complex Urban Spatial Systems: Application of the Paradigm of Bounded Rationality, Master Thesis at National Chung Hsing University Urban Planning Institute, (in Chinese).
Green, D.G. 1993. *Complex Systems: From Biology to Computation*. Amsterdam: IOS Press.
Holland, J.H. 1995. *Hidden Order: How Adaptation Builds Complexity Reading*. Massachusetts: Cambridge: Blackwell.
Kauffman, S. 1995. *At Home in the Universe: The Search for the Laws of Self-Organization and Complexity*. New York: Oxford University Press.
Kreps, D.M. 1990. *Game Theory and Economic Model*. New York: Oxford University Press.
Krugman, P. 1996. *The Self-organizing Economy*. Oxford: Blackwell Publishers.
Lai, S.K., and J. Chen. 1996. The Impact of Information Collection on the Simulated Behaviors in 1-D Cellular Automata: A Computer Simulation Based on the Spatial Model of Prisoner's Dilemma, Proceedings of Taiwan Institute of Urban Planning, pp. 4–14 (in Chinese).

Lai, S.K. 1998. "A Property Rights Based Interpretation of Land Development Behavior." *Land Economics Annual Publication* 9: pp. 1–11.

Lai, S.K. 2003. "On Transition Rules of Complex Structures in One-Dimensional Cellular Automata: Some Implications for Urban Change." *The Annals of Regional Science* 37(2): pp. 337–352.

Lin, R. 1998. Exploration of Self-Organization of Urban Land Use Pattern based on Semi-Fractal Spatial Index of Mixed Land Use, Master Thesis at National Chung Hsing University Urban Planning Institute, (in Chinese).

Nowak, M.A., and R.M. May. 1993. "The Spatial Dilemmas of Evolution." *International Journal of Bifurcation and Chaos* 3(1): pp. 35–78.

Robin, M.H., and W.R. Melvin. 1987. *Rational Choice*. Chicago: The University of Chicago Press.

Simon, H.A. 1955. "On A Class of Skew Distribution Function." *Biometrika* 52: pp. 425–40.

Tobler, W.R. 1979. Cellular Geography. In *Philosophy in Geography*. S. Gale, G. Olsson, and D. Reidel (eds): Dordrecht.

White, R., and G. Engelen. 1993. " Cellular Automata and Fractal Urban Form: A Cellular Modelling Approach to the Evolution of Urban Land-Use Pattern." *Environment and Planning B* 25: pp. 1175–99.

Wolfram, S. 1984. "Cellular Automata as Models of Complexity." *Nature* 311: pp. 419–24.

Wolfram, S. 1994. Universality and Complexity in Cellular Automata. In *Cellular Automata and Complexity*. ed. S Wolfram, New York: Addison-Wesley.

Chapter 12
Planning in Complex Spatial and Temporal Systems: A Simulation Framework[1]

1 Introduction

Planners are confident that their planning affects not only behaviors in organizations, but also outcomes. There is, however, little backing for this confidence. Surprisingly little is known about planning processes and how they affect organizations. One approach to gaining understanding of planning behaviors in organizations is to develop and analyze simulation models. The framework presented here builds on two streams of previous work: the garbage-can models of organizational behavior presented by Cohen et al. (1972) and the spatial evolution models of Nowak and May (1993). Our objective is to develop a framework sufficient to investigate the implications of introducing planning behaviors into complex organizational systems evolving in space and time. Our primary focus for this chapter is on devising simulations from which we might discover general principles about the effects of planning the behavior of organizations. Additional work will be necessary to determine the external validity of these simulations, that is, to interpret concrete situations in terms of such principles.

We focus on the planning activities of considering related choices (Hopkins, 2001), setting aside for this chapter planning with respect to uncertainty about planning objectives, environments, and available alternatives. Information that reduces uncertainty arises from some regularity about observed phenomena that permits prediction across actors, space, or time. The level of planning investment can be measured by the number of comparisons and judgments made in gathering information about related choices while making a plan, as manifested by the manipulation of these choices. Plans are sets of decisions, which are contingent on outcomes resulting from prior decisions and system behavior based on exogenous parameters. Plans persist in time and space. As decisions become actions yielding outcomes, further contingent decisions can be enacted. These contingent decisions are, however, part of the persistent plan. Revising a plan thus implies changing the contingencies on which ensuing decisions are based.

We construct the elements of this simulation framework in sequence. Planning is understood here as gathering information to reduce uncertainty (e.g., Friend and Hickling, 2005; Schaeffer and Hopkins, 1987). Section 2 explains the garbage-

---

[1] This chapter has been published in *Geospatial Techniques in Urban Planning* 2012.

can model and develops one definition of planning as manipulation of decision situations within that framework. Section 3 explains the spatial process of urban modeling and the spatial framework in terms of evolutionary planning behavior in a prisoner's dilemma game. Section 4 introduces an idea of how these two types of models can be integrated and the questions that might be addressed by analysis of such simulations. Section 5 concludes.

2 Planning Behaviors in the Planning Process

As everyone knows, scientific technology is developing day and night. Since computer models have emerged, there are various models developed for scientific research. While one of them, namely agent-based modeling (ABM), has been proven to be an effective way to simulate activities in which entities participate (Torrens, 2007), this kind of simulation is expected to provide a valuable tool for exploring the effectiveness of policy measures in complex environments (Jager and Mosler, 2007). Before discussing planning the behavior of organizations and its effects on a complex urban society, we should take a retrospective glance reviewing the current research on ABM with respect to urban social systems.

2.1 Agent-based Modeling

2.1.1 ABM for Planning Support Systems
In the last decades, influenced by rapid urbanization, the relationships between policies, the location and intensity of urban activities, and related urban environmental problems have become a hot topic for planners and researchers (Chin, 2002; Ewing, 1994, 1997; Neuman, 2005). This research is always carried out using statistical analysis or investigated in ways such that the variability of entities' activities and the influences between different entities cannot be represented particularly well. When computer models were first constructed for urban systems, they were built for testing the impacts of urban plans and policies rather than for scientific understanding purposes (Batty, 2008). The basic argument was that given a good theory, a model would be constructed based on it, which would then be validated and, if acceptable, used in policymaking (Batty, 1976). Topical examples can be gleaned from urban growth simulations, in which the spatial process of urban growth can be visualized and represented in a very realistic way using cellular automata (CA) models. These can be used to support decision-making (Batty et al., 1997, 1999; Clarke and Gaydos, 1998; Wu, 2002; Li and Yeh, 2000; Fang et al., 2005).

Now ABM is becoming the dominant paradigm in social simulations due primarily to its priority on reflecting agents' choices in complex systems. Researchers employ ABM for planning support and decision-making on urban policies. One example is a role-playing approach introduced by Ligtenberg, in which a complex spatial system including a multi-actor spatial planning process can be simulated for spatial planning support (Ligtenberg, 2010). Furthermore, in regard to the highly complex process of making urban policy decisions, a multi-agent paradigm has been built to develop an intelligent and flexible planning support system, within which three types of agents, including interface agents who improve the user-system interaction, tool agents to support the use and management of models, and domain agents to provide access to specialized knowledge, were created (Saarloos et al., 2008). Researchers also utilize ABM to simulate urban development processes. As described by a CityDev model, the economic activities of agents (e.g., family, industrial firms, and developers) that produce goods by using other goods and trade their goods on the markets have been simulated to visualize urban development processes resulting from urban policies (Semboloni, 2004).

In China, one of the countries around the world whose urbanization is taking place at an unprecedented rate, the conflict between human activities and urban environments is very serious. Agent-based simulation has easily gained much attention from Chinese researchers. Some of these researchers have improved traditional urban growth models by building up a set of spatial-temporal land resource allocation rules and developing a dynamic urban expansion model based on a multi-agent system (MAS) to simulate the interactions among different agents, such as residents, farmers, and governments (Zhang et al., 2010). This work is able to reflect basic urban growth characteristics, explain the reasons for the urban growth process and explain the effects of agents' behavior on urban growth. MAS simulations have shown a higher precision than cellular automata models, which suggests that these models could provide land-use decision-making support to government and urban planners. Meanwhile, other researchers have focused on solving urban transportation problems using ABM. One example is a qualitative model of a multi-lane environment that has been built to simulate several cars acting in a multi-lane circuit (Claramunt and Jiang, 2001). This work is an illustrative example of a constrained frame of reference. The potential of this model is that it was illustrated and calibrated using an agent-based prototype, within which the modeling objects were individual cars.

2.1.2 Residential Motility Simulation
In a study of ABM challenges for geospatial simulation, seven challenges for ABM work were illustrated, including the purpose of model building, the independent theory of model rooting-in, and interactions among agents (Crooks et al., 2008). Within this work, ABMs have been utilized to model different urban systems problems, such as residential location, urban emergence evaluation, and residential segregation. Similar studies have been carried out on this topic such as a MASUS model (Multi-Agent Simulator for Urban Segregation) which provides a virtual laboratory for exploring the impacts of different contextual mechanisms on the emergence of segregation patterns (Feitosa et al., 2010). A population dynamic model in which inhabitants can change their residential behavior depending on the properties of their neighborhood, neighbors and the whole city has been built (Benenson, 1998). A micro-simulation model for residential location choice has been developed, in

which the Monte Carlo method was employed to model individual decision rules and an Artificial Neural Network (ANN) theory has been utilized to determine individual location choice (Raju et al., 1998). It is apparent that the principle of ABM has brought numerous researchers into the field of residential mobility simulation. Since residential location has been abundantly simulated, some researchers have begun to consider the environmental influences and landscape changes caused by household residential location choice. A framework called HI-LIFE, to be used for simulating and modeling residential demand for new housing by considering household interactions taking life cycle stages into account, was argued for in 2009 (Fontaine and Rounsevell, 2009). Within this work, household residential location choices have been simulated to predict regional landscape pressure in the future. Furthermore, an ABM framework integrating spatial economic and policy decisions, energy and fuel use, air pollution emissions and assimilation has been developed for urban sustainability assessments (Zellner et al., 2008).

2.1.3 Land and Housing Market Simulations
For researchers to use ABM to simulate land and housing markets is quite usual now. In research by D.C. Parker, a local land market was portrayed as a special conceptual residential market, and the stakeholders and households were agents within it. This research combined traditional deductive optimization models of behavior at the agent level with inductive models of price expectation formation (Parker and Filatova, 2008). As implemented in this research, households make decisions on their housing behavior by evaluating the house utility and finally determining their willingness to pay for it. Another researcher simulated relocation processes and price setting in an urban housing market through modeling households' decision-making on relocation based on perceptions of housing market probabilities (Ettema, 2011). In this study, utility was also an important factor for households' preference evaluations.

Such simulations can be quite helpful for local governments making policies affecting urban housing and land markets or making decisions about related policies. However, there is still little exploration into planning behaviors using ABM approaches.

2.2 Simulation of Planning Behaviors in the Planning Process

2.2.1 Limitations of Current Urban Models
We reviewed some typical simulations of urban policy or urban phenomena based on the ABM approach described above. These studies are typically aimed at helping planners or decision-makers work out special planning policies. Within these models, urban policies are mostly imported as simulation factors, viewing the policies as preconditions for simulation. These simulations concentrate mainly on representing possible urban changes that could be influenced by policy implementation. However, there is too little information about how a policymaking process could be implemented and how would it influence organizations. Thus, our

focus has come to be how to support policymakers with practical planning behavior models, through which planning behaviors can be automatically introduced into complex organizational systems evolving in space and time.

2.2.2 The Garbage-can Model

To solve the problem discussed above, we introduce the garbage-can model. The garbage-can model of organizational planning behavior allows structuring of planning issues so that control is to be investigated, rather than merely imposed externally. It is thus particularly appropriate for investigating planning in organizations. Planning interventions or actions are at least partially substitutable for aspects of organizational design. Both affect the coordination of decisions. Thus to investigate planning, we must be able to manipulate aspects of organizational design and of planning interventions in that design. We first explain the original garbage-can model and then introduce planning as an extension of the model.

The original formulation of the garbage-can model of organizational choice considers four elements: choices, solutions, problems, and decision-makers (Cohen et al., 1972). Choices are situations in which decisions can be made, that is, commitments are made to take certain actions. In organizations, votes to spend money or signatures on forms to hire or fire persons are examples of actions on choices. Solutions are actions that might be taken, such as tax schedules that might be levied or land developments that might be approved. Solutions are things that choices can commit to enact, things we have the capacity to do directly. Problems are issues that are likely to persist and that decision-makers are concerned with resolving, such as homelessness, unfair housing practices, congested highways, or flooding. Note that choices enact solutions; they do not solve problems. We cannot merely choose not to have homelessness. We cannot "decide a problem." We can choose to spend money on shelters or to hire social workers, which may or may not affect the persistence of homelessness as a problem. Decision-makers are units of capacity to take action in choice situations.

A garbage can is a choice opportunity where the elements meet in a partially unpredictable way. Solutions, problems, and decision-makers are thrown into a garbage can and something happens. There is, however, no simple mapping of decision-makers to problems or of solutions to problems. Further, an organization has many interacting garbage cans, many interacting choice opportunities. The original model was used to investigate universities as an example of "organized anarchy." Structure as control can be increased from this starting point, however, which makes possible the investigation of a wide range of types and degrees of organizational structure (e.g., Padgett, 1980). Planning and organizational design are at least partially substitutable strategies for affecting organizational decision-making. Organizational design and planning are both means for "coordinating" related decisions. Thus the garbage-can model provides a useful starting point for investigating planning behaviors in organizations.

The major assumption of the models is that streams of the four elements are independent of each other. Solutions may thus occur before the problems these solutions might resolve are recognized. Choice opportunities may occur because regular meetings yield decision-maker status, independent of whether solutions are available.

Cohen et al. (1972) reported their results by focusing on four statistics: decision style, problem activity, problem latency, and decision difficulty. The three decision styles were resolution, oversight, and flight. Resolution meant that a choice taken resolved all the problems that were thrown into the garbage can at that choice opportunity. If a decision was taken for a choice to which no problems were attached, it was classified as oversight. All other situations constituted flight. Cohen et al. were able to demonstrate the sensitivity of organizational behavior to various access structures and decision structures.

The decision process was quite sensitive to net energy load. Net energy load is the difference between the total energy required for a problem to be resolved and that available from decision-makers. With the general formulation of a decision process considering net energy load, Cohen et al. (1972) ran a simulation addressing four variables: net energy load, access structure, decision structure, and energy distribution. Different net energy loads, roughly analogous to organizational capacity in the form of decision-makers relative to organizational demand, should yield differences in organizational behavior and outcomes. Access structure is the relationship between problems and choices. A zero-one matrix defines which problems can be resolved by which choices. Different access structures vary in the number of choices that can resolve particular problems. Decision structure defines which decision-makers can address which choices and thus how the total energy capacity of the organization can be brought to bear in resolving choices.

2.2.3 Planning Behaviors in Garbage-can Models

The original garbage-can model implies that the organization does not have control over the occurrence of problems and choices. In particular, the organization is not capable of generating choice opportunities to deal with problems that have just arisen in a given time step. The arrival of choice opportunities and the arrival of problems are both random. One way of introducing planning to the model is to allow the organization to purposefully create choice opportunities for resolving problems. This choice-problem dependence is a matter of degree with one extreme being the case of the original garbage can and the other extreme a complete mapping of arriving problems to created choice opportunities. This is equivalent to being able to compare garbage cans and choose one to act in at each time period of the simulation. What effect would the ability to choose among choice opportunities over time so as to match current problems have on the simulation results?

Lai (1998, 2003) ran a prototypical simulation to illustrate this approach. He assumed that, at a given time step, the planner is able to acquire complete information about the structure of the organization, except for the arrival of problems in that time period. The planner knows the decision structure and access structure, and the relationships among the elements. Thus the planner can predict which decision-makers and problems will be in which garbage cans (choice opportunities) and how much energy will be accumulated in and spent by decision-makers in each one. Choice opportunities in this case are related choices that the planner can select from based on the difference between the energy required to make a decision and the energy available from decision-makers. The planning criterion is thus to select the choice opportunity (the garbage can) that results in the smallest energy deficit. Planning thus defined involves choosing the entry times for choices, without considering problems, decision-makers, or solutions. Simulation results were sensitive to interventions based on this definition of planning. In the pilot study, such planning resulted in increasing the efficiency with which choices were made, meaning more choices were made with less energy expended, but fewer problems were resolved. Problems, choices, and decision-makers tended to remain attached to each other in the case where planning occurred more than in the case without planning.

Lai's work was only tentative because of the small size of the simulations. Also, his scheme is only one way of introducing planning into the original model. Control as structure over other elements could also be considered. A combination of partial controls in experimental design on the four elements might yield planning possibilities that would result in more useful analyses of simulation results. Regardless of these details, Lai (1998, 2003) was able to demonstrate the possibility of gleaning instructive results for understanding planning effects because he showed that it is possible to add structure to decision-making without increasing the organization's ability to resolve problems. The result suggests that this simulation modeling approach incorporates sufficient degrees of freedom to discover counterintuitive results.

3 Incorporation of Spatial Relationships

All planning behaviors have to be conducted within a certain urban space. Thus, there is no doubt that when planners try to make a plan, there will be interaction between the urban area and planning behaviors. How to better represent the spatial process of planning behavior is now a problem. In this section, we first review how spatial processes are explored using the CA and ABM approaches in current research reports and then present two examples for discussion on how spatial datasets can be integrated into ABM simulations. We present a possible solution using a prisoner's dilemma game to simulate spatial evolution in planning behaviors, such as planning in organizations promoted by the garbage-can model.

3.1 Spatial Process of Urban Modeling

3.1.1 Urban Modeling and Spatial Processes
In urban modeling, spatial processes can be simulated through automata. There are automata of different types, but simply put, each automaton can be defined as a discrete processing mechanism with internal states. When the state of one

automaton has been changed by its own characteristics or through input from outside conditions, such as urban policies, this change will be transmitted to other automata through a predetermined transition rule. Thus, researchers can represent a spatial process by defining the spatial features of automata and the transition rule between them. A typical application of this principle is CA simulation, in which a real urban space is modeled as a cell in the simulation. Each cell has its own spatial characteristics, and urban policies can be input as simulation conditions. Changing conditions will finally result in a cell state change. This type of model has been used in research simulating strategic spatial plans, with cells' spatial attributes including landscape, land-use zoning, slope, urban plan, and land price (Ma et al., 2010). These attributes will determine the state value of a cell, and so, along with the transition rule, determine any changes of state it may undergo.

Spatial processes within ABM can be achieved through the interaction between agents and space. Spatial information for a simulation model can be gained by coupling geographic information systems with the model. Some researchers in this field have argued for a simulation approach named the geographic automata system, in which a MAS can be combined with CA and which takes advantages of GI Science to model complex geographic systems that are comprised of infrastructure features and human objects (Torrens and Benenson, 2005). Within geosimulation, the most common implementation of multi-agent models is for the agents to act as objects within a spatial framework (Albrecht, 2005; Benenson and Torrens, 2004). This approach also can be employed for residential mobility simulation (Torrens, 2007).

As most simulations of residential location do, the spatial features of a cell are utilized to calculate the location utility for agents. Thus, the interaction between agents and space can be within the simulation model. As in the research on residential pressure on landscape change we reviewed before, regional space is represented by a regular lattice of grid cells indexed by their geographic coordinates (i, j) in the matrix space {I×J}. Each cell is considered to be a homogenous land unit with key spatial information including three groups, *like available properties, land accessibility, and environmental amenities*. Interaction between agents and space takes place as agents choose their new location by evaluating the utility of cells. Household location change will further change the landscape of a cell. Thereby, landscape pressure can be evaluated (Fontaine and Rounsevell, 2009).

3.1.2 GIS and Spatial Data Sets
The ABM simulations can be run on a platform combining geographic information systems and ABM or CA, the former being the ArcGIS system of ESRI whereas the latter is an agent-based or CA software such as StarLogo, created by MIT or AUGH, developed by Cecchini (1996). Two examples of such coupling are provided here. In the first example, a land-use change model was constructed with the StarLogo software programmed by MIT coupled with GIS (Lai and Han, 2009). The research assessed the probability of development based on economic property right indices, and the probability of possible land uses allowed in the

zoning system was embedded in the simulation rules. Finally, the research used parameters developed over 100 generations of a genetic algorithm method to calibrate the simulation model. The main results from this research are as follows: (1) using the parameters gained from the genetic algorithm method, the model was indeed able to simulate, at least partially, the pattern of land uses for the Taipei metropolitan area; (2) the zoning system in the simulated area does influence the appearance and pattern of land uses. It limits the development of industrial land use and affects the fractal pattern of commercial land use; and (3) after comparing the spatial patterns of simulation results and conducting one-way ANOVA analysis, it can be concluded that zoning affects specific locations, but not the fractal pattern of land uses.

Figure 12.1 shows the logic of how the use type of a particular parcel (cell) is determined. Note that the use types are checked against zoning regulations in which mixed uses are allowed. Figure 12.2 is a sample illustration of the simulation and Figure 12.3 is the interface.

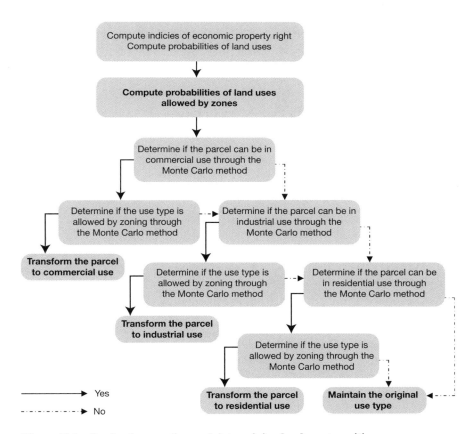

Figure 12.1 Logic of computing and determining land-use transitions

216   *Urban Complexity and Planning*

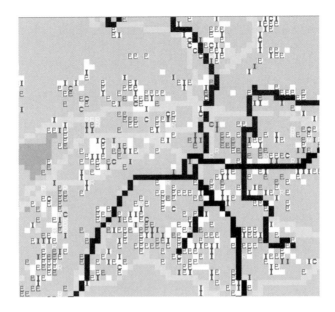

Figure 12.2 Sample simulation plot. (Black = road; blue = transit line; I = industrial; C = commercial; R = residential; E = vacant)

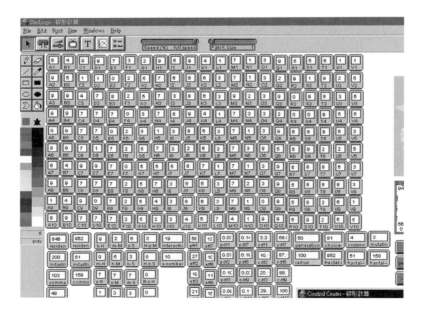

Figure 12.3 Simulation interface. Rules of the genetic algorithm (upper buttons) and the simulated maps and necessary data (lower buttons) are displayed

Planning in Complex Spatial and Temporal Systems 217

In the second example, research was conducted, grounded on a microscopic simulation approach to studying how decisions made locally gives rise to global patterns (Lai and Chen, 1999). CA provides the simplest bottom-up way to study discrete systems and complex urban spatial systems. Based on the coupling of a CA model and GIS of a small town in central Taiwan, Minjian Township, the research focused on an agent-based simulation approach to considering land-use and transportation networks as two traits of the evolution of complex urban spatial systems. The simulation views land development decisions as simple rules characterized by the degrees of complexity and diversity. Three factors, the numbers of transition rules (N), the diversity of transition rules (D), and the numbers of classifications of the transition rules (n), are derived from theories of measures of complexity and evolution in general system theory (GST). Simulating systems behavior based on the transition rules classified and sorting out the results by the three factors show that when the diversity of rules increases, the urban structure will grow in a complex, fractal way. Figure 12.4 shows the simulation framework and two illustrations of the simulation are given in Figure 12.5. Note that the simulation was run on the AUGH platform (Cecchini, 1996). Both rules of the simulation in Figure 12.5 are for high diversity, measured by and derived from different levels of complexity.

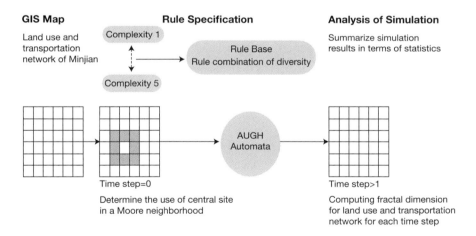

Figure 12.4 Simulation framework (complexity 1 through 5 represent degrees of complexity as measured by fractals)

Figure 12.5 Coupling of a CA model with GIS to explore land use and transportation interaction (yellow = residential; red = commercial; gray = road; blue = river)

3.2 Space Evolution in Planning Behavior

3.2.1 Prisoner's Dilemma Game in Space
Planning in the context of urban development, both physical and social, must acknowledge the significance of spatial effects of association and competition. Recent work on evolution of behavior, characterized as games in space, provides one starting point for incorporating space in simulations (Nowak, 2006). Here, we first present the model of Nowak and May (1993) and then introduce planning to the model. Allen and Sanglier (1981) considered some aspects of urban spatial evolution in a similar framework.

Nowak and May (1993) investigated the spatial evolution of a set of actors in a square lattice as actors in a sequence of a prisoner's dilemma game. The prisoner's dilemma game presents each player with two options: cooperate or defect. The payoffs are determined by the combination of plays such that the values of the payoffs for player one decrease in the following order $DC > CC > DD > CD$ where C signifies cooperate and D signifies defect. The first strategy is the action of player one, and the second is the action of player two. Player two faces a symmetric situation. The dilemma is that it is in each player's individual interest to defect regardless of the action of the other, but in doing so they both end up worse off, since DD has a lower payoff for each player than CC. Interaction among players (agents) in a spatial configuration based on this simple decision rule generates complex spatial patterns given different relative payoff levels. The effects of spatial configurations can be investigated by comparing the results of non-spatial sequences of a prisoner's dilemma game.

Arthur (1994) interpreted a similar sequence in terms of increasing returns to market share. He showed that if the payoff for adopting a strategy increases with the number of agents adopting the same strategy, it is impossible to predict the eventual evolutionary outcome of the resulting trajectory of market share. One typical illustration of this phenomenon is the adoption of particular computer software packages. The payoff increases with the number of other adopters because of the greater likelihood of additional compatible packages, knowledgeable users, and continuing upgrades. Similarly, consumers seem to have made choices about Betamax versus VHS in video formats at least partially on the basis of likelihood of available videotapes to play rather than on picture quality.

3.2.2 Planning in a Spatial Evolution Game

The payoff in the prisoner's dilemma game will then vary depending on the number of agents in the "neighborhood" choosing a particular option: cooperate or defect. This combination can be described using the fractal concept of space (see Mandelbrot, 1983; Batty and Longley, 1994; Batty, 2005). This approach allows simulations to characterize spatial relations across continuous dimensions, which can represent a richer variety of urban geographic relationships or organizational structures more effectively than Euclidean space.

Consider a continuum of space-filling agents residing in a fractal space of dimension who act based on the payoff in the prisoner's dilemma game and the principles of garbage-can simulation. Each agent makes one of two choices, defect or cooperate, as in the usual prisoner's dilemma game. The payoffs, however, are not fixed, but depend on the numbers of these choices adopted in the system. The payoffs for player one are depicted below, where (p,q) denotes the initial payoff or preference for choice p made by an agent interacting with another agent making choice q; r is the rate of change of return relative to the number of agents making a particular choice; and n(p) is the total number of agents choosing choice p. The rate r can be positive, negative, or zero, representing increasing, decreasing, or constant rates of return, respectively. Note that $a(d,c) > a(c,c) > a(d,d) > a(c,d)$.

Table 12.1   Payoff matrix

Player 2 Player 1	Cooperate	Defect
Cooperate	$a(c,c) + rn(c)$	$a(c,d) + rn(c)$
Defect	$a(d,c) + rn(d)$	$a(d,d) + rn(d)$

The agent chooses for the next time step so that it yields the maximum payoff based on the choices among its neighbors at the current time step. The neighbors are the agents, including the agent under consideration, located within a radius R from the site where the agent is located in fractal space. The agent can also make a choice by selecting the maximum payoff among the agents located within its "neighborhood" or the square lattice over time period T. R and T are thus indicative of planning investment in space and in time according to our definition. That is, they denote the scope of related choices considered in space and time, respectively. Let M (R,k) be agents standing for the mass of the fractal subspace with radius R and center k. We have M (R,k) = uR(D) where u is a uniform density and D is a fractal dimension (Mandelbrot, 1983). The total payoff for an agent j located at the center of M(R,j) is the sum of the payoffs for that agent interacting with all agents i in M(R,j), including j itself. That is:

P(j,t,R,T) = $\sum \sum$ [(a(c(j,t),c(i,t))+ rn(c(j,t))],

where P(j,t,R,T) is the cumulative payoff function for j over time period T at time t within M(R,j), and c(j,t) is the choice made by j at time t.

The first summation is over t of elements of the set T and the second is over i elements of the set M(R,j). The decision rule for any agent k at time t+1 is to adopt the choice made by the agents in k's neighborhood that yields the maximum payoff. That is:

c(k,t+1) = c(j | Max P(j,t,R,T)), for j is an agent of M(R,k).

This form of simulation of spatially structured behavior provides a basis for incorporating space into a simulation model similar to the garbage-can model discussed above.

4 Idea for Integrating the Garbage-can Model with a Spatial Evolution Game for Planning Simulation

To incorporate the garbage-can model into a spatial model, consider a continuum of decision-makers (agents) in a fractal space. There are finite numbers of problems and choices. Define a decision structure of relationships among decision-makers and choices, an access structure of relationships between problems and choices, and a solution structure between solutions and problems. These zero-one matrices of relationships have the same meaning and range of forms as in the original garbage-can model and are givens external to each simulation run. These structures can be varied as described earlier to discover their effects on choice-making behavior.

The initial payoffs for all decision-makers are the same, but these payoffs vary with respect to two variables in the simulation. The first variable is the number of agents that adopted that choice in the particular time step of the simulation. The second variable is the problems associated with that choice at that time. Because the problems arrive in a random sequence, the payoffs are subject to random fluctuations and the evolution is not deterministic. The payoff table is therefore different from that of the prisoner's dilemma game because in the spatial version there is interaction among the agents involved. The decision rule for an agent adopting a particular choice is the same as that in our spatial model: the best choice is the one that yields the maximum payoff considering the choices among the agent's neighbors in space and time.

This spatial version of the prisoner's dilemma model can then be used to consider the effects of space on a garbage-can model that also incorporates planning behaviors as suggested in Figure 12.6. We have not yet run such simulations in a structured way so as to test the sensitivity of this model to spatial scope or temporal consideration of related choices. We can identify, however, the types of questions that might be addressed. Different types of organizational structures, from strictly hierarchical to "matrix" structures could be considered as partial substitutes for planning intervention. For example, does a hierarchical organizational structure benefit less from planning than a "matrix" organization? Does planning that is focused on considering more related choices (i.e. more garbage cans) yield more problem resolutions than planning focused on generating solutions for fewer choices (garbage cans)? What differences arise from increasing the size of the neighborhood in space relative to increasing the size of the neighborhood in time? A spatial version of the garbage-can model has been provided (Lai, 2006), and the simulation framework suggested here can be considered as a sequel to that model.

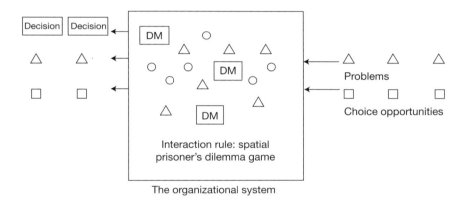

Figure 12.6 Relationship between the garbage can model and the prisoner's dilemma game model (DM = decision maker)

5 Conclusions

We have proposed modified versions of two previously proposed simulation models to allow consideration of the effects of planning in complex, spatial, temporal organizational systems. We have extended the garbage-can model of Cohen, March, and Olsen so as to consider a particular definition of planning behavior. Recent simulation runs suggest that the revised model is sensitive to these planning interventions. We have also proposed a revised version of the prisoner's dilemma spatial game, taking into account space and planning. In particular we have considered increasing returns, planning investments, and fractal space. Such simulations can be coupled with GIS to yield policy implications for real world situations. The major work of running structured sets of simulations so as to discover and elucidate systemic principles remains.

Simulations of this type are of interest because of the abstract form of questions that can be considered. The intent is not to simulate concrete, specific cases, but to understand the functioning of systems. The simulation result is encouraging in that it implies planning interventions might increase the efficiency of choice making without increasing the number of problems resolved. This suggests that useful, counterintuitive properties might be discovered. Such systemic understanding must then be interpreted in concrete terms for organizational behavior.

References

Albrecht, J. 2005 "A new age for geosimulation." *Transactions in GIS*, 9(4): 451–4.
Allen, P. M., and M. Sanglier. 1981. "Urban evolution, self-organization, and decision-making." *Environment and Planning A* 13: 167–83.
Arthur, W.B. 1994. *Increasing Returns and Path Dependence in the Economy*. Ann Arbor: The University of Michigan Press.
Arthur, W.B. 1989. "Competing technologies, increasing returns, and lock-in by historical events." *The Economic Journal* 99: 116–31.
Batty, M., and P. Longley. 1994. *Fractal Cities*. New York: Academic Press.
Batty, M., H. Couclelis, M. Eichen. 1997. "Urban Systems as Cellular Automata." *Environment and Planning B: Planning and Design* 24(2): 159–64.
Batty, M. 2005. *Cities and Complexity: Understanding Cities with Cellular Automata, Agent-Based Models, and Fractals*. Cambridge, Massachusetts: The MIT Press.
Batty, M. 2008. Fifty years of urban modelling: Macro statics to micro dynamics. In S. Albeverio, D. Andrey, P. Giordano, and A. Vancheri, eds, *The Dynamics of Complex Urban Systems: An Interdisciplinary Approach*, Physica-Verlag, Heidelberg, DE (2008), pp. 1–20.
Batty, M. 1976. *Urban Modelling: Algorithms, Calibrations, Predictions*. Cambridge University Press, Cambridge, UK.
Batty, M., Y. Xie, and Z. Sun. 1999. "Modeling urban dynamics through GIS-based cellular automata." *Computers, Environment and Urban Systems* 23(3): 205–33.
Benenson, I. 1998. "Multi-agent simulations of residential dynamics in the city." *Computers, Environment and Urban Systems* 22(1): 25–42.
Benenson, I, and P.M. Torrens. 2004 "Geosimulation: Object-based modelling of urban phenomena." *Computers Environment & Urban Systems* 28: 1–8.
Cecchini, A. 1996. "Urban modeling by means of cellular automata: generalized urban automata with the help on-line (AUGH) model." *Environment and Planning B* 23: 721–32.
Chin, N. 2002. Unearthing the roots of urban sprawl: A critical analysis of form function and methodology, Centre for Advanced Spatial Analysis (CASA) Working Paper Series. London: University College London.

Claramunt, C., and B. Jiang. 2001. "A qualitative model for the simulation of traffic behaviours in a multi-lane environment." *Geographical Sciences* 11 (1): 29–42.

Clarke, K.C., and L.J. Gaydos. 1998 "Loose-coupling of a cellular automaton model and GIS: long-term growth prediction for the San Francisco and Washington/Baltimore." *International Journal of Geographical Information Science* 12(7): 699–714.

Cohen, M.D., J.G. March, and J.P. Olsen. 1972. "A garbage can model of organizational choice." *Administrative Science Quarterly* 17(1): 1–25.

Crooks A., C. Castle, and M. Batty. 2008. "Key challenges in agent-based modelling for geo-spatial simulation." *Computers, Environment and Urban Systems* 32(6): 417–30.

Ettema, D. 2011. "A multi-agent model of urban processes: Modelling relocation processes and price setting in housing markets." *Computers, Environment and Urban Systems* 35(1): 1–11.

Ewing, Reid H. 1994. "Characteristics, causes and effects of sprawl: A literature review." *Environmental and Urban Issues* 21(2): 1–15.

Ewing, Reid H. 1997. "Is Los Angeles-style sprawl desirable?" *Journal of American, Planning Association* 63(1): 107–26.

Fang, S., G. Gertner, Z. Sun, and A. Anderson. 2005. "The impact of interactions in spatial simulation of the dynamics of urban sprawl." *Landscape and Urban Planning* 73(4): 294–306.

Feitosa Flávia F., Bao Quang, and Paul L.G. Vlek. 2010. "Multi-agent simulator for urban segregation (MASUS): A tool to explore alternatives for promoting inclusive cities." *Computers, Environment and Urban Systems*, in press.

Filatova T., D.C. Parker, and V.D.A. Veen. 2008 "Agent-Based Urban Land Markets: Agent's Pricing Behavior, Land Prices and Urban Land Use Change." *Journal of Artificial Societies and Social Simulation* 12(13) <http://jasss.soc.surrey.ac.uk/12/1/3.html>.

Fontaine, C.M., and M.D.A. Rounsevell. 2009. "An agent-based approach to model future residential pressure on a regional landscape." *Landscape Ecology* 24: 1237–54.

Friend, J., and A. Hickling. 2005. *Planning under Pressure: The Strategic Choice Approach*. New York: Elsevier Butterworth Heinemann.

Hopkins, L.D. 2001. *Urban Development: The Logic of Making Plans*. London: Island Press.

Jager, W., H.J. Mosler. 2007. "Simulating Human Behavior for Understanding and Managing Environmental Resource Use." *Social Issues* 63(1): 97–116.

Jiang, B. 2000. "Agent-based approach to modeling environmental and urban systems within GIS." Proceedings of 9th international symposium on spatial data handling. 1–12.

Lai, Shih-Kung. 1998. "From organized anarchy to controlled structure: effects of planning on the garbage-can processes." *Environment and Planning B: Planning and Design* 25: 85–102.

Lai, Shih-Kung. 2003. "Effects of planning on the garbage-can decision processes: a reformulation and extension." *Environment and Planning B: Planning and Design* 30: 379–89.

Lai, Shih-Kung. 2006. "A spatial garbage-can model." *Environment and Planning B: Planning and Design* 33 (1): 141–56.

Lai, Shih-Kung, and Chen, Yo-Jen. 1999. "A dynamic exploration into land uses and transportation networks interaction based on cellular automata simulations." Paper presented at the 1999 International Symposium of City Planning, Tainan, Taiwan.

Lai, Shih-Kung, and Haoying Han. 2009. *Complexity: New Perspectives on Urban Planning*. Beijing: China Architecture and Building Press (in Chinese).

Li, X., and A.G.O. Yeh. 2000. "Modeling sustainable urban development by the integration of constrained cellular automata and GIS." *International Journal of Geographical Information Science* 14(2): 131–52.

Ligtenberg, A., et al., 2010. "Validation of an agent-based model for spatial planning: A role-playing approach." *Computers, Environment and Urban Systems* 34(5):424–34.

May, Y., Z. Shen, Y. Long, M. Kawakami, K. Wang, and K. Suzuki, 2010 "Urban Growth Simulation for Spatial Strategic Plan of Chuangdong Area, China." 18th International Conference on GeoInformatics, pp 1–6.

Mandelbrot, B.B. 1983. *The Fractal Geometry of Nature*. New York: W.H. Freeman.

Neuman, M. 2005. "The compact city fallacy." *Planning Education and Research* 25(1): 11–26.

Nowak, M.A. 2006. *Evolutionary Dynamics: Exploring the Equations of Life*. Cambridge, Massachusetts: The Belknap Press of Harvard University Press.

Nowak, M.A., and R.M. May. 1993. "The spatial dilemmas of evolution." *International Journal of Bifurcation and Chaos* 3(1): 35–78.

Padgett, J.F. 1980. "Managing garbage can hierarchies." *Administrative Science Quarterly* 25(4): 583–604.

Parker, D.C., and T. Filatova. 2008. "A conceptual design for a bilateral agent-based and market with heterogeneous economic agents." *Computers, Environment and Urban Systems* 32(6): 454–63.

Raju, K.A., P.K Sikdar, and S.L Dhingra. 1998 "Micro-simulation of residential location choice and its variation." *Environment and Urban Systems* 22(3): 203–18.

Saarloos, D.J.M., T.A. Arentze, A.W.J. Borgers, and H.J.P. Timmermans. 2008. "A multi-agent paradigm as structuring principle for planning support systems." *Computers, Environment and Urban Systems* 32(1): 29–40.

Schaeffer, P.V., and L.D. Hopkins. 1987. "Planning behavior: The economics of information and land development." *Environment and Planning A* 19: 1211–32.

Semboloni, F., J. Assfalg, S. Armeni, R. Gianassi, and F. Marsoni, 2004 "CityDev, an interactive multi-agents urban model on the web." *Computers, Environment and Urban Systems* 28(1–2): 45–64.

Torrens, P.M. 2007 "A Geographic Automata Model of Residential Mobility." *Environment and Planning B: Planning and Design* 34: 200–222.

Torrens, P.M., and I. Beneson. 2005. "Geographic Automata Systems." *International Journal of Geographical Information Science* 19(4): 385–412.

Torrens, P.M. 2007. "A geographic automata model of residential mobility." *Environment and Planning B: Planning and Design* 34: 200–222.

Wu, F. 2002 "Calibration of stochastic cellular automata: the application to rural-urban land conversions." *International Journal of Geograghic Information Science* 16(8): 795–818.

Zellner, M.L., T.L. Theis, A.T. Karunanithi, A.S. Garmestani, and H. Cabezas. 2008. "A new framework for urban sustainability assessments: Linking complexity, information and policy." *Computers, Environment and Urban Systems* 32(6): 474–88.

Zhang, H., Y.N. Zeng, B. Ling, and X.J. Yu. 2010. "Modelling urban expansion using a multi agent-based model in the city of Changsha." *Geographical Sciences* 20(4): 540–56.

Chapter 13

Decision Network: A Planning Tool for Making Multiple, Linked Decisions[1]

1 Introduction

Making plans and acting accordingly are fundamental to the urban planning profession. Few would argue against the presumption that making plans is helpful in coping with urban phenomena because planning for urban development characterized by interdependence, indivisibility, irreversibility, and imperfect foresight yields benefits to planners (Hopkins, 2001). However, the question remains unsatisfactorily answered as to whether making plans can really help us in coping with complex urban systems. Instead of addressing the issue directly, in the present book we will develop an analytical planning tool called *Decision Network* based on the presumption that making plans matters and yields benefits to the user in terms of his or her preferences.

Most planning situations are composed of multiple, linked decisions. The essential idea of making plans is therefore to coordinate linked decisions in order to achieve desired goals. Though this conception is crucial in making plans, little has been discussed in the planning literature about how it should be explored and how planning tools can be developed based on this conception (exception including, however, Hopkins 2001). Planning and design are distinct in that the former takes into account contingencies, whereas the latter focuses on arrangement of actions. A decision (planning) support system must therefore be capable of helping the planner to coordinate contingent decisions in context, relationship, and sequence. Commonly applied decision or planning aids enhance only part, if not all, of these aspects: the garbage-can model (Cohen et al., 1972) on context, the strategic choice approach (Friend and Hickling, 2005) on relationship, and decision tree (Raiffa, 1968) on sequence. In the present chapter, we present a planning tool, *Decision Network*, that blends the three techniques into a coherent framework, so that all three aspects of decisions are taken into account.

In Section 2, we will review the three planning tools under consideration. In Section 3, the conceptual framework of the planning tool of *Decision Network* will be provided. In Section 4, we will demonstrate using a hypothetical numerical example how *Decision Network* functions. In Section 5, we will discuss some

---

1 This chapter has been published in *Environment and Planning B: Planning and Design* 2011, Vol. 38, pages 115–28.

possible applications, extensions, and limitations of the planning tool. We conclude in Section 6.

2 Three Commonly used Techniques for Decision Analysis

In this section, three commonly used decision techniques are reviewed from which *Decision Network* developed in Section 3 is derived, namely, the garbage-can model (Cohen et al. 1972), the strategic choice approach (Friend and Hickling, 2005), and decision tree (Raiffa, 1968).

The garbage-can model is a description of the chaotic choice behavior in organized anarchies. It stresses how decisions are made in a particular context or garbage can in terms of problems, solutions, and decision-makers. The model views the decision process in an organization as four independent streams: streams of problems, solutions, decision-makers, and choice opportunities or decision situations. These four elements interact in an unpredictable, chaotic way and if problems, solutions, and decision-makers meet in a particular choice opportunity, a decision may or may not be made, depending on whether the energy supplied exceeds that demanded. In addition to the interaction of the four streams of elements, there are structural constraints confining who are eligible for making decisions where and which problems can be brought to bear with which choice opportunities. Given the simple conception of the organizational choice behavior, the system generates extremely complex, unpredictable behavior that yields interesting, robust patterns. For example, the model predicts that most decisions are made without solving problems. However, when a structure as manifested by planning is imposed on the system, something different happens (Lai, 1998). In particular, order emerges from chaos in that the system seems tamed by the imposed structure so that problems and decision-makers tend to be attached to certain fixed choice opportunities through time. However, fewer problems are solved with planning than without planning, resulting in speedy decision-making. In short, the garbage-can model focuses on the context where decisions emerge, rather than relationship and sequence of these decisions, but it is useful in making sense of real and simulated dynamic decision processes (e.g., Kingdon, 2003; Fioretti and Lomi, 2008a; 2008b) and provides a conceptual basis for the planning tool developed in the present chapter, as will be shown in Section 3.

The strategic choice approach, on the other hand, addresses the relationship among decisions and has evolved as a practical computerized means of tackling interrelated decisions under uncertainty (Friend, 1993). It can be conceived at best as a design approach to planning in that actions are predetermined through comparing combinations of interrelated decisions derived from the relationship among decisions, without worrying about the contingencies. The technique normally starts with a shaping model in which a decision graph is constructed to represent the relationships among decision areas. A decision area in the strategic choice approach is similar to a choice opportunity in the garbage-can model in that both represent decision situations except that a decision area only expresses options under consideration, whereas a choice opportunity specifies the context in which a decision may or may not be made. Once a decision graph is constructed, the strategic choice approach enters into a designing mode by eliminating incompatible combinations of options across decision areas. The remaining combinations of options, or decision schemes, are subject to a multi-attribute evaluation analysis in the comparing mode, in order to rank order these decision schemes according to a set of pre-specified criteria. Once the decision schemes are ranked, in the final stage of the strategic choice approach, the choosing mode, a tentative action plan is made taking into account uncertainties and robustness of the selected decisions in relation to the ensuing ones. The four-stage process may proceed in a non-linear fashion so the decision-maker can start from any one working mode to another, without following the order as specified. In short, the strategic choice approach views the planning process as continuous and focuses on the relationship among decisions, rather than the context where decisions emerge and the sequence in which these decisions are considered, but it provides a solid logic of a rational process for the planning tool developed here, as will be shown in Section 3.

Decision tree is a widely used tool for making rational decisions. It is developed based on the sound theoretical basis of the subjective expected utility model; therefore, unlike the garbage-can model, it is normative in nature. A decision tree is composed of three components: decision nodes, chance nodes, and arcs connecting these nodes. Like choice opportunity in the garbage-can model and decision area in the strategic choice approach, a decision node is a decision situation that is under the control of the decision-maker with possible alternatives emanating from that node to represent different possible paths in the tree. A chance node is something that cannot be controlled by the decision-maker, with possible states emanating from that node to represent possible outcomes of an uncertain event. The arcs connecting these nodes represent the sequential logic of these events as a manifestation of causal links of the decision problem under consideration. The arcs emanating from the chance node are assigned subjective probabilities to indicate the likelihoods that the associated states would come about. Each path of the decision tree, that is, a sequence of decision and chance nodes, is associated with a utility at the right end of the tree to indicate the preference for the outcome of that path. Once the decision tree is constructed, a computational process of folding back to calculate the expected utilities associated with the decision nodes is implemented in order to determine the best path in the tree that maximizes the overall expected utility. The selected path is, to some extent, a plan that leads the decision-maker to make choices along the unfolding events. Much has been built on the notion of decision tree since its conception, including multi-attribute utility theory (Keeney and Raiffa, 1993) and influence diagrams (Oliver and Smith, 1990). In short, decision tree focuses on the sequential logic of decisions, rather than the context where decisions emerge and the relationship among these decisions, but it provides a sound theoretical basis for making rational decisions for the planning tool developed in the present chapter, as will be shown in Section 3.

3 The Conceptual Framework

None of the three models reviewed in the previous section alone can cope completely with a planning problem of intertwined decisions. The garbage-can model is regarded as a description of how decisions come about in a certain context; the strategic choice approach focuses on figuring out the relationship among decisions, ignoring the dynamic aspects of other interacting elements; and decision tree emphasizes the causal sequences of decisions by assuming a single decision-maker. In order to take advantage of the merits of all three models, in our view the context, relationship, and sequence of decisions are all important aspects that an effective planning tool must cover. The planning tool, *Decision Network*, is aimed at addressing all these considerations for the planner faced with complex, interrelated decisions. *Decision Network* is composed of a network of decision nodes. Like a decision area in the strategic choice approach, each node is an emergent decision situation with a finite number of options in it (see Figure 13.1). Like a choice opportunity in garbage-can model, each decision situation is associated with four inputs, that is, decision-makers, problems, solutions, and places. Like an arc in decision tree, an outcome emanating from the decision situation under consideration to another serves as one of the four inputs of the latter, thus forming a network (see Figure 13.2). Each option within a decision situation is associated with a utility measurement. Each

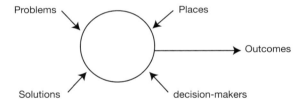

Figure 13.1   A decision situation

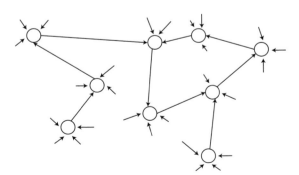

Figure 13.2   A decision network

decision situation is also associated with a probability, meaning that it is emergent and that the decision situation may or may not be realized or encountered by the planner. Given the conceptual framework, the problem is then to find a path of plan in the decision network that maximizes the subjective expected utility. The logic of this construct can be formalized mathematically and a hypothetical numerical example is given in the next section to demonstrate how the logic works.

4 A Numerical Example

In order to demonstrate how *Decision Network* works, in this section we provide a hypothetical numerical example as an illustration. Consider a network of decisions of five decision situations, three problems, two decision-makers and four solutions or alternatives. A decision situation is an opportunity where decisions may or may not be made, reminiscent of the decision node in a decision tree or the decision area in the strategic choice approach. The decision situation can be a formal meeting or forum or an informal gathering where problems, solutions, and decision-maker(s) are brought to bear to discuss issues under consideration. A meeting in deciding a zoning change or issuing a construction permit is a decision situation. A public hearing for approving urban development plans is another case in point. These decision situations can be either deterministic or stochastic in that some decision situations can be planned and controlled ahead of time, while others are emergent depending on contingencies of the environment. We do not know when and where developers and land owners would meet to decide when and where to invest in land development, but we do know that some decision opportunities will come up where developers will discuss plans for land development with the local government. To clarify, we denote the deterministic decision situations as decision nodes and the stochastic decision situations as chance nodes. Assume that three of the five decision situations are deterministic decision nodes with a probability of one that they will definitely occur, while the remaining two are stochastic chance nodes with various probabilities of occurrence. Assume further that the probabilities that chance nodes of decision situation 4 and 5 will occur are 0.7 and 0.5, respectively. These probabilities are subjective rather than frequencist probabilities to indicate the decision maker's degree of belief in what would happen (Savage, 1972).

Problems incur negative utilities, or disutilities, in that they cause effects which are not desired by the decision-maker. On the other hand, solutions are things the decision-maker can act on and result in positive utilities, or simply utilities, in that they constitute the alternatives available to the decision-maker to solve problems. Traffic congestion is a problem because it causes time delay when traveling in and between cities. Road construction is a solution to the traffic congestion problem because it prevents the traffic flow from being congested. Decision-makers bring expertise and resources to decision situations in solving problems, so their presence in decision situations incurs positive utilities. In deciding which route to construct the road, transportation planners make careful evaluation of alternative routes and choose the one to act on that is most effective in relieving the traffic congestion problem. The variables and parameters of the decision network problem are summarized in Table 13.1.

In addition to the variables and parameters as shown in Table 13.1, there are three structures in which these variables are related to each other: access structure, decision structure, and solution structure. The access structure specifies which problem is associated with which decision situation. Some problems can only be attended to in certain decision situations. In the land development context, for example, acquisition of land, at least in China, can only be brought to bear in decision situations in which the local government is involved. A matrix is used to identify this structure with rows as problems and decision situations as columns. A "1" in the matrix denotes that the problem in the corresponding row can be considered in the associated decision situation in the corresponding column, whereas a "0" cannot. In this numerical example, the access structure is given as below. Note that Problem 1 can be attended to in either Decision Node 2 or Chance Node 5, but not both simultaneously.

Access structure

p\d	1	2	3	4	5
1	0	1	0	0	1
2	0	0	0	1	0
3	0	0	1	0	0

Similarly, the decision structure specifies which decision-maker has authority to participate in which decision situation. Some decision-makers have greater authority in that they are eligible for participating in more decision situations than others, though, in reality, higher-level decision-makers only have time for more important decisions. The higher profile officials in the local government are eligible for participating in a wider range of forums, such as public hearings and household associations, than those with lower rank. The decision structure can be represented by a matrix similar to the access structure and for this a numerical example is given below. Note that Decision-maker 1 has more access to decision situations (totally three of them) than Decision-maker 2 who is associated with only two decision situations. Unlike problems which can be present in only one decision situation, we further assume that a decision-maker can participate in more than one decision situation because problems disappear once resolved, whereas decision-makers persist over time.

Decision structure

dm\d	1	2	3	4	5
1	0	1	1	0	1
2	1	0	0	1	0

Table 13.1 Variables and parameters of the hypothetical decision network problem

Variable	Terminology	Notation	Probability	Utility
Decision situations	Decision Node 1	d_1	1.0	n. a.
	Decision Node 2	d_2	1.0	n. a.
	Decision Node 3	d_3	1.0	n. a.
	Chance Node 4	d_4	0.7	n. a.
	Chance Node 5	d_5	0.5	n. a.
Problems	Problem 1	p_1	n. a.	-0.6
	Problem 2	p_2	n. a.	-0.5
	Problem 3	p_3	n. a.	-0.7
Solutions	Solution 1	s_1	n. a.	0.6
	Solution 2	s_2	n. a.	0.3
	Solution 3	s_3	n. a.	0.7
	Solution 4	s_4	n. a.	0.5
Decision-makers	Decision-maker 1	dm_1	n. a.	0.7
	Decision-maker 2	dm_2	n. a.	0.3

Viewing the solutions as alternatives available in solving problems, the solution structure specifies which solution is available to which decision situation. Solutions are usually specialized and generated specifically for particular decision situations. For example, shelters constructed for the homeless cannot be used for schools. Therefore, similar to the access structure where problems are decision specific, solutions can be associated with more than one decision situation, but they can be used in only one decision situation. The solution structure for this numerical example is given below. Note that Solution 1 is available to either Decision Nodes 2 or 3, but not both at the same time. Note also that, to simplify, we do not consider here the relationship between problems and solutions, assuming that all problems can be solved by any solution.

Solution structure

s\d	1	2	3	4	5
1	0	1	1	0	0
2	1	0	0	0	0
3	0	0	0	1	0
4	0	0	1	0	1

Given the variables and parameters in Table 13.1 and the access, decision, and solution structures depicted earlier, the decision-maker is faced with a planning problem of multiple, linked decisions in determining which problems and solutions should be associated with which decision situations in order to maximize the overall expected utility. This problem can be represented by a decision network denoted as G_0 as shown in Figure 13.3.

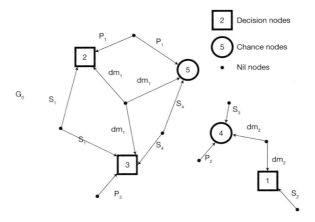

Figure 13.3 The decision network of G_0 for the numerical example

The directed graph in Figure 13.3 is composed of nodes that specify decisions and arcs that connect these nodes. There are three types of nodes: decision nodes, chance nodes, and nil nodes. Decision nodes, represented as squares, are deterministic decision situations with probabilities of occurrence equal to one; chance nodes of circles are stochastic decision situations with probabilities of occurrence greater than zero and less than one; and nil nodes shown as dots are auxiliary ones for analytic purposes. The arcs emanating from the nil nodes represent the associative relationship in the matrices of the structures. For example, in Figure 13.3, there are two arcs labeled as p_1 emanating from a nil node to Decision Node 2 and Chance Node 5, respectively, which means that in the access structure, Problem 1 has two 1's associated with Decision Node 2 and Chance Node 5 respectively. Note that the graph is not completely connected in that Decision Node 4 and Chance Node 1 form an independent cluster. Note also that though the decision situations are not directly connected with each other; they are interdependent indirectly through the connection of problems, solutions, and decision-makers.

Because problems and solutions can only be connected to one decision or chance node, to solve the network problem is to seek a combination of how p_1, s_1, and s_4 are connected to respective, single decision or chance nodes. Since the number of such possible connections for p_1, s_1, or s_4 each is two, there are totally $2 \times 2 \times 2 = 8$ combinations of such connections. Let $u(d_i)$ denote the expected utility by summing up all utilities that are associated with the elements connected to decision situation i; $p(d_j)$ the probability that decision situation j would occur; $u(s_k)$, $u(p_l)$, and $u(dm_m)$ the utilities associated with Solution k, Problem l, and Decision-maker m; and $u(G_n)$ the overall utility for graph n by summing up across all the decision and chance nodes their expected utilities. We can compute the respective overall utilities for the graphs derived from the eight combinations of the p_1, s_1, and s_4 connections as follows. Since $u(d_1)$ and $u(d_4)$ remain fixed across these eight graphs, we can first calculate them as:

$u(d_1) = p(d_1)[u(s_2) + u(dm_2)] = 1.0(0.3 + 0.3) = 0.6$; and
$u(d_4) = p(d_4)[u(p_2) + u(s_3) + u(dm_2)] = 0.7(-0.5 + 0.7 + 0.3) = 0.35$.

The calculation for the overall utility of each graph proceeds as follows:

For G_1, p_1 is connected to d_5, s_1 connected to d_2, and s_4 connected to d_5.
$u(d_2) = p(d_2)[u(s_1) + u(dm_1)] = 1.0(0.6 + 0.7) = 1.3$;
$u(d_3) = p(d_3)[u(p_3) + u(dm_1)] = 1.0(-0.7 + 0.7) = 0.0$;
$u(d_5) = p(d_5)[u(p_1) + u(s_4) + u(dm_1)] = 0.5(-0.6 + 0.5 + 0.7) = 0.3$; and
$u(G_1) = 0.6 + 0.35 + 1.3 + 0.0 + 0.3 = 2.55$.

Similarly, for G_2, p_1 is connected to d_2, s_1 connected to d_2, and s_4 connected to d_5. A close examination will find that $u(G_2) = 0.6 + 0.35 + 0.7 + 0.0 + 0.6 = 2.25$. For G_3 where p_1 is connected to d_5, s_1 to d_3, and s_4 to d_5, and $u(G_3) = 0.6 + 0.35 + 0.7 + 0.6 + 0.3 = 2.55$. For G_4 where p_1 is connected to d_2, s_1 to d_3, and s_4 to d_5, and $u(G_4) = 0.6 + 0.35 + 0.1 + 0.6 + 0.6 = 2.25$. For G_5 where p_1 is connected to d_5, s_1 to d_2, and s_4 to d_3, and $u(G_5) = 0.6 + 0.35 + 1.4 + 0.5 + 0.05 = 2.80^*$. For G_6 where p_1 is connected to d_2, s_1 to d_3, and s_4 to d_3, and $u(G_6) = 0.6 + 0.35 + 0.1 + 1.1 + 0.35 = 2.50$. For G_7 where p_1 is connected to d_2, s_1 to d_2, and s_4 to d_3, and $u(G_7) = 0.6 + 0.35 + 0.7 + 0.5 + 0.35 = 2.50$. Finally, for G_8 where p_1 is connected to d_5, s_1 to d_3, and s_4 to d_3, and $u(G_8) = 0.6 + 0.35 + 0.7 + 1.1 + 0.05 = 2.80^*$.

Apparently, G_5 and G_8 yield the highest overall utility of 2.80, and are thus the solutions to the decision network problem. More specifically, Problem 1 should be considered in Chance Node 5, Solution 4 in Decision Node 3, and Solution 1 in either Decision Node 2 or 3. Note that there are four pairs of overall utilities in the eight graphs because with the connections for p_1 and s_4 as given, the connection choice to a deterministic decision node for s_1 does not affect the overall utility due to linearity of the decision rule. Figures 13.4 and 13.5 show the graphs of decision network for G_5 and G_8, respectively.

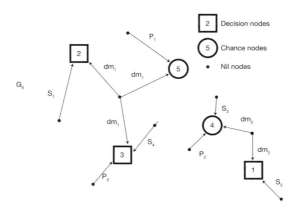

Figure 13.4 The decision network of G_5 for the numerical example

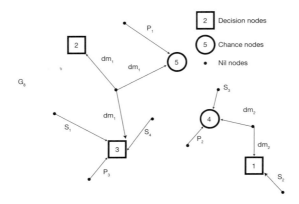

Figure 13.5   The decision network of G_8 for the numerical example

5   Spatial Application and Possible Extensions

The comprehensive planning approach to managing urban growth as manifested by limiting cities in compact forms is being widely applied. Urban growth boundaries (UGBs) are probably the best known approach in the US. In contrast, urban construction boundaries (UCBs) in China have an implementing mechanism similar to the UGBs in the US and have been implemented as legal boundaries of managing urban growth. However, the effectiveness of UCBs in containing urban growth in China has been criticized (Han, et al., 2009) partly because UCBs, once derived from city master plans (CMPs), are not capable of controlling land development through the existing planning system. We do not intend to delve into the issues of UCBs here, but in order to illustrate spatially and realistically how *Decision Network* works as depicted in the previous section, consider the making of the UCBs expansion decisions in a hypothetical scenario as shown in Figure 13.6 and Table 13.2. Figure 13.6 shows the urban development patterns before and after the setting of the UCBs for a hypothetical city. It is assumed that, because of the ineffective control of the UCBs on land development behavior, newly developed areas could fall inside (A1) and outside (A2) the UCBs, with some vacant land left unused (A3). Table 13.2 depicts the elements of the decision network problem and the corresponding variables and parameters with the description of the implication and situations of the decision and chance nodes. For example, Decision Node 1 is the decision situation where routine meetings are held with the mayor and planners participating in determining whether to issue the development permit to a developer on a site within the UCBs, under the conditions that the area of land developed outside the UCBs is greater than that inside and that the area of vacant land left undeveloped is greater than or equal to the area of land developed outside the UCBs. The three chance nodes are simply the decision situations in relation to the revision of the UCBs based on different possible futures of the urban development pattern. Three distinct problems include over-development in the rural area, lack of land for large investment within the UCBs, and infrastructure expansion outside the UCBs. Three levels of solutions are considered: status quo, moderate revision of the UCBs, and significant revision of the UCBs. Decision-makers include the mayor, developers, and planners, each of whom is associated with distinct utility. Note that utility could be defined in relation to property right (Barzel, 1997) and that the relationship between the elements requires the model to specify the structural constraints as depicted earlier, that is, access, decision, and solution structures. Once these structures are specified, the remaining task is to compute the optimal connection of these elements in order to find out the best actions as depicted in the numerical example.

The decision network tool presented in the present book is still in its initial stage, but the conceptual framework and the numerical example depicted here illustrate in effect how the tool works. In order for *Decision Network* to solve the real world problems, more complicated network structures could be added to the simple version. For example an outcome structure could be created that relates one decision situation to another so that the decision outcome from the former can serve as an input element, such as a problem or a solution, into the latter. This way, decision situations are directly connected. In addition, a spatial structure that relates decision situations to places can be considered so that the tool can be applied to solve spatial planning problems. Furthermore, the relationship between problems and solutions can be specified in the solution structure so that solutions are problem-specific.

The numerical example shows the detailed, but cumbersome, steps to search for the optimal solution to the decision network problem in an algebraic way.

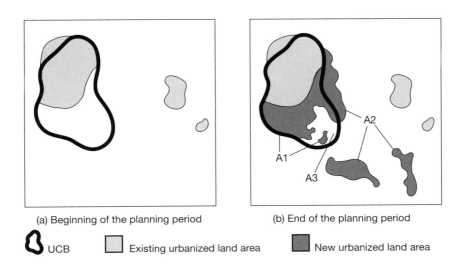

Figure 13.6 **A hypothetical example of delineating UCBs**

Table 13.2 The variables and parameters for the hypothetical example of delineating UCBs

Variable	Terminology	Notation	Probability	Utility	Actual conditions	Implication	Situation
Decision situations	Decision Node 1	d_1	1.0	n. a.	A2≤A1 and A2≤A3	Currently slow growth outside the UCBs and enough size of the UCBs	Routine meeting for better control
	Chance Node 1	d_2	0.5	n. a.	A3<A2<A1	Relatively fast growth outside the UCBs and insufficient size of the UCBs	Meeting on whether the UCBs should be expanded
	Chance Node 2	d_3	0.25	n. a.	A1≤A2≤A3	Ineffective implementation, but enough size of the UCBs	Meeting on how to control urban growth outside the UCBs
	Chance Node 3	d_4	0.25	n. a.	A1≤A2 and A3<A2	Ineffective implementation and insufficient size of the UCBs	Meeting on whether the UCBs should be comprehensively revised
Problems	Problem 1	p_1	n. a.	-0.6	Over-expansion of rural settlements		
	Problem 2	p_2	n. a.	-0.5	Need of large private projects for large area of land which cannot be found within the UCBs		
	Problem 3	p_3	n. a.	-0.7	Inevitable occupation of land outside the UCBs by large public infrastructures such as roads and airports		

Table 13.2 Concluded

Variable	Terminology	Notation	Probability	Utility	Actual conditions	Implication	Situation
Solutions	Solution 1	s_1	n. a.	0.3	Status quo		
	Solution 2	s_2	n. a.	0.5	Small revision of the UCBs without comprehensive change of the CMP		
	Solution 3	s_3	n. a.	0.7	Re-establish the UCBs by comprehensively revising the CMP		
Decision-makers	Decision-maker 1	dm_1	n. a.	0.7	Urban planners		
	Decision-maker 2	dm_2	n. a.	0.3	Developers		
	Decision-maker 3	dm_3	n. a.	0.4	Mayor		

A more efficient solution algorithm can be found by formulating the problem in a more rigorous, general way (e.g., Kirkwood's (1993) approach to sequential decisions of influence diagram). Once the decision network problem is formalized and efficiently solved, it can be implemented through computer programming languages serving as a decision support system or, even better, if coupled with geographic information systems, serving as a planning support system.

In the current formulation, uncertainties are narrowly assumed to be captured by subjective probabilities to indicate the decision-maker's degree of belief in the occurrence of decision situations. This notion of uncertainties is derived directly from subjective expected utility theory (Savage, 1972). A broader interpretation of contingencies would include different types of uncertainty, including the uncertainties about environment, values, and related decisions (Friend and Hickling, 2005). Hopkins (2001) argues that there is also uncertainty about available alternatives in making plans. These contingencies could be captured by decision weights in place of probabilities. For example, Kahneman and Tversky (1979) propose a weighting function that transforms probabilities into decision weights to capture the decision-maker's attitude in relation to the impact of events on the desirability of prospects, not merely the perceived likelihood of these events. Krantz and Kunreuther (2007) suggest a plan/goal approach in contrast to the traditional strategy/event approach to decision-making under uncertainty and interpret probabilities in the strategy/event approach also as decision weights. These different interpretations of contingencies could be incorporated into the current formulation of *Decision Network* to enrich the content of the tool and enhance its usefulness.

In short, *Decision Network* can provide advice not only on which actions to take now in the light of other related decision situations, but also the scope of the plan if we take into account decision cost. Robustness can be analyzed similar to the strategic choice approach so that the action taken now can remain optimal within several possible futures. One of the limitations of *Decision Network* in the current formulation is that the model is static. In a world full of uncertainties, a dynamic model may represent more realistically how the world works. There may be three possible ways to address, in principle, the dynamics of the world. Firstly, following the strategic choice approach, the formulation of the decision network model could be revised when new information arises to incorporate the flow of and the relationship between decision-makers, problems, and solutions. For example, some problems drop out of the decision network formulation after they have been solved, whereas some higher-level decision-makers remain in the scene even after decision situations have changed. Secondly, computerized simulations could be constructed to complement the decision network formulation in order to emulate the dynamic characteristics of the complex decision processes in the real world (e.g., Lai, 1998; 2003; 2006). Thirdly, the current formulation of *Decision Network* presented here can readily be transformed into a linear programming problem with the maximization of the overall expected utility as the objective function. Dynamic programming techniques could be used to extend the current linear programming formulation in order to address a sequence of decision network formulations that cope with the changing conditions over time (e.g., Cooper and Cooper, 1981). None of the three ways of addressing the dynamic world is easy, but they serve as a starting point for *Decision Network* to attain more realism. Note in particular that linear programming cannot be used directly as a model for urban development (Hopkins, 1979); rather it should be considered as a metaphor for the logic of design, or plan for that matter, in the face of complexity (Simon, 1996)

6 Conclusions

Planners for urban development and decision-makers in complex environments are faced with multiple, linked decisions at the same time. Making single, independent decisions as commonly perceived in decision analysis is insufficient in dealing with the complexity. *Decision Network* is aimed at providing a tool for planning to make multiple, linked decisions. The potential applications of *Decision Network* are not limited to urban planning. It can be a useful planning tool if the decision-maker is faced with more than one decision. Therefore, *Decision Network* is most effective in a complex environment in which decisions are interrelated. The potential clients who might seek *Decision Network* for advice may include urban planners, city managers, policy analysts, and business managers, among others. In addition, *Decision Network* can serve as the kernel for a larger planning support system that addresses spatial problems by coupling it with geographic information systems. In the present book, we have depicted a conceptual framework with a numerical example of an analytical tool for planning that takes into account context, relationship, and sequence of decisions. Much can be built on this framework for further explorations.

Acknowledgements

The author is grateful to Professor Lewis D. Hopkins for his helpful insight into the conceptual relationship between the garbage can model, the strategic choice approach, and decision tree.

References

Barzel, Y. 1997. *Economic Analysis of Property Rights*. Cambridge University Press, Cambridge.
Cohen, M.D., J.G. March, and J.P. Olsen. 1972. "A garbage can model of organizational choice." *Administrative Science Quarterly* 17(1): 1–25.
Cooper, L., and M. Cooper. M. 1981. *Introduction to Dynamic Programming*. Pergamon Press, New York.

Fioretti, G., and A. Lomi. 2008a. "An agent-based representation of the garbage can model of organizational choice." *The Journal of Artificial Societies and Social Simulation* 11(1) 1 http://jasss.soc.surrey.ac.uk/11/1/1.html.

Fioretti, G., and A. Lomi. 2008b. "The garbage can model of organizational choice: an agent-based reconstruction." *Simulation Modelling Practice and Theory* 16(2): 192–217.

Friend, J.K. 1993. "The strategic choice approach in environmental policy making." *The Environmental Professional* 15: 164–75.

Friend, J., and A. Hickling. 2005. *Planning under Pressure: The Strategic Choice Approach, Third Edition.* Elsevier Butterworth-Heinemann, London.

Han, H., S-K. Lai, A. Dang A., Z. Tan, and C. Wu. 2009. "Effectiveness of urban construction boundaries in Beijing: an assessment." *Journal of Zhejiang University SCIENCE A* 10(9): 1285–95.

Hopkins, L.D. 1979. "Quadratic versus linear models for urban land use plan design." *Environment and Planning A* 11(3): 291–8.

Hopkins, L.D. 2001. *Urban Development: The Logic of Making Plans.* Island Press, London.

Kahneman, D., and A. Tversky. 1979. "Prospect theory: an analysis of decision under risk." *Econometrica* 47(2): 263–91.

Keeney, R.L., and H. Raiffa. 1993. *Decisions with Multiple Objectives: Preferences and Value Tradeoffs.* Cambridge University Press, Cambridge.

Kingdon, J.W. 2003. *Agendas, alternatives, and Public Policies.* Longman, New York.

Kirkwood, C.W. 1993. "An algebraic approach to formulating and solving large models for sequential decisions under uncertainty." *Management Science* 39(7): 900–913.

Krantz, D.H., and H.C. Kunreuther. 2007. "Goals and plans in decision making." *Judgment and Decision Making* 2(3): 137–68.

Lai, S-K. 1998. " From organized anarchy to controlled structure: effects of planning on the garbage can decision processes." *Environment and Planning B: Planning and Design* 16: 155–70.

Lai, S-K. 2003. "Effects of planning on the garbage-can decision processes: a reformulation and extension." *Environment and Planning B: Planning and Design* 30(3): 379–89.

Lai, S-K. 2006. "A spatial garbage-can model." *Environment and Planning B: Planning and Design* 33(1): 141–56.

Oliver, R.M., and Smith, J.Q. 1990. *Influence Diagrams, Belief Nets and Decision Analysis.* John Wiley & Sons, New York.

Raiffa, H. 1968. *Decision Analysis: Introductory Lectures on Choices under Uncertainty.* Addison-Wesley, Reading, MA.

Savage, L.J. 1972. *The Foundations of Statistics.* Dover, Mineola, NY.

Simon, H.A. 1996. *The Sciences of the Artificial.* The MIT Press, Cambridge, MA.

Chapter 14
Effectiveness of Plans in the Face of Complexity

1 Introduction

The claim that plans are useful or effective for improving the efficiency of cities surprisingly lacks both theoretical and empirical backing. The question of effectiveness of plans is therefore a fundamental one worth pursuing in order to provide a foundation, theoretical or empirical or both, for the urban planning profession. The main distinction of the urban planning profession from other professions that apply planning techniques is that the former deals with large, complex systems, whereas the latter focus on smaller, simpler ones, including business administration. Attempts to address the question of effectiveness of plans have been scattered in the literature and recently reviewed by Hopkins (2012), but no conclusive answer has yet been provided while more open questions are left to be explored. The reader is encouraged to refer to Hopkins's literature review for cited work there.

The main reason why planning effectiveness is difficult to assess is partly because cities are complex systems, and it is difficult to distinguish consequences resulting from plans from consequences resulting from other interventions, such as policies, projects, institutions, and programs, as well as natural evolution, such as land market and environmental settings. Elsewhere, I have shown that plans considering multiple, linked decisions yield higher expected payoffs than considering these decisions independently (Han and Lai, 2009), that making plans has effects on complex organizational processes (Lai, 1998; 2003), and that effects of plans on urban growth boundaries are at best difficult to distinguish from effects of other activities (Han et al., 2009).

The present chapter intends to tackle this question through axiomatic theorem construction. Drawing from Hopkins's (2001) insight that urban development decisions are interdependent, irreversible, indivisible, and with imperfect foresight, I will show in an axiomatic system that the four I's together constitute a sufficient condition for complex systems, including cities, and a necessary condition under which plans work. The two lemmas lead to a conclusive theorem that plans are effective for improving the performance of complex systems. Section 2 depicts a model of cities from which our axiomatic system is derived. Section 3 defines some preliminaries. Section 4 proceeds to construct the axiomatic system. I conclude in Section 5.

2 The Model

I set out to consider cities as complex, dynamic networks of decisions (Batty, 2001; 2008), rather than interdependent agents interacting with buildings because agents make decisions which yield outcomes affecting urban development. Considering cities as complex networks of decisions blends the activities and physical settings into a whole, rather than treating the two sets of elements as separate, independent entities as traditionally perceived in urban studies research. The interaction between the activities and physical settings is thus taken into account explicitly in our model. Activities are roughly analogous to making and realizing decisions that shape and are shaped by the physical settings. The traditional urban planning problem of land-use activities vs. transportation facilities is a case in point. In other words, I consider cities as complex systems of linked decisions.

There is no accepted definition of "complex systems" yet, but a consensus has emerged that "complex systems" are distinct from systems that are either in the phase of order or chaos; that is, complex systems are always at the edge of chaos (e.g., Waldrop, 1992; Kauffman, 1995). Therefore, by "complex" we mean that the pattern of how these decisions are connected in the networks is neither ordered nor random. An ordered distribution depicts that a decision is connected to a fixed number of other decisions in a given topological pattern in a network. A random distribution implies that any decision may be connected to any other decisions in the network. This conception of complex systems coincides with Watts and Strogatz's (1998) notion of "small worlds." In a small world, the nodes in a network are both closely connected with short path lengths and highly clustered with high clustering coefficients. According to Watts and Strogatz (1998), there can be three regimes of network topological structures, independent, uniform, and clustered, as shown in Figure 14.1.

In an independent network, each decision is disconnected from any other decision. In a uniform network, the decisions can be either orderly connected with each decision which is in turn connected to a fixed number of neighboring

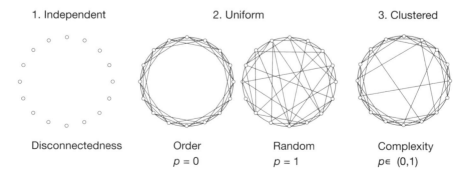

Figure 14.1 A typology of network topological structures

decisions, or randomly connected with each decision connected to any other decision. A parameter p is given to such a network, showing the probability under which a decision is reconnected randomly to any other decision in the network, given a fixed number of connections; thus an ordered network has a p value of zero, while a random network is given the value of one. In a complex network, the p value is assigned to an interval between zero and unity, so that the decisions are clustered with loose connections to a few decisions that are topologically far away from the decisions (Watts and Strogatz, 1998). Roughly speaking, the ordered distribution connotes order while the random distribution implies chaos; therefore complex systems are defined here as networks of decisions whose topological structures fall within the order and chaos spectrum. This interpretation is intuitively appealing because cities are not in order and never in chaos. We can observe spatially clustered activities that evolve over time and sometimes self-organize themselves into partial order, or organized complexity (Jacobs, 1993).

The internal working of networks of decisions can best be depicted by the garbage-can model proposed by Cohen et al. (1972). Considering organizational choice behavior as four interacting streams of elements, that is, problems, solutions, decision-makers, and decision situations within certain structural constraints, Cohen et al. were able to construct a series of computer experiments to observe how the organizational choice behavior responds to external changes, such as the relations between problems and decision situations and between decision-makers and decision situations. Based on the garbage-can model, I have shown elsewhere that planning as manifested by optimization matters; in particular, planning results in order of organizational choice behavior with reduced numbers of problems solved (Lai, 1998; 2003). The garbage-can model has also been extended into modeling how cities work by incorporating the spatial dimension (Lai, 2006).

Following Cohen et al. (1972), the term "decisions" used here begs a careful definition. In particular, these decisions are emergent, transient situations where decision-makers, problems, solutions, and places meet and something happens (Lai, 2006). I use "decisions" and "decision situations" interchangeably in this chapter. Two decisions are connected if the choice made in one decision affects the consequences of the choice made in the other, or vice versa. This definition of interdependence is different from that focusing solely on interrelationship between choices without regard to how systems work (e.g., Friend and Hickling, 2005). The distinction is subtle but important because the mechanisms in which the systems work are taken into account in my definition. It does not require that an outcome of a decision becomes an input of another, which is a strong case of connectivity. Thus, one can imagine that a city is composed of a giant network of such decisions whose pattern keeps evolving over time and space. An action is an act to be taken in a decision. A consequence is the outcome resulting from one or more than one decision. A plan is a set of connected decisions in order to achieve desired outcomes.

3 Preliminaries

Based on the model of cities as networks of decisions just depicted, the following definitions are given.

Definition 1   Dependent Connectedness Relation D

Let x and y belong to a non-empty set of decisions X. x and y are dependently connected, denoted as xDy or (x, y) ∈ D, if and only if the choice in x depends on the consequences resulting from the choice in y, but not vice versa.

Note that the decisions belonging to the relation of *D* is one-way connected. Given this fundamental relation of *D* and let *x* and *y* belong to *X*, we can identify four types of rations between decisions as follows:

Dependent Connectedness D: (x, y) ∈ D ∧ (y, x) ∉ D.
Converse of Dependent Connectedness C: (y, x) ∈ D ∧ (x, y) ∉ D.
Mutually Dependent Connectedness M: (x, y) ∈ D ∧ (y, x) ∈ D.
Mutually Independent Connectedness I: (x, y) ∉ D ∧ (y, x) ∉ D.

In particular, we define an interdependence relation *R* as one that belongs to *D*, *C*, or *M*. In the context of the garbage-can model (Cohen et al., 1972) as depicted earlier, we assume that if two decision situations, or decisions, are connected, then they may have common problems, decision-makers, or solutions that could be attached to them. In other words, if two decisions are connected, then the two decisions may be competing for problems, decision-makers, or solutions. The results of such competition of one decision will cause different consequences that in turn affect the choices in the other decision. Consider the locational choices of a highway and a shopping mall, both competing for locations with good accessibility (solutions). The locational choice of either decision will result in consequences that affect the choice of the other. Therefore, they are mutually connected. The same logic applies to the competition for problems and decision-makers. That is:

Definition 2   Interdependence Relation R

Let x and y belong to a non-empty set of decisions X. x and y are interdependent, denoted as xRy or (x, y) ∈ R, if and only if the choice in x depends consequentially on the choice in y, and/or vice versa.

In a complex network as defined in Section 2, decisions may be clustered, forming subunits of the system. In the societal context, for example, these clusters of decisions can be firms, governments, voluntary groups, or any other type of organizations. To simplify and follow Watts and Strogatz (1998), let us consider a circular network of decisions as shown in Figure 14.2.

We define a clustered set as a fixed number of decisions topologically centered on a particular decision *i*. For example, as shown in Figure 14.2, x_{i-3}, x_{i-2}, x_{i-1}, x_i,

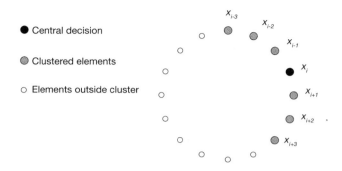

Figure 14.2 A simplified circular network of decisions

x_{i+1}, x_{i+2}, and x_{i+3} are a clustered set of six elements centered on x_i with k equal to three, the number of neighboring decisions.

Definition 3   Clustered Set

$C_i = \{x_{i-k}, x_{i-k+1}, \ldots, x_{i-2}, x_{i-1}, x_i, x_{i+1}, x_{i+2}, \ldots, x_{i+k-1}, x_{i+k}\}$.

Note that the decisions within a cluster can be connected to elements either inside or outside the cluster, resulting in different degrees of clustering as shown in Figure 14.3. In Figure 14.3, given the clustered set with k equal to three, the two topological structures depict different degrees of clustering with the network on the left (with 12 links within the cluster) more clustered than the one on the right (with nine links within the cluster).

Given the above relational and structural definitions of complex network systems, we now characterize in concrete terms interdependence, irreversibility, indivisibility, and imperfect foresight, or the four I's (Hopkins, 2001). In addition to interdependence relation between decisions R, there are also interdependence relations between clustered sets S, or special interdependence. That is, special interdependence S exists if and only if at least two decisions in two mutually exclusive clustered sets are connected respectively. Thus, we have:

Definition 4   Special Interdependence S

Let $C_i \wedge C_j = \phi$. C_i and C_j are specially interdependent if and only if $\exists\, x_i \in C_i$, $\exists\, x_j \in C_j$, and $(x_i, x_j) \in R$.

Indivisibility and irreversibility are related to the notion of increasing returns and path dependence, respectively (Arthur, 1994). In particular, increasing returns are a special, continuous case of indivisibility which results from agglomeration economy, while path dependence implies irreversibility. Both indivisibility and irreversibility imply that a clustered set of decisions are completely connected, meaning that each decision in the set is connected to every other decision in the

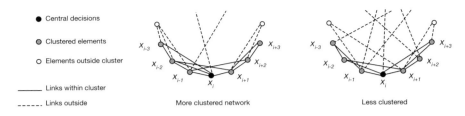

Figure 14.3 Networks with different degrees of clustering

same set. Otherwise, the disconnected decisions are divisible and reversible. To simplify, we set aside the case where irreversibility results from chains or subsets of connections in the clustered set. Therefore, we have:

Definition 5 Indivisibility and Irreversibility

C_i *is indivisible and irreversible if and only if* $\forall\ x_i, x_j \in C_i$ *and* $x_i \# x_j$, *so that* $(x_i, x_j) \in R$.

The definition of imperfect foresight is defined here to simply mean that whether a decision takes place is probabilistic. That is, decision situations are stochastic and may or may not occur. Once a decision situation comes to existence, choices in it are made with uncertain consequences. All such uncertainties are assumed to be captured by the probability p of whether the decision situation comes about. Let p stand for a probability function, and we have:

Definition 6 Imperfect Foresight

x is imperfectly foresighted if and only if $0 < p(x) < 1$, $x \in X$.
In mathematical terms, we have:

Definition 7 Independent Network

$\forall\ x, y \in X, (x, y) \notin R$.

Definition 8 Ordered Network

$\forall\ C$, *let* $x, y \in C$ *and* $x \neq y$. $(x, y) \in R$.

Definition 9: Random Network

$\forall\ C, \exists\ x, y \in C$ *and* $x \neq y$. $(x, y) \notin R$.

Definition 10 Complex Network

A complex network is neither an ordered nor a random network.

It can be derived from these definitions that in a complex network there exists at least both one ordered clustered set and one unordered clustered set.

Given the structural definitions of complex networks systems, we define plans as:

Definition 11   Plans

Given a network of decisions, a plan is an assignment of problems, decision-makers, and solutions to connected decisions in order to yield the maximum expected utility.

A detailed application of this conception of plans to decision networks can be found in Han and Lai (2009). Drawing on the garbage-can model (Cohen et al., 1972), Han and Lai (2009) developed a logic for formulating and solving large, complex problems by making multiple, linked decisions. In their formulation, problems, solutions, and decision-makers are assigned to decision situations in order to yield the maximum total expected utility of the system under consideration, whereas in the original garbage-can model, these four elements interact in a random way and something happens. For example, if certain problems (associated with negative utility, or disutility), solutions, and decision-makers (the two associated with positive utility, or utility) meet in a particular decision situation and satisfy certain structural constraints, and the net expected utility is positive, then a decision is made and the attached problems solved. This descriptive formulation of how organizational choice behavior works is intuitively appealing because these processes are in chaos rather than in order. Han and Lai (2009), based on previous simulations on effects of plans (Lai, 1998; 2003), consider a set of such decision situations as a network competing for problems, solutions, and decision-makers. A plan is defined as assigning these elements to the decision situations under consideration in order to maximize the total expected utility of the network.

4   The Theorem

Given the structural definitions of complex network systems in Section 3, we now proceed to prove that interdependence, irreversibility, indivisibility, and imperfect foresight give rise to complexity and that plans work in such complex network systems. To simplify, we assume that the number of decisions in the network is n, that is, $|X| = n$, and that the total number of links of connected decisions in the network is fixed. Since the number of links reaches the maximum of nk in the case of ordered network, where k stands for half of the number of the neighboring decisions for each central node, $|R| = nk$ for the network. In addition, following Han and Lai (2009), a problem or solution can be associated with only one decision. Lemma 1 shows that interdependence, indivisibility, and irreversibility constitute the sufficient condition for complex systems.

Lemma 1

Interdependence, indivisibility, and irreversibility are the sufficient condition for complexity

Proof:

The strategy of the proof includes three parts. First, we prove that special interdependence implies the impossibility of an ordered network. Second, we prove that indivisibility and irreversibility imply the impossibility of a random network. Third, with the two parts given, we can prove that interdependence, indivisibility, and irreversibility together necessitate the existence of complex systems.

Part 1:

If there exists special interdependence in the network, then $\exists x_h \notin C_i$ so that $(x_i, x_h) \in R$, for $x_i \in C_i$ and $x_h \in C_h$. Since the total number of links is fixed at nk, that is, $|R| = nk$, there must exist $C_h \neq C_i$ so that $\exists (x_h, x_g) \notin R$, where $x_h, x_g \in C_h$ and $x_h \neq x_g$, or $\exists (x_i, x_j) \notin R$, where $x_i, x_j \in C_i$ and $x_i \neq x_j$, which leads the network to an unordered one. In words, if there exists special interdependence, then at least one clustered set is not ordered because the total number of links is fixed, resulting in an unordered network.

Part 2:

According to Definition 5, because of indivisibility and irreversibility, for each clustered set C_i, there exists for the central decision i $(x_i, x_j) \in R$, $x_j \neq x_i$, for all $x_j \in C_i$, excluding the possibility that the network is random.

Part 3:

From Part 1 and Part 2, since special interdependence relation S, between clustered sets that are derived from interdependence relation R, implies the impossibility of an ordered network and indivisibility and irreversibility imply the impossibility of a random network, we can conclude that given the interdependence relations between decisions and clustered sets respectively, if there also exist indivisibility and irreversibility, the network is neither ordered nor random, and must be complex.

Lemma 2

That plans work implies that decisions are interdependent, indivisible, irreversible, and imperfectly foresighted.

Proof:

The strategy of the proof also includes three parts. First, we prove that plans work in terms of increasing the total expected utility of the network implies special interdependence. Second, we prove that plans work implies indivisibility and irreversibility. From Part 1 and Part 2, we can conclude that that plans work implies the four I's.

Part 1:

In the general case and following Han and Lai (2009), as shown in Figure 14.4, the central decision x_i of a clustered set is originally connected to x_{i-3} in that set by assigning a problem with negative utility to that decision (the diagram on the left). There must exist a decision x_h outside the clustered set in the network with the minimum probability $p(x_h) < p(x_i)$ and $p(x_h) < p(x_{i-3})$ so that if x_i is reconnected to x_h through a plan by reassigning that problem to x_h (Definition 11), then the total expected utility of the network will be increased by the amount of minus $u(p(x_{i-3})-p(x_h))$, where u is the negative utility associated with that problem. For this logic to obtain, the network must be specially interdependent (Definition 4). Note that the same logic of proof applies to assigning solutions with positive utility.

In the special case where there is more than one decision with the minimum probability of occurring, assume that these decisions are evenly scattered in the network and that the network is ordered as shown in the simplified diagram of Figure 14.5.

Reconnecting the decision in the clustered set with the minimum probability of occurring from x_i to the one that is outside the clustered set is still desirable because this would reduce the connection cost of the network due to shortened path length (Watts and Strogatz, 1998).

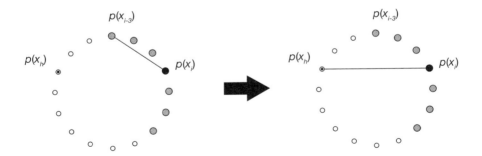

Figure 14.4 How plans of reassigning problems affect the topological structure of the network

252   *Urban Complexity and Planning*

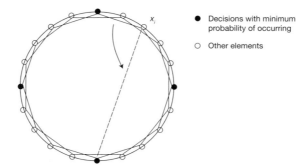

Figure 14.5   The special case of more than one decision with the minimum probability of occurring

Part 2:

In the general case, suppose x_i is the decision with the minimum probability of occurring in a clustered set as shown in Figure 14.6.

Let $x_i \in C_i$ be the decision with the minimum probability of occurring so that $p(x_i) < p(x_{i-3})$ and $p(x_i) < p(x_h)$, where $x_h \notin C_i$. Reconnecting x_{i+3} from x_h to x_i by assigning the problem from x_{i-3} to x_i instead of x_h will increase the total expected utility of the network from $up(x_h)$ to $up(x_i)$. The resulting network must be an ordered one which in turn implies indivisibility and irreversibility (Definition 5).

In the special case where there is more than one decision with the minimum probability of occurring and the network is random as shown in the simplified diagram of Figure 14.7, reconnecting x_{i-2} from a decision outside the clustered set with x_i as the central decision to x_i by reassigning the associated problem will not change the total expected utility of the network, but is still desirable because such reconnection would result in the transformation of the random network to a small world network with smaller cost of connection (Watts and Strogatz, 1998).

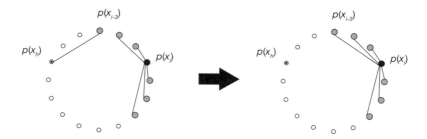

Figure 14.6   Effects of plans as defined here on the total expected utility of the network

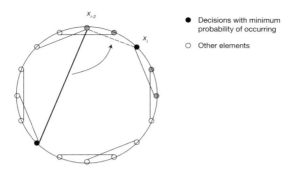

Figure 14.7   Effects of plans on the special case of random network

Part 3:

From Part 1 and Part 2, we can conclude that for plans to work by reconnecting decisions through problems or solutions assignment to increase the total expected utility of the network as depicted from Figures 14.4 through 14.7, the resulting topological structure of the network must imply the four I's.

Theorem: Plans work in complex network systems
From Lemma 1 and Lemma 2, we can conclude that plans work implies complex systems.
Proof:
The theorem obtains through logical inference from Lemmas 1 and 2 since the four I's imply complexity and effectiveness of plans implies the four I's.

5   Conclusions

That plans work for urban development is a claim that lacks theoretical and empirical backing. In the present book, based on a model of cities as networks of decisions, we provide a partial answer to this fundamental question by proving axiomatically that plans work in complex network systems of which cities are a manifestation. The theorem reached from the axiomatic system provides a foundation for practicing planning in complexity. In particular, it implies that plan-based actions that consider multiple, linked decisions are more effective than decision-based actions that treat these decisions as independent, in particular in the face of complex systems. The theorem prompts a future reassessment of the validity of the traditional choice theory in economics that seems to be built on a simple, artificial world, rather than a complex, real one.

References

Alexander, C. 1965. "A city is not a tree." *Architectural Forum* 122(1): 58–61.
Arthur, B. 1994. *Increasing Returns and Path Dependence in the Economy*. Ann Arbor, Michigan: University of Michigan Press.
Batty, M. 2001. "Cities as small worlds." *Environment and Planning B: Planning and Design* 28: 637–8.
Batty, M. 2008. "Wither network science?" *Environment and Planning B: Planning and Design* 35: 569–71.
Cohen, M.D., J.G. March, and J.P. Olsen. 1972. "A garbage can model of organizational choice." *Administrative Science Quarterly* 17: 1–25.
Friend, J., and A. Hickling. 2005. *Planning under Pressure: The Strategic Choice Approach*. London: Elsevier Butterworth-Heinemann.
Han, H-Y., and S-K. Lai. 2009. "Decision network: a planning tool for making multiple, linked decisions." paper submitted to Environment and Planning B: Planning and Design for possible publication.
Hopkins, L.D. 2001. *Urban Development: The Logic of Making Plans*. New York: Island Press.
Hopkins, L.D. (2012). "Plan assessment: making and using plans well." in R. Crane and R. Weber (eds), *Oxford Handbook of Urban Planning*. Oxford, UK: Oxford University Press.
Jacobs, J. 1993. *The Death and Life of Great American Cities*. New York: The Modern Library.
Kauffman, S. 1995. *At Home in the Universe: The Search for Laws of Self-Organization and Complexity*. New York: Oxford University Press.
Lai, S-K. 1998. "From organized anarchy to controlled structure: effects of planning on the garbage-can decision processes." *Environment and Planning B: Planning and Design* 25: 85–102.
Lai, S-K. 2003. "Effects of planning on the garbage-can decision processes: a reformulation and extension." *Environment and Planning B: Planning and Design* 30 (3):, 379–89.
Lai, S-K. 2006. "A spatial garbage can model." *Environment and Planning B: Planning and Design* 33(1): 141–56.
Watts, D.J., and S.H. Strogatz. 1998. "Collective dynamics of 'small-world' networks." *Nature*, 393: 440–442.
Waldrop, M.M. 1992. *Complexity: The Merging Science at the Edge of Order and Chaos*. New York: Touchstone.
Wolfram, S. 2002. *A New Kind of Science*. Champaign, Illinois: Wolfram Media.

Index

Page numbers in *italics* refer to figures and tables.

access structures 4, 27, 43, 54, 212
   ABM and SGCM *see* spatial garbage can model (SGCM), agent-based approach
   Decision Network tool 232
   land development firms case study 12, 15, *16*, *17–18*, 18
   SGCM 44–45, *52*, 52–53, *53*
activities 39, 44, 63, 208, 209, 244
activities decisions 40–41
adaptability 62, 76
   see also land development behavior simulation
adaptive efficiency 69
agenda setting 55
agent-based modeling (ABM) 39–40, 61
   applied to SGCM *see* spatial garbage can model (SGCM), agent-based approach
   land and housing market simulations 210
   literature review 62–64, *64*
   planning behaviors simulation 210–213
   for planning support systems 208–209
   residential motility simulation 209–210
   spatial processes 214, 214–215, *215*, *216*
agents 62
agglomeration 136, 138, 147, 152
   see also firm location simulation
aggregation behavior 152–153
aggregation strength 155, 158, 161, 162, 164
Alexander, C. 81, 84
ANOVA analyses
   agent-based SGCM 75

   Graeco-Latin Square simulation 52–53, *53*
   for modified garbage-can model 29–30, *35–37*
Arthur, W.B. 135–136, 137, 152–153, 166, 170–171, 190–192, 218–219
artificial life 80
association 43
attraction models *see* location attraction models simulation
AUGH platform 217, *217*
automata theory 82
autonomy 62
Axelrod, R. 101–102

Bak, P. 190, 196
bar experiment 191–192, *192*
Barabási, A-L. 184
Barzel, Y. 130
Bayesian approach 123, 124, 126
Bayesian theorem 124
Benenson, I. 63
between-subjects effects 73, *74*
Bonabeau, E. 184
Boolean networks 203–204
Boolean rule 203
bottom-up approach 79, 80, 121–122, 187, 217
bounded rationality 54, 190–193, *192*
   see also land development behavior simulation
bulletin board mystery 135

canoe metaphor 44
capabilities 69, 105, 120
Caruso, G. 131–132
Casti, J.L. 192

cellular automata (CA) 81–82, 100, 122, 187–188
  classes 86, *87*, *108*, 108–109, *109*
  elementary 121, 122–123, 123–124, 125–127, *128*, 132
  evolution patterns 107–109, *108*, *109*, 203
  one-dimensional *see* one-dimensional cellular automata
  and prisoner's dilemma 102–104, *104*
  spatial processes 214, 217, *218*
  see also land development behavior simulation
central place theory 169
chance nodes 229, 231–236, *233*, *234*, *235*, *236*, *238*
chaos 203, 204, 244, 245
Chapin, F.S. 187
characteristic transition rule 82, *88*, 88
Chen, K. 190, 196
China 164–165, *165*, 209
choice opportunities 3, 4, 6, *26*, 42, 212, 213
Christaller, Walter 169
cities
  assumptions about 120–121
  creative 119, 120, 132
  as decision networks 244–245
  as discrete dynamical systems 120–121, 123
  frequency-size distribution 137
  growth rates 89
  linear 79
  as organized anarchy 39–42, 63
  regularity 137
  relationships between elements 120
  safe 120, 132–133
  SGCM perspective 61, 63
  as system capable of computation 121–122
CityDev model 63
clustered sets 247, *248*
co-evolution 57
Cohen, M.D. 3, 4–6, 25, 43, 212, 245
competing technologies model 136, 137–138, *138*
competition 43, 218, 246
complex adaptive systems 80, 192

complex network systems 244–245, 253
complex networks 248–249
complex spatial systems 46, 47, 62, 79, 89, 148
complex structures 81, 103
complex systems 244
complexity science 169, 188–190
  see also land development behavior simulation
complexity theory 61, 80–81
comprehensive planning 236
comprehensive rationalism 54
computer simulations 1, 80, 99, 101, 208
cones 125
connectedness 246
contingencies 207, 227, 240
Conway, J.H. 102
cooperation 43, 102
Creative Cities Network 132
creativity 119, 132

decision analysis techniques 228–229
  see also Decision Network tool
decision areas 228–229
decision arrays 66, 67
decision costs 20–21, 26–27, 31, 32–34
decision difficulty 6, 9, 14, 15, 18, 21, 31, 33
decision horizons 28
decision-maker activity 9, 15, 31
decision-makers 1–2, *2*, 40, 44
  in garbage-can model 3, 4, 42, 211
  motivations 20
  in SGCM 46, 63
decision-making 55
Decision Network tool 227–228
  conceptual framework *230*, 230–231
  numerical example 231–235, *233*, *234*, *235*, *236*
  spatial applications and extensions 236–237, *237*, *238*–*239*, 240–241
decision nodes 229, 231–236, *233*, *234*, *235*, *236*, *238*
decision situations 40, 41, 44, 56, 63, 245
decision structures 4, 27, 43, 120, 212
  ABM and SGCM *see* spatial garbage can model (SGCM), agent-based approach
  Decision Network tool 232

land development firms case study 12, 15, *16*
    SGCM 44–45, 46, 52, *52*, 54, 57–58
decision styles 6, 43, 212
decision time horizons 7–8
decision tree model 229
decisions
    clustered sets 247, *248*
    complex networks 248–249
    connected 245, 246, 249
    contingent 1, 55, 119, 207, 227
    defined 245
    imperfect foresight 248
    independent networks 248
    indivisibility and irreversibility 248
    interdependence 246–247, *247*
    linked 55, 227, 241, 253
    network structures *244*, 244–245
    ordered networks 248
    random networks 248
    related 4, 7, 55
    special interdependence 247–248
decreasing returns 136, 170
defection 103–104, *104*, 219, *219*
dependent connectedness relation 246
deterministic finite automaton (DFA) 83–84, *85*, 92–93, *93*
developers
    prisoner's dilemma 101, 104
    see also land development behavior simulation
development decisions 39, 40, 55, 61, 79, 243
    see also land development behavior simulation
development patterns 40, 61
development potential 155–156, 158
development process 34n2, 40–41, 63
distance cost 139, 147, 148
disturbances 51, 56–57
disutility 20, 28, 30, 31, 32, 33, 130–131, 231
diversity 132, 175, 217
domain agents 63

earthquakes 152, 171
econometrics 187
economics 100, 136, 138, 152, 170, 187, 203

effectiveness of plans 243, 253
    axiomatic system
        definitions 246–249, *247*, *248*
        model *244*, 244–245
        proof *251*, 251–253, *252*, *253*
        theorem 249–250
elementary cellular automata 121, 122–123, 123–124, 125–127, *128*, 132
elements 3, 40
emergence 189
energy 7, 47–48, *48*, 51, 55, 65, 213
    see also net energy loads; total net energy
energy distributions 4, 15, *16*, *17–18*, 18–19, 27, 43, 212
energy loads 27
energy-time plots 48, *49*, *50*
Engelen, G. 188, 196
entropy 69–70, 71–72, *72*, 76, 124, 125, 126, 127
equilibrium 80, 100, 136, 190, 192, 203, 204
event-driven system 126, 127, 132
events 1, 40, 63–64, 145, 147–148, 190

facilities 39, 40, 41, 152
finite automata 83–84, *84*
Fioretti, G. 67
firm location simulation
    conclusions 148
    discussion 147–148
    research design 138–140, *139*, *140*
    results 140–141, *141*, *142*, *143*, 143–145, *144*, *146*
flight 6, 11, 43, 212
fluid participation 3
forecasting 125
four Is 121, 131, 243, 249–253
fractals 204

"game of life" 62, 102
game theory 101
garbage-can model 3–6, 20–22, 42–43, 211–212
    decision analysis 228, 245
    decision process 26
    effects of planning simulation 7–11, *9*, *10*

land development firms case study
    11–15, *13*, *14*, *16*, *17*, *17–18*,
    18–19, *19*
  modified 26–27, 33–34
    ANOVA analysis 29–30, *35–37*
    implications 31–33
    simulation design 27–29, *29*
    simulation results 29–31
    statistics and variables *30*
  planning behavior simulations
    212–213
  planning in 6–7
  and prisoner's dilemma 220–221, *221*
  spatial *see* spatial garbage can model
    (SGCM)
Gibrat, Robert 172
Gibrat's Law 172
GIS (geographic information systems)
    214–215, *215*, *216*, *217*, 217, *218*
Graeco-Latin Square simulation 47–48,
    48, *49*, *50*, 51–53, *52*, *53*
growth rates 89, *160*, 161, 182

Hanley, P.F. 63
Hillier, B. 80
homo economicus assumption 187
Hopkins, L.D. 3, 34, 44, 63, 100, 121,
    123, 240, 243
Hsueh, M-S. 182

IDs (identifications) 65–66, 67
imperfect foresight 34n2, 121, 131, 248,
    249–253
increasing returns 136–137, 138, 152–153,
    170, 218–219, 247
  see also location attraction models
    simulation; power law distribution
incrementalism 54
independent networks 244, 248
individual behaviors 189, 192, 193, 204
indivisibility 34n2, 121, 131, 247, 248,
    249–253
information
  collecting/gathering 1, 2, 32, 100–101,
    102, 105–106, 123
  incomplete/imperfect 80, 101
  manipulation 100, 101, 105
information content 127, 132

information economics 100
institutional design 62, 73, 76, 120,
    128–130, *129*, 132–133
institutional structures 54, 56, 128–130,
    129
institutions 128–129
intelligence 119
interaction
  between actors/agents/elements 39–40,
    41, 46, 61, 62, 79, 80, 148
  between decisions 41, 61, 79
  between garbage cans 4
  global-local 189
  local 79, 188–189
  see also prisoner's dilemma
interdependence 34n2, 113, 131, 245,
    246–247, *247*, 249–253
interdependence relation 246–247
irreversibility 34n2, 121, 131, 247, 248,
    249–253
issues 44

Kahneman, D. 240
Kauffman, S. 203, 204
Kingdon, J.W. 55
Krantz, D.H. 240
Krugman, P. 137, 152, 171, 172, 182, 204
Kunreuther, H.C. 240

Lai, S-K. 3, 7, 55, 62, 63, 100–101, 122,
    131, 182, 212
land and housing market simulations 210
land development behavior simulation
  conclusions 204–205
  discussion 202–204
  research design 193–197, *194*, *196*,
    197
  results 197–198, *198*, *199*, *200*,
    200–202, *201*, *202*
land development firms case study 11–15,
    13, *14*, *16*, *17*, *17–18*, 18–19, *19*
land-use/transportation dilemma 41, 56,
    125
land uses 88, 130, 188, 196, 214–215, *215*,
    216
Li, X. 63
Ligtenberg, A. 62, 63, 208
localization economics 152

location *see* firm location simulation; location attraction models simulation; spatial garbage can model (SGCM)
location attraction models simulation
  conclusions 166–167
  discussion 164–166, *165*
  mathematical simulation calculation 161–164, *162*, *163*
  research design 153–156, *155*, *156*
  results *157*, 157–161, *158*, *159*, *160*
locational patterns 136–137
lock-in processes 147, 148, 170
logic 123, 190, 191
Lomi, A. 67

March, J.G. 25, 221
MASUS model (Multi-Agent Simulator for Urban Segregation) 209
mathematical deduction 81
mathematical models 39, 99, 100, 101, 135–136, 177–182
May, R.M. 103–104, 105, *196*, 218–219
metaplanning 2
mixed attraction *see* location attraction models simulation
mobility 62
Morgenstern, O. 102
multi-agent system (MAS) 209, 214

nearly decomposable systems 81
neighborhood attraction *see* location attraction models simulation
net energy loads 4, 14, *14*, *17–18*, 18, 43, 212
network topological structures *244*, 244
Neumann, J. von 62, 81, 102
non-deterministic finite automaton (NDFA) 83–85, *84*, 92–93
non-linear dynamics 189
North, D.C. 69
Nowak, M.A. 103–104, 105, *196*, 218–219

Olsen, J.P. 25, 221
one-dimensional cellular automata 79–82, 90, 99–100, 131–132
  implications and discussion 88–89
  model 82–85, *84*, *85*
prisoner's dilemma 102–104, 114
  discussion 112–114, *113*
  evolution rules 114–115, *115*, *116*
  research design 104–107, *106*, *107*
  results 107–112, *108*, *109*, *110*, *112*
  simulation design and observations 86–88, *87*, *88*
order 69–70, 125–127, *128*, 135, 137, 138, 188
ordered networks 248
organizational choice 14, 42
organizational choice behavior 14, 26, 33, 245, 249
organizational design 4, 43, 211
organizational performance 19, 21, 32, 33
organized anarchy 3, 4, 39
oversight 6, 43, 67, 68, 69, 212

Parker, D.C. 210
payoff matrix 103–104, *104*
perfect rationality 54
permit system 56, 130
physical environment 58, 79
planning
  as computation in a universal system 123–125
  conventional 54
  defining 1–2, 27, 55, 100–101, 119
  and order 125–127, *128*
  problem-focused 120, 130–131
  regimes 126
  types 1–2, *2*
planning activities 1, 2, 119
planning behaviors 207–208
  ABM approach 210–211
  garbage-can model 212–213
  spatial relationships 213–215, *215*, *216*, *217*, 217–221, *218*, *219*, *221*
planning horizon 124
planning investments 2, 120, 124, 132, 207
  planning effects simulations 7–11, 20–21, 28–29, *29*, 30, 31, 32–34
planning scopes 127, 132
planning theory 54
plans 99, 123, 207, 249
  see also effectiveness of plans
polarization 158, 163, 182

population dynamic model 209
positive feedback 136, 170, 189
power law 137, 148, 151, 152, 169–172, *171*, 203, 204
  equation 201
  increasing returns approach
    conclusions 166–167
    discussion 164–166, *165*
    mathematical simulation calculation 161–164, *162*, *163*
    research design 153–156, *155*
    results *156*, *157*, 157–161, *158*, *159*, *160*
    see also location attraction models simulation
power law distribution 182–184, *183*
  Bak and Chen study 190, 196
  criticality simulation 200
  mathematical approximation 176–181, *179*
  self-organization simulation 201, 202, 204
  simulation 172–176, *173*, *174*, *175*, 175, *176*
  White and Engelen study 188, 196
primary cities 152, 158, *160*, 160–161, 166
principle of computational equivalence 122–123, 132
prisoner's dilemma 101–102
  and garbage-can model 220–221, *221*
  and one-dimensional CA *see* one-dimensional cellular automata, prisoner's dilemma
  payoff matrix 103–104, *104*
  spatial processes 218–221, *221*
  and two-dimensional CA 195–196
probability mechanisms 137
problem activity 8, 13, 14, 15, 18, 21, 29, 30, 33
problem disutility 20–21, 30, 31, 32–34
problem latency
  ANOVA analysis 35
  garbage-can model
    conclusions 21, 33
    simulation 1 8, *9*, 9
    simulation 2 14, *14*, 15, 18
    simulation 3 29, *30*, 31
problem significance 20–21

problem-solving 32, 73, 76, 120, 130, 133
problems, defined 3, 40, 42, 211

random networks 248
random system 126, 127
rank-size rule 137, 152, 169, 170, *171*, *183*
regimes of planning 126–127
regularity 137
regulations and rules 39, 41, 57, 64, 215
residential motility simulation 209–210
resolution 6, 43, 69, 212
responsiveness 62
role-playing approach 62, 208–209
rule 76 83–84, *84*, *85*, 85, 92–93, *93*
rules and regulations 39, 41, 57, 64, 215

sand particles 190
sand piles 171, 190
scale attraction *see* location attraction models simulation
scaling behavior 89
Schaeffer, P. 100, 123
self-organization 62, 69, 120, 125, 145, 188–190, 203–205
self-organized criticality 190
  see also land development behavior simulation
semi-lattice rules 85, 88
semi-lattices 81, 82–84, *85*, 85, 87, *88*, 89, 94, *94–97*
Simon, H. 81
Simon, H.A. 137, 151, 172, 181–182, 190
Simon's model 172, 181–182
small worlds 244
sociality 62
solution structures 73, 120, 212, 237
  ABM and SGCM *see* spatial garbage can model (SGCM), agent-based approach
  Decision Network tool 232, 233
  SGCM 44–45, 52, *52*, 54, 57–58
solutions, defined 3, 40, 42, 44, 211
spatial arrays 66
spatial change 125, 132
spatial evolution 86, 90, 99, 101, 103, 122, 136, 148, 169
spatial garbage can model (SGCM) 41–42, 43–46, *47*, 53–58, 61, 63–64, *64*

agent-based approach 75–76
    decision-making rule 68, *68*
    research design 65–70, *68, 70*
    results *71*, 71–74, *72, 73, 74, 75*
    simulation design of Graeco-Latin Square 47–48, *48, 49, 50*, 51–53, *52, 53*
spatial modeling 43–44, 213–214
    ABM approach 214–215, *215, 216*
    CA approach 217, *218*
    game in space approach 218–220, *219*
    garbage-can model 220–221, *221*
spatial processes 213–214
spatial structures 120
    ABM and SGCM *see* spatial garbage can model (SGCM), agent-based approach
    SGCM 44–45, 46, *52*, 52, 54, 57–58
special interdependence 247–248
Stanley, M.H.R. 89
strategic choice approach 228–229, 230
stream of opportunities model 44
Strogatz, S.H. 244
subjective expected utility (SEU) 190
systems approach 80, 81

Taipei, Taiwan 145, 148, 215
    see also land development firms case study
Taiwan 145, 148, 164–165, *165*, 182–183, 215, 217
    see also land development firms case study; location attraction models simulation
Tang, C.I. 7
Tobler, W.R. 187
top-down approach 79, 80
total net energy
    ABM and SGCM *68*, 68, 69, 70, 73–74, *74*, 76
    SGCM 47, 48, *48, 49, 50*, 51, 52, 53, 57–58
transition rules 81, 86, 88–90, 122, 123, 217
    classification 87, *87*, 94, *94–97*
    types 84–85
transportation/land-use dilemma 41, 56, 125, 244

tree rules 84, 87, 88
Tversky, A. 240
two-dimensional cellular automata 89, 104, 193, 195–196, *196*
typology of planning contexts 2

uncertainty 80, 101, 240
    reducing 1, 99, 100, 101, 207
unclear technology 3
United States (US) 89, 164, 165, *183*, 183, 204
universal computation 120–121, 122–123, 125, 131, 132
urban change 79–82
    see also one-dimensional cellular automata
urban construction boundaries (UCBs) 236–237, *237, 238–239*
urban development process 34*n*2, 40–41
urban economics 138, 187
urban growth 209, 236
urban growth boundaries (UGBs) 236
urban planning profession 243
urban settlement formation 151, 164, 166
    see also location attraction models simulation
urban spatial evolution *see* spatial evolution
urban spatial systems 79, 122
utilities 131, 229, 231

"v" shape curves 48, *49, 50*, 51, 56
video tape example 170
von Neumann machine 62

walkable communities 56
Watts, D.J. 244
White, R. 188, 196
Wolfram, S. 203
    CA research 81
        256 rules 103
        CA categories 86, 107–109, 202
        elementary CA 122, 125
        one-dimensional CA 112
        complex phenomena 99

Zipf, G.K. 137, 145, 152, 169, 172
zoning 41, 56, 64, 130, 215